MADAGASCA

Marxist Regimes Series

Series editor: Bogdan Szajkowski,
Department of Sociology, University College,
Cardiff

Further Titles

MADAGASCAR

Politics, Economics and Society

Maureen Covell

 Frances Pinter (Publishers),
London and New York

First published in Great Britain in 1987 by
Frances Pinter (Publishers) Limited
25 Floral Street, London WC2E 9DS

British Library Cataloguing in Publication Data

Covell, Maureen
   Madagascar: politics, economics and
   society.—(Marxist regimes series).
   1. Madagascar—Social conditions
   I. Title. II. Series
   969´.105   HN799.A8
   ISBN 0-86187-426-9
   ISBN 0-86187-427-7 Pbk

Typeset by Joshua Associates Limited, Oxford
Printed by SRP Ltd, Exeter, England

Editor's Preface

Madagascar, an archipeligo in the western part of the Indian Ocean, occupies an important strategic position in an area which has been the subject of great power rivalries for more than a decade now. The particular variety of Malagasy Marxist adaptations has been shaped by the country's rich history, culture and complex social networks. Principally these factors, rather than a single ideology, have played the main role in the formation of current political structures and economic options.

This, the first comprehensive study in English since 1975 of Madagascar's politics, economics and society, gives a detailed analysis of the country's development from pre-colonial times to the present. The monograph is a timely and a very important contribution to the overall analysis of Marxist experiments. It gives the reader a unique insight on the problems, dilemmas and limited options facing most countries in the developing world.

The study of Marxist regimes has commonly been equated with the study of communist political systems. There were several historical and methodological reasons for this. For many years it was not difficult to distinguish the eight regimes in Eastern Europe and four in Asia which resoundingly claimed adherence to the tenets of Marxism and more particularly to their Soviet interpretation—Marxism–Leninism. These regimes, variously called 'People's Republic', 'People's Democratic Republic', or 'Democratic Republic', claimed to have derived their inspiration from the Soviet Union to which, indeed, in the overwhelming number of cases they owed their establishment.

To many scholars and analysts these regimes represented a multiplication of and geographical extension of the 'Soviet model' and consequently of the Soviet sphere of influence. Although there were clearly substantial similarities between the Soviet Union and the people's democracies, especially in the initial phases of their development, these were often overstressed at the expense of noticing the differences between these political systems.

It took a few years for scholars to realize that generalizing the particular, i.e., applying the Soviet experience to other states ruled by elites which claimed to be guided by 'scientific socialism', was not good enough. The relative simplicity of the assumption of a cohesive communist bloc was questioned after the expulsion of Yugoslavia from the Communist Information Bureau in 1948 and in particular after the workers' riots in Poznań in 1956 and the Hungarian revolution of the same year. By the mid-1960s, the totalitarian model of communist politics, which until then had been very much in force, began to crumble. As some of these regimes articulated demands for a distinctive path of socialist development, many specialists studying these systems began to notice that the cohesiveness of the communist bloc was less apparent than had been claimed before.

Also by the mid-1960s, in the newly independent African states 'democratic' multi-party states were turning into one-party states or military dictatorships, thus questioning the inherent superiority of liberal democracy, capitalism and the values that went with it. Scholars now began to ponder on the simple contrast between multi-party democracy and a one-party totalitarian rule that had satisfied an earlier generation.

More importantly, however, by the beginning of that decade Cuba had a revolution without Soviet help, a revolution which subsequently became to many political elites in the Third World not only an inspiration but a clear military, political and ideological example to follow. Apart from its romantic appeal, to many nationalist movements the Cuban revolution also demonstrated a novel way of conducting and winning a nationalist, anti-imperialist war and accepting Marxism as the state ideology without a vanguard communist party. The Cuban precedent was subsequently followed in one respect or another by scores of Third World regimes, which used the adoption of 'scientific socialism' tied to the tradition of Marxist thought as a form of mobilization, legitimation or association with the prestigious symbols and powerful high-status regimes such as the Soviet Union, China, Cuba and Vietnam.

Despite all these changes the study of Marxist regimes remains in its infancy and continues to be hampered by constant and not always pertinent comparison with the Soviet Union, thus somewhat blurring the important underlying common theme—the 'scientific theory' of the laws of development of human society and human history. This doctrine is claimed by the leadership of these regimes to consist of the discovery of objective causal relationships; it is used to analyse the contradictions which arise between goals and actuality in the pursuit of a common destiny. Thus the political elites of these countries have been and continue to be influenced in both their ideology and their political practice by Marxism more than any other current of social thought and political practice.

The growth in the number and global significance, as well as the ideological political and economic impact, of Marxist regimes has presented scholars and students with an increasing challenge. In meeting this challenge, social scientists on both sides of the political divide have put forward a dazzling profusion of terms, models, programmes and varieties of interpretation. It is against the background of this profusion that the present comprehensive series on Marxist regimes is offered.

This collection of monographs is envisaged as a series of multi-disciplinary textbooks on the governments, politics, economics and society of these countries. Each of the monographs was prepared by a specialist on the country concerned. Thus, over fifty scholars from all over the world have contributed monographs which were based on first-hand knowledge. The geographical diversity of the authors, combined with the fact that as a group they represent many disciplines of social science, gives their individual analyses and the series as a whole an additional dimension.

Each of the scholars who contributed to this series was asked to analyse such topics as the political culture, the governmental structure, the ruling party, other mass organizations, party-state relations, the policy process, the economy, domestic and foreign relations together with any features peculiar to the country under discussion.

This series does not aim at assigning authenticity or authority to any single one of the political systems included in it. It shows that, depending on a variety of historical, cultural, ethnic and political factors, the pursuit of goals derived from the tenets of Marxism has produced different political forms at different times and in different places. It also illustrates the rich diversity among these societies, where attempts to achieve a synthesis between goals derived from Marxism on the one hand, and national realities on the other, have often meant distinctive approaches and solutions to the problems of social, political and economic development.

*University College
Cardiff*

Bogdan Szajkowski

Contents

List of Illustrations and Tables

Madagascar

Preface

This book is an attempt to describe and understand a country and political system about which only too little is known in English. I have been particularly insistent on putting the Malagasy experience of Marxism in its historical and societal context, since one of the chief points of interest of the experience has been the attempt of the Malagasy to integrate their society and its traditions with Marxism. My interest in Madagascar and the Malagasy dates from 1968, when I first arrived in the island to begin research on my dissertation. I spent over a year there, in the capital, Antananarivo, and in two other cities, Fianarantsoa and Toliary, and met with a kindness that I have been very slow in repaying.

During my stay in Madagascar, and even earlier, in the year I spent in Paris before going to Madagascar, I was able to meet some of the people who were to participate in the events of 1972, and the construction of a Marxist regime after 1975. Their arguments, as well as my own observations in Madagascar, convinced me of the need for a change of regime and an attempt to construct 'something better'. Many other people also helped with the research for the original dissertation: Willette, Holding, Ignace, Vincent, Raymond, Roland, and the people and officials of several neighbourhoods in Fianarantsoa and Toliary. They (and other Malagasy) might not agree with my descriptions and evaluations of their experience, but I hope they will believe that I wish them well.

Many people have contributed to the existence of this book. First, of course, is the editor of this series, Bogdan Szajkowski, to whom I am grateful for the chance to write it. I am also grateful to him, and to the managing editor of the series, Heather Bliss, for their extreme patience in the matter of deadlines. With time, we may all forget how many I have missed! While I was doing the research for this book, many people, both Malagasy and non-Malagasy, kindly agreed to talk to me, on the condition that I not name them. I hope they consider the book an adequate repayment for their contributions, which were essential to its existence.

One of the most enduring Malagasy values is an attachment to the family, taken in its widest sense to include both immediate kin and more distant relatives, and both the dead and the living. I have been very fortunate in my family attachments, and this book, such as it is, is for my family in the larger sense of the word.

Basic Data

Official name	Democratic Republic of Madagascar
Population	9.9 million (1984)
Population density	14 inhabitants per sq. km. overall, but varies greatly from region to region
Population growth (% p.a.)	3.1
Urban population (%)	21
Total labour force	4.55 million
Life expectancy	Male, 51 years; female, 54 years
Infant death rate (per 1,000)	110
Child death rate (per 1,000)	22
Ethnic groups	Merina, Betsileo, Betsimisaraka
Capital	Antananarivo
Land area	587,000 sq. km., of which 55% arable
Official language	The constitution does not name an official language. Malagasy is the national language.
Other main languages	French
Administrative division	6 provinces
Membership of international organizations	United Nations, Organization of African Unity, Non-Aligned Movement
Foreign relations	
Political structure	
Constitution	Adopted by referendum, December, 1975
Highest legislative body	National Popular Assembly
Highest executive body	Supreme Council of the Revolution

Prime Minister	Desiré Rakotoarijoana (since 1977)
President	Didier Ratsiraka (since 1975)
Ruling party	Vanguard of the Malagasy Revolution (Arema) in conjunction with other members of the National Front for the Defence of the Revolution
Secretary general	Didier Ratsiraka
Party membership	Uncertain

Growth indicators (% p.a.)

	1965–73	1970–82	1973–83
National income	3.5	less than half 1965–75 figure)	0.2
Industry		3.0	0.7
Agriculture		0.3	0.3
Food production per capita			0.5

Trade and balance of payments

Exports	(1985) US$316 million
Imports	(1985) US$469 million
Exports at % of GNP	10.8
Main exports	Coffee, cloves, cotton products, sugar
Main imports (%)	Petroleum (29.4), food (22.3; rice alone; 18.5), machinery and equipment (21.4)
Destination of exports (%)	Socialist countries (7.5), non-socialist countries (92.5)
Main trading partners	France, Indonesia, United States, Japan
Foreign debt	(1984) US$1,867 million
Foreign aid	(1984) US$156 million

Main natural resources	Chrome, graphite, mica; some possibility of petroleum

Food self-sufficiency	Shortages of rice and other staples. Population grew by 32% from 1970–84, rice production by 8.5%. There is

unexploited land, and most observers agree that food production could be expanded.

Armed forces	30,000, including a para-military gendarmerie of 8,000. Military service of 18 months is compulsory, but not all are called up. Most conscripts are used on development projects and to help staff the state education system.

Education and health
  School system   Six years basic education, secondary, university
  Primary school enrolment   92% of school-age children are enrolled
  Secondary school enrolment   14% of age group enrolled
  Higher education   1% of age group 20–24 enrolled in University of Madagascar and six Regional University Centres
  Adult literacy (%)   50
  Population per hospital bed   410
  Population per physician   10,780

Economy
  GNP   (1980) US$689 million
  GNP per capita $260
  GNP by %
    Agriculture   43
    Industry   15
    Services   42
  State budget   (1984) US$600 million
    Defence expenditure % of state
    budget   30 of recurrent budget
  Monetary unit   Malagasy franc (ariary)

Main crops   Rice, cotton, sugar cane, coffee, cloves

Land tenure   Individual, some state farms, some share-cropping

Main religions	Christianity (about 50%)

Transport
   Rail network   860 km.
   Road network   Paved: 3,957 km.; unpaved: 10,170 km.

Population Forecasting

The following data are projections produced by Poptran, University College Cardiff Population Centre, from United Nations Assessment Data published in 1980, and are reproduced here to provide some basis of comparison with other countries covered by the Marxist Regimes Series.

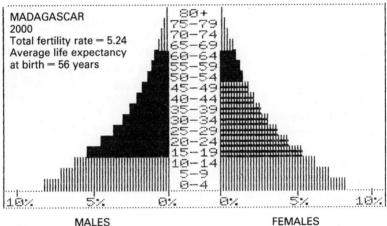

MADAGASCAR
2000
Total fertility rate = 5.24
Average life expectancy
at birth = 56 years

MALES   FEMALES

Projected Data for Madagascar 2000

Total population ('000)	15,204
Males ('000)	7,525
Females ('000)	7,679
Total fertility rate	5.24
Life expectancy (male)	54.2 years
Life expectancy (female)	57.8 years
Crude birth rate	39.1

Crude death rate	11.9
Annual growth rate	2.72%
Under 15s	43.27%
Over 65s	3.44%
Women aged 15–49	23.32%
Doubling time	26 years
Population density	26 per sq. km.
Urban population	31.5%

Glossary

anciens combattants	former soldiers
andevo	a slave caste
andriana	nobles
baccalauréate	examination at the end of secondary schooling. Those who pass are entitled to go to university
chefs de canton	local level bureaucrats
colons	settlers
côtiers	inhabitants of regions outside the central plateaux
decentralized collectivities	units of local government
Deuxième Bureau	Security and information office
fady	taboo
fanjakana	Governing power and those associated with it
faritany	province
firaisampokontany	district
fivondronampokontany	region
fokonolona	inhabitants of a village or neighbourhood
fokontany	village, urban neighbourhood
hova	commoners
indigénat	legal code applied to non-French citizens in the colonial period. This category included almost all Malagasy
loi cadre	1956 law granting internal autonomy to French African colonies
lycée	secondary school that prepared students for the baccalauréate examination
mainty	a slave caste
menalamba	lit., The Red Shawls; 1896 revolt against imposition of French rule
Merina	pronounced to rhyme with 'cairn'
notables	local inhabitants of some importance, used by the central power as intermediaries with the rest of the population
originaires	people born in a given region, of a family from that region

prefect	agent of the central administration, responsible for a 'region'
quartier	neighbourhood
ray amn'dreny	lit. 'fathers and mothers', in practice a council of the male elders of a *fokonolona*
sans partis	independent of party
sous préfet	agent of the central administration, responsible for a 'district'
tanety	hillside

List of Abbreviations

AEOM	(Association des Etudiants d'Origine Malgache) Association of Students of Malagasy Origin
AKFM	(Akoton'ny Kongresi 'ni Fahaleovantenan Madagasikara) Independence Congress Party of Madagascar
ANP	(Assemblée Nationale Populaire) National Popular Assembly
Arema	(Antokin'ny Revolisiona Malagasy) Vanguard of the Malagasy Revolution
CGT	(Comité de grève des travailleurs) Workers' strike committee
CEG	(Collège d'Enseignement Général) Comprehensive Education College (first two years of secondary education)
CIMELTA	One of the oldest industrial firms in Madagascar, specializing in heavy machinery
CMD	(Conseil Militaire de Développement) Military Development Council
CMM	Compagnie Marseillaise de Madagascar
CNPD	(Conseil National Populaire de Développement) People's National Development Council
CSR	(Conseil Suprème de la Révolution) Supreme Council of the Revolution
DGID	(Direction Générale d'Information et de Documentation) Directorate General for Information and Documentation (presidential security and information services)
FISEMA	(Firaisana Sendikaly Malagasy) Malagasy Union Federation; AKFM affiliated union under First Republic
*FJKM	Council of Christian Churches of Madagascar
FNDR	(Front National pour la Défense de la Révolution Socialiste Malgache) National Front for the Defence of the Malagasy Socialist Revolution

FRS	(Forces Républicaines de Sécurité) Republican Security Forces
GIMOI	Groupe Interuniversitaire pour Madagascar et l'Océan Indien
GMP	(Groupe Mobile de Police) Mobile Police Group (1972–5 version of FRS)
IMF	International Monetary Fund
ITOM	*Industries et Travaux d'Outre-Mer* (see Bibliography)
JINA	(Jeunesse Nationaliste) Secret society indirectly affiliated with the MDRM
LOI	*Lettre de l'Ocean Indien* (see Bibliography)
MDRM	(Mouvement Démocratique de la Rénovation Malgache) Democratic Movement for Malagasy Renewal
MFM	(Mpitolona ho amin'ny Fanjakana ny Madinika) Party for Proletarian Power
Monima	(Madagasikara Otronin'ny Malagasy) lit., Madagascar upheld by the Malagasies, or Party of Malagasy Solidarity
OCAM	(Organisation Commune Africaine et Malgache) Malagasy-African Common Organization
OFPS	*Options Fondamentales pour la Planification Socialiste* (see Bibliography)
OMNIS	(Office Militaire Nationale pour les Industries Stratégiques) National Military Office for Strategic Industries
OMPIRA	(Office Militaire pour la Production Agricole) Military Office for Agricultural Production
PADESM	(Parti des Desherités de Madagascar) Party of the Disinherited of Madagascar
PANAMA	(Parti Nationaliste Malgache) Secret society indirectly affiliated with the MDRM
PSD	(Parti Social Democrate) Social Democratic Party
RDM	République Démocratique Malgache (see Bibliography)
RFEPA	*Revue Française d'Etudes Politiques Africaines* (see Bibliography)
*SEREMA	Union affiliated with Arema
SINPA	(Société d'Intérêt National de Commercialisation des Produits Agricoles) National Interest Society for the Commercialization of Agricultural Products

SNTP	(Société Nationale de Travaux Publiques) National Public Works Society
SONACO	(Société National de Commerce Extérieure) National Society for Foreign Trade
TTS	(Tanora Tonga Saina) lit. 'Aware Youth', Revolutionary Youth
UDECMA	(Union des Démocrates Chrétiens de Madagascar) Union of Malagasy Christian Democrats
Vonjy	(Vonjy Iray Tsy Mivaky) National Unity Party
VS Monima	(Vondrona Socialista Monima) Monima Socialist Union Split from Monima Ka-miviombio, 1977
VVS	(Vy Vato Sakelika) Iron, Stone, Network. Secret society disbanded by the French 1917
ZOAM (ZWAM)	(Zatovo orin'asa anivon'ny Madagasikara) Unemployed youth of Madagascar (Earlier Zatovo Western Andevo Malagasy Youth Slave Cowboys of Madagascar)
ZWAM	*See* ZOAM

1 Introduction

On 15 June 1975, the Malagasy Republic became the Democratic Republic of Madagascar. The island's new head of state, naval captain Didier Ratsiraka, declared that scientific socialism was the only solution to the country's problems, and announced the formation of a regime based on the principles of humanist Marxism. In December a national referendum adopted a constitution for 'a new type of state expressing the interests of the laboring masses' (Democratic Republic of Madagascar, *Constitution*, Preamble). The proclamation of the new republic was the culmination of a process that had begun with the collapse of the first post-colonial regime in 1972 under the pressures of peasant revolts, urban riots, and the refusal of the armed forces to continue defending it. The 1972 'May Revolution' was followed by three years of turmoil in which successive combinations of civilian and military forces attempted to strike a balance between the groups involved in the uprising and their opponents and create a stable governing coalition. Ratsiraka's predecessor had been assassinated after less than a week in office, and Ratsiraka himself only came to power after four months of intensive bargaining conducted behind the screen of a temporary collective military government.

The period since Ratsiraka's accession to power has been marked by both turmoil and stability, while policy initiatives have been sufficiently varied that the regime has attackers and defenders on both left and right. The persistence of the regime and of its most important members has made it one of Africa's most long-lived. On the other hand, the 1972 revolution marked an important change in the nature of Malagasy society: social cleavages and tensions once hidden by a 'peaceful if melancholy' appearance have, since May 1972, broken out in periodic urban riots and rural revolts, with violent government countermeasures (see Valette, 1969; Serre, 1975). In the summer of 1985 government troops attacked the headquarters of opposition movements grouped under the banner of martials arts societies, accusing them of plotting to overthrow the regime and substitute a state based on the principles of religion and Kung Fu.

Government pronouncements and initiatives have also followed a course that is far from straightforward. In the period immediately following 1975, much of the economy was nationalized, a new mass party, the Avant Guard of the Malagasy Revolution (Arema) was established, and the process of increasing diplomatic and military links with other Marxist regimes, particularly the Soviet Union and North Korea, was accelerated. Since 1980 the regime has promised measures to reintroduce elements of private enterprise into the economy, the revolutionary vanguard has been urged to study Descartes and the Bible as well as Marx, and Madagascar's foreign policy has received accolades from Ronald Reagan for its 'real non-alignment'. Interpreters of the politics of revolutionary Madagascar have argued: that the first set of policies did not represent a real change and therefore that the post-1980 'reversal' is just the dropping of the façade; that there was a real attempt at change that has been abandoned, and that there was an attempt at change that continues, with post 1980 policies being simply a temporary—and limited—concession to economic pressures.

It is the purpose of this book to examine events in Madagascar since 1975 from three points of view. First, the adoption of scientific socialism made the country an early member of the growing number of self-identified African Marxist regimes. The appearance and multiplication of these regimes has led to the development of a large body of literature on the meaning of this choice, the reasons for it and its consequences. Madagascar is often considered an 'ambiguous' or 'peripheral' member of this category (Young, 1982b, p. 50; Wiles, 1982, p. 14). However, it is one of the few scientific socialist regimes of military origin to have come to power with the support of a civilian party with strong Marxist leanings and in conjunction with popular, if not revolutionary uprisings. Second, the current government is a combined civil–military regime with important civilian participation and a functioning multi-party system. Here, too, it is one of a growing number of regimes that cannot be categorized simply as 'military rule', even though the armed forces are an essential component of the ruling coalition. Finally, the regime is, of course, Malagasy. The society of Madagascar is a complex web of divisions and connections. Changes of regime have added new layers without obliterating the old ones. The history of group relations in the island has created a set of problems that any regime, of whatever coloration, must deal with and that limits the ability of governments to set the political agenda solely in function of their ideological predispositions. These problems are not necessarily unique to Madagascar: indeed, the most central one, that of the relationship between state and society, is receiving increasing attention in several contexts. However, the particular form they take in Madagascar is tightly rooted in the island's history.

The Analysis of African Marxist Regimes

When the new Malagasy regime declared its adherence to scientific socialism in 1975 African Marxist regimes were so rare as to constitute exceptions rather than a category. Benin, Congo and Somalia were the only other examples, and of these only Somalia had excited much strategic or theoretical interest. Since then self-proclaimed Marxist or radical states of both military and guerrilla origin have become sufficiently numerous to constitute a separate category of analysis with a growing body of literature centered on a series of practical and theoretical questions. How Marxist are these regimes? Under what circumstances do they come into existence? What difference does the adoption of a Marxist label make to domestic and foreign policies? What difference does it make to their populations?

Answering the question 'how Marxist or socialist are these states' has become complicated by the growing vagueness of the meaning of Marxism. The last three decades have seen a loosening of the empirical signification of the term as the socialist camp has split and split again, and as it has been joined by an increasing variety of states, most of whom lack one or more of the classic attributes of a Marxist state (see Waller & Szajkowski, 1981, pp. 14–15; Young, 1982b, p. 25). While it might be extreme to argue that 'what now goes under the name of 'Marxism–Leninism' has now become a grab bag of theories in which something can be found to deal with most conditions' (Ottaway and Ottaway, 1981, p. 200) few of the newcomers to the socialist camp have felt obliged to adopt in totality policies such as class struggle with the proletariat as ideal referent, collectivization of agriculture, opposition to religion or even the creation of a monopolistic vanguard party. Indeed, as Crawford Young points out, this decline of ideological uniformity was probably 'the crucial prologue to the birth of the Afro-Marxist state'. In place of uniformity, Young argues, a great variety of sources of 'radical thought' has come into existence. These include Western communist parties, the 'radical anti-imperialist Third World milieux' of the European Left, in which May 1968 is a referent as significant as October 1917, and, of course, Third World countries themselves whose experience might well be more interesting than that of the 'Second World' of established developed Marxist regimes (Young, 1982b, pp. 25–7). The ideas developed in these sources include an identification of imperialism and neo-colonialism as more immediate foes than internal class enemies, an emphasis on transformation in agriculture as more important than rapid industrialization, and, in the place of alliances with the proletariat, a reliance on a coalition of state-based actors (including the army), selected intellectuals and a heterogeneous although usually urban collection of 'radical' groups. Most significantly, in spite of the emphasis on the universality of uniform scientific socialism, national specificity is insisted upon and even glorified.

All this means that the question 'how Marxist' should probably be recast into a series of questions, the first being 'what meaning does the regime itself give to Marxism?' Although some writers have argued that an emphasis on national specificity is a major distinguishing characteristic of Africa's 'first wave' non-Marxist socialist regimes (for example, Jowitt, 1979, pp. 151–4) others have maintained that, on the contrary, it is impossible to understand Third World Marxist regimes without taking into account their countries own 'rich and distinctive political traditions and the aspiration to create a socialism that will accord with their own circumstances' (Waller & Szajkowski, 1981, pp. 14–15). It seems more interesting to compare a regime's policy initiatives with its ideological pronouncements, especially in the case of Madagascar where the new regime has been prolific in both, than to compare either with an ideal type of 'the socialist state'. Models of socialism proposed for this latter comparison seem unusually stringent, with non-Marxist scholars being, if anything, more demanding of claimants to the Marxist–Leninist label than Marxists. The existence of these models, and the common finding that self-declared radical states often fall short of matching them and that their elites may well be engaged in something quite other than 'the construction of socialism' does direct attention to the concrete results of policy and its impact on the population and relations between state and population. Evaluating regimes on the basis of the fit between ideology and results, is, of course, a more difficult undertaking since more factors intervene in the connection between policy and results than in the connection between ideology and policy.

The Functions of Ideology

In his discussion of the reasons why African elites might adopt Marxist ideology, Kenneth Jowitt remarks, almost as an aside, that an additional reason 'may be the belief among certain African elites that Leninist regimes have specific techniques, experiences and resources relevant to their problems' (Jowitt, 1979, p. 143). This is a point that deserves further exploration, and it will be discussed when I consider the development of radical discourse and analysis in Madagascar. Here it should be pointed out that Jowitt, like many writers who examine this topic, tends to concentrate on what might be called the 'utilitarian' functions of ideology. Finding many such functions they argue that the obvious usefulness of the adoption of Marxism–Leninism to an African elite in search of a legitimizing and organizing principle means that any commitment to the content of the ideology is probably lacking. At one extreme this line of analysis argues that the ideology serves only to cloak a situation in which the real commitment of the elite is to its own power, its continued prosperity and the pleasure of its factional disputes (see, for example, Decalo, 1979). These analyses rarely look at the other side of the ledger: the dysfunctions of a use of ideology with its stress on goals and performance as the basis for legitimization and the choice of as specific and divisive an ideology as Marxism for this role. We tend to think that 'talk is cheap': in fact, it can be very costly in terms of both internal and external support. However, Madagascar does constitute an interesting case for those who wish to argue that the adoption of an ideology, of whatever content, serves a whole range of functions for rulers. The proclamation of the Democratic Republic of Madagascar in 1975 was not the first time that a Malagasy state had converted to an alien ideology. In 1869, the Queen, Prime Minister and court of the Merina monarchy, which at the time controlled most of the island, were baptized as Christians. Historians allow some role for personal conviction in this event, but the Prime Minister in particular was almost certainly motivated largely by reasons of state policy. These reasons included a desire to create a bond with important foreign powers, the development of a new basis for the identification and unification of a state elite that was still in the process of formation, and the cultivation of support from important groups in the Malagasy population (see Raison-Jourde, 1983). However, the choice also created problems for the monarchy, and a comparison of the two events underlines the importance of examining the dysfunctions as well as the functions of ideology.

Can an Army be Revolutionary?

Most discussions of the characteristics of military rule argue that armies are particularly unlikely to be revolutionary. Studies that treat the army as a corporate, institutionalized body separated from society argue that by the time officers reach a rank in which they are likely to participate in military government, they will have acquired a rational–technological orientation that is apolitical, distrustful of the type of popular mobilization necessary to make a revolution, and probably, in Western-trained armies, anti-communist as well (see, for example, Feit, 1973). Coming to the same conclusion from another extreme is the current image of African armies as composed of self-seeking officers, riddled with factional disputes and so non-institutionalized that they cannot keep themselves together, let alone run a revolution. Ideology becomes only one more weapon in materialistic factionalism (Decalo, 1976). Class analysis adds its own negative to the argument by claiming that the military must be characterized as a bourgeoise or petit-bourgeois institution: unlikely or a least uncertain revolutionaries (see, for example, the debate on the Ethiopian Derg. The heading for this section is adapted from Lefort, 1981, p. 157; see also Halliday and Molyneux, 1981, pp. 35-7. For an argument stressing the importance of civilian alliances in determining the direction of 'radical' military rule, see Knauss, 1980). These lines of argument fall into contrasting errors. The first two exaggerate an army's degree of isolation from its society. Both assume that the military has considerable autonomy, leaving it free to preserve a corporate ethos in the first case, and to indulge in its factional games in the second. Not all armies have this degree of isolation. In many countries 'the armed forces cannot be defined only as a monolithic hierarchical organization with its own ethos. All the divisions of the civilian political system appear in them, crystallized and personalized around representative individuals' (Roquie, 1981, p. 157). The Malagasy army represents an example of an army with fragmented boundaries. The entry of political issues from the larger society has broken its institutional cohesion but this entry has also limited, although not eliminated, the play of personalistic factional intrigue. Class analysis seems to err in the other direction, in denying the army the autonomy to make alliances with groups in society outside the classes to which the officers belong whether by birth or by their military position. Unless one takes the extreme position that nothing short of an alliance with a full-blown proletariat can be revolutionary, a military-based elite's choice of civilian groups to include in its governing coalition can give an important indication of its intended political direction. Moreover, all three approaches appear to ignore the significance of the role of the army as the predominant means of political change in countries like Madagascar. The socially ambitious might well pursue their goals through a military career, but so might aspiring politicians and revolutionaries.

State and Society

Issues of ideology and the control and exercise of power are closely related to a third issue, that of the relationship between state and society. New regimes do not begin in a new world, and even elites whose goals include changes in state, society and the relations between them must deal with groups and attitudes shaped by previous regimes. In Madagascar, the relationship between state and society has historically been so adversarial that state action requiring any kind of popular participation is extremely difficult. As Naomi Chazan points out, the capacity of a state to maintain its position of legitimacy depends on 'reciprocity within an agreed on political framework' (Chazan, 1983, p. 350). The states of Madagascar have historically had problems achieving both the reciprocity and the agreed framework. The Merina empire, which ruled two-thirds of the island in the nineteenth century was imposed on many of its subjects and increasingly exploitative of nearly all. The colonial regime that was installed after 1896 was even less legitimate and resistance to it culminated in a rebellion in 1947 that cost 80,000 to 100,000 lives in a population of four million. In reaction to the existence and practices of these states the Malagasy political culture developed a conception of state power as intrusion, the term *fanjakana* representing this power in all its manifestations. A contrasting ideal of 'Malagasy rule' that included a rejection of state structures external to the local community survived independence and has been, if anything, re-inforced by the policies of post-colonial regimes.

Another source of tension between state and society lies in the fact that the existence of any given state is not equally advantageous to all groups in society. A state 'is created by political groups interested in establishing domination and control, and this involves struggles with other political and socio-economic groups having different interests' (Callaghy, 1984, p. xi). Moreover, states are characterized by and often create a state backed system of stratification—of unequal access not only to political power but also to 'quality of life and mobility' (Schatzberg, 1980). This has been as true in Madagascar as elsewhere. The rural ideal of 'Malagasy rule' found an urban echo in the 1972 slogan of the *Fanjakana Madinika*, the republic of the humble. The radical populism of these two rejections of the hierarchical state constituted a serious rival to the scientific socialism and democratic centralism of other participants in the May revolution.

A final source of tension between state and society lies in the difficulty the state has in controlling its own agents. A state is rarely a homogeneous entity and the different groups that make up its totality often have different and competing interests, to say nothing of interests that might conflict with the requirements of the perpetuation of the state. The adoption of an official state ideology might be seen as an attempt to unify these groups, but it can also divide them. Problems of corruption, or simply of translating political will into action have plagued the successive regimes of Madagascar. The current Marxist regime is facing a crisis of control over its components and over society that is less severe than similar crises elsewhere in Africa, but still important. This does not represent the collapse of 'the once mighty colonial state' (Callaghy, 1984) since the colonial state in Madagascar was not particularly effective when it turned its attention to matters outside the narrow sphere of self-perpetuation. However, the problem, while characteristic of regimes in Madagascar, has passed into crisis since 1972. The loss of state efficacy, the attempts of those at the head of the state to reassert control, and the conflict between the need for control and the attempt to introduce a particular ideological direction constitute one of the major themes of present day Malagasy politics.

2 Geographical and Historical Background

'Madagascar is not an island, but an archipelago'. This saying captures an important aspect of the country, whose geography and history have combined to produce a society of considerable diversity with a disarticulated economy and a non-articulated communications system. The population is small in relation to the size of the country and unevenly distributed, with densities ranging from seven persons per square kilometre in Toliaray province to over forty in the countryside around Antananarivo (*Les options fondamentales pour la planification socialiste*, 1978, p. 29).

The island itself can best be thought of as a wedge, with the sharply sloping side to the east and the gradual slope to the west. The mountains that form the apex run the length of the island, reaching over 1,500 metres in the north, where they form an important barrier between the province of Antseranana and the rest of the country. The east coast is also an area of heavy rainfall with frequent cyclones and the combination of rainfall and declivity make the maintenance of any type of transportation system difficult. The south of the island is in a rain shadow and has a desert climate and a widely scattered population. The west coast, from Morombe to just north of Mahajanga receives less rainfall than the east, but profits from the presence of a series of rivers that rise in the higher parts of the island to provide water and alluvial deposits for agriculture. In the interior lies the region known as the plateaux, a mountainous area where again topography makes the construction and maintenance of transportation systems difficult (*Atlas de Madagascar*, 1969; Bastian, 1967; *Area Handbook*, 1973).

Government policies have not overcome, and have often exacerbated geographic problems. The pre-colonial states of Madagascar often refused to build roads, as a deliberate part of their defence strategy. The colonial regime did build roads and railroads, but as a function of its own political and economic priorities. Toamasina was developed as the main port, in spite of the dangers of cyclones and the difficulties of creating a network of hinterland roads under east coast conditions, because of its proximity to Réunion. The best port in Madagascar, and one of the best in the Indian Ocean, is in the north of the island, at Antseranana. Its location, facing the east coast and horn of continental Africa, led to its development as a naval base rather than as a commercial port. The ports of the west coast are subject to considerable silting, and the primacy of Toamasina means that the necessary maintenance work has been neglected by both colonial and post-colonial governments. The road and railroad systems hardly constitute a system in the sense of an interconnected whole. With the exception of the plateaux network they drain hinterlands to ports rather than linking regions. Small paved stretches around administrative centres or the home villages of former cabinet ministers testify to the importance of political criteria in the creation of the system. None of the roads is as good as it looks on the map. The 500 kilometre trip from Antananarivo to Mahajanga never took less than eight hours, it now takes three days—when it is possible.

Economy

The Malagasy economy is dominated by agriculture, which occupies about 84 per cent of the active population and accounts for almost all exports. (World Bank, 1979; *LOI*, 1985; Hugon, 1977. Figures for population and employment are estimates. The last Malagasy census was held in 1975, and most of its results were never published.) Agriculture itself is dominated by rice (see Table 6.1) which is the main food crop and which, with cattle, is the only agricultural product traded within the island. There have been perennial shortages since the mid-1960s, and managing supplies has been a major priority and major problem for successive regimes since then. The other important agricultural products of the island are all export crops. The production of coffee was quickly dominated by small Malagasy producers, but sugar, vanilla and cloves are grown both by individual producers and on large plantations, once the property of *colons* or commercial companies, and still worked by migrant labourers from the south. The plateaux play almost no role in this export-oriented agriculture, and agricultural production and trade parallels and reinforces the pattern of communications, making the island an archipelago of economically distinct and isolated regions. There are some major exceptions including the trade in rice and cattle, labour migrations from south to north, and the illegal trade in rum and Indian hemp.

The non-agricultural sector of the economy is dominated by services. Industrial production employs about 50,000 people and is concentrated in the Antananarivo–Antsirabe area, with some installations in Mahajanga (textiles) and Antseranana (naval repair). The 'informal sector' is estimated to employ at least as many people as industry and the administration employs as many as either (Hugon, 1982; World Bank, 1979). Even combined, these sectors do not begin to absorb the numbers joining the work-force every year. The government controls or participates in many industries; the rest are dominated by foreign or non-Malagasy local capital. Of the seven major export-oriented enterprises one is government owned and one has 1 per cent Malagasy participation. The rest are non-Malagasy (British Overseas Board of Trade, 1984).

Population

There are many competing theories about the origin of the Malagasy population and the time of its arrival on the island (Deschamps, 1972; Kent, 1970; Kottak, 1980; Valette, 1974). The debate among them has so far proved inconclusive, and has acquired political overtones. The population, language and culture are a mixture in which Indonesian and African elements predominate with some Indian and Arab influences. The Malagasy language, spoken throughout the island, is largely Malayo-Polynesian, and linguistic analysis suggests that it came from the eastern part of the Indonesian archipelago, separating from the original some 1500 to 2000 years ago (Kottak, 1980, p. 40). There are two versions of the subsequent journey to Madagascar and settlement of the island. The first, which stresses the underlying unity of the population, argues that the proto-Malagasy migrated to the island over a long period of time, following a coastal route along India, across the southern tip of the Arabian peninsula and down the east coast of Africa, settling for varying periods along the way. According to this theory, the elements of the Malagasy mix arrived on the island at the same time, already blended. Current differences in dialect, customs and self-identification are simply variations on an underlying common theme.

The second theory stresses the diversity of the island's population and argues that those common elements that do exist were developed on the island from the interaction of different groups arriving at different times. The Malayo-Polynesians arrived first and made their way to the plateaux, conquering and absorbing the few indigenous groups they encountered. Later immigration and the slave trade brought the Africans, while the much less important traces of Indian and Arab influence are also the result of separate migrations. According to this theory differences in appearance, dialect and custom represent original differences that have been only imperfectly assimilated into a 'Malagasy' culture. More recently, attempts have been made to combine the two theories, giving most weight to the first. Competing theories do point to the combination of unity and diversity of

Madagascar's population and their competition to the degree to which unity and diversity are political constructs (Simon, 1974).

Ethnicity is also a manipulable construct. Most current analyses of 'the ethnic variable' emphasize the degree to which it is indeed a variable, changing over time and from context to context, depending on conscious political activities of mobilization and organization for its importance, and Madagascar is an excellent illustration of the argument (Young, 1982a). There are eighteen official 'ethnic groups' used as census categories, (see Table 2.1) but this form of identification hardly constitutes a key to Malagasy politics. The groups themselves are riddled with internal subdivisions and several are, in fact, political constructions created from smaller groups in the eighteenth and nineteenth centuries: the Merina, Sakalava and Betsimisaraka are the most important of these. Others, such as the Betsileo and Bara were first grouped together as administrative subdivisions of the nineteenth-century Merina empire. Variations in the basic Malagasy culture do exist, but the different dimensions do not co-vary or constitute cultural wholes connected to specific local groups. In general, locality and extended family are more important bases for solidary action than ethnicity.

Another common way of categorizing the Malagasy population, again clearly the result of a combination of historical events and political interest, is

Table 2.1 Malagasy 'ethnic groups'

Group name	% of population	Group name	% of population
Merina	26.1	Sihanaka	2.4
Betsimisaraka	14.9	Antanosy	2.3
Betsileo	12.0	Mahafaly	1.6
Tsimihety	7.2	Antaifasy	1.2
Sakalava	5.8	Makoa	1.1
Antandroy	5.3	Bezanozano	0.8
Antaisaka	5.0	Antakarana	0.6
Tanala	3.8	Antambahoaka	0.4
Antaimoro	3.4	Others	1.1
Bara	3.3		

Source: Area Handbook, 1973, based on figures from the Institut National de la Statistique. Thompson (1987) gives the following figures, based on 1974 and 1975 estimates, for the major groups: Merina, 26.2 per cent; Betsimisaraka, 14.9 per cent; Betsileo, 12.1 per cent. Tsimihety, 7.3 per cent; Sakalava, 6.2 per cent; Antandroy, 5.4 per cent; Antaisaka, 5.3 per cent.

the distinction between *côtier* and Merina or *côtier* and people of the plateaux. The Betsileo occupy an ambiguous position, being of the plateaux but not Merina and the varying circumstances under which one or the other aspect of this dual identity is important illustrate the manipulability of the construct. The distinction between Merina and *côtier* (many of whom do not live anywhere near a coast) is the result of the existence and politics of the Merina empire, the differential distribution of education that dates from imperial times, and the policies of the colonial regime and its successor government who tried to mobilize support by portraying themselves as defenders against 'Merina domination'. The conflict cannot be reduced either to ethnic or class competition, but has elements of both (see Tronchon, 1975. The Merina are sometimes, erroneously, called Hova, one of the castes into which the group is divided).

Most groups are further divided into endogamous castes. A basic division between descendants of slaves and descendants of free men runs through the majority of ethnic groups, and often the free castes are further divided into nobles and commoners. In societies that had monarchs, noble and commoner castes are also divided according to the closeness of specific clans to the royal family. These traditional hierarchies have interacted with subsequent systems of stratification in complex ways that vary from group to group and region to region. The freeman–slave division has been the one most often translated into modern economic status (see, for example, Bloch, 1971).

Some analysts combine ethnic, traditional and modern stratification to argue the importance of a 'Merina bourgeoisie' composed of descendants of noble and important commoner families who dominated nineteenth century Merina society by their control of land, slaves and trade (Archer, 1976). This position has been perpetuated as slaves became sharecroppers, money was invested in real estate and small businesses, and preferred access to education was translated into high positions in the colonial and post-colonial administrations. Like the 'Merina–*côtier*' division this is a political as well as analytic category, with enough reality at its basis to make attacks on the 'Merina bourgeoisie' an occasionally useful basis for political mobilization. However, the economic and political development of Madagascar, especially since independence, has reduced the usefulness of the concept as an analytic category. One of the major changes in Malagasy society since the mid-1950s, continuing and if anything accelerating since the 1972 Revolution and the 1975 adoption of Marxism–Leninism has been the accession of Malagasies from all regions to what might be roughly called modern bourgeois status. The whole interest of the period lies, not in a triumphant self-perpetuation of the upper classes of Antananarivo, but in the interplay of various lines of cleavage as changing coalitions formed, dissolved and reformed in the pursuit of political and economic power.

Early Political History

The eighteenth and nineteenth centuries in Madagascar were a period of multiple attempts at state-building, increased interaction among different political units in the island, and growing contact between these units and the European dominated international economic and political system. The processes were interrelated. Internal factors were an important element in state-building but the desire to profit from growing international trade also played a role in the development first of the Sakalava and Betsimisaraka federations on the west and east coasts, and later of the Betsileo and Merina monarchies in the interior. (For accounts of early state-building in the non-Merina groups of Madagascar, see Feeley-Harnik, 1982; Kent, 1970; Kottak, 1980.) This trade became important in the mid-eighteenth century with the introduction of sugar production in Réunion and the development of the plantation economy of the Mascarenes and, while it included some agricultural commodities, it increasingly took the form of the exchange of slaves taken in raids on neighbouring groups for a range of goods, including weapons. As a result, participation in and domination of the trade became a matter of political as well as economic survival for the Malagasy groups involved (Campbell, 1981). Connections with European powers, especially Britain and France, were used both in the competition among political units on the island and by aspiring dominant groups within societies. The outside powers' interest in the island varied with their changing economic and strategic interests in the area until the end of the century, when it was caught in the overall scramble for African possessions. Madagascar was annexed by the French in 1896.

Of the various states that developed in pre-colonial Madagascar, the Merina empire, whose capital was Antananarivo, came to dominate. Although studies of other groups make it clear that the processes of centralization, stratification, extraction and ideological manipulation that were involved in the creation of the Merina monarchy also occurred in these units, it was the Merina rulers who developed a form of organization that most closely resembled that of a modern state. More specifically, the consolidation of the monarchy involved the transfer of power and legitimacy from local units to the centre, the development of a stratification system whose upper levels owed their position to their relationships with the monarchy, and an attempt to control other sources of power in the society. The specific changes all contributed to the separation of state from society. (There is an abundant and growing literature on the Merina empire. Some basic sources are Callet, n.d. Délivré, 1974; Kent, 1970; Raison-Jourde, 1983; Bloch, 1971; Berg, 1981.)

The basic pre-monarchical political unit of Merina society was the *fokonolona*. The vagueness of the literal meaning of the term, 'a group of people' corresponds to an elasticity in the concept itself, which originally meant a group of people claiming descent from a common ancestor. By the end of the eighteenth century it had come to mean the human community inhabiting a particular geographic area, usually a village. Land belonged to the *fokonolona* rather than the individual, members owed it labour, and it had extensive powers of social control including the right to impose the death penalty. *Fokonolona* decisions were made by the *ray aman'dreny* (fathers and mothers, in practice a group of male elders) of the community. This was not exactly village democracy, since the *fokonolona* were stratified by age, sex, relative prosperity, and the overlying caste system. However, power was embedded in its social context, and amenable to the countervailing forces available in a face-to-face society. The creation of a centralized state entailed the transfer to the monarch of the *fokonolona*'s control over both land and people. In particular the duty of the individual to participate in works of common interest and in the defence of the *fokonolona* was transferred to the central state. These changes, the first 'reform of the *fokonolona*', marked the beginnings of a change in the institution from an instrument of self-government to an instrument for central control of local areas and extraction of their resources. As the monarchy expanded beyond the boundaries of Imerina and became the Merina empire, the system, or variants of it, was introduced in the conquered territories. The fact of conquest added to the adversarial nature of the relationship created by the extractive activities of the state. By the end of the nineteenth century, as the resources of the empire were strained by its attempts at further expansion and the requirements of defence against the French, its demands on the local units increased at the same time as its ability to maintain local peace and security declined. As a result, the *fokonolona* turned in on themselves and attempted to revive the functions of self-policing and self-defence that they had performed before the days of the monarchy. This history left a lasting contradiction in the nature of the *fokonolona* and other local units. They were both the means through which central governments attempted to control the behaviour of the population, and a means by which the population attempted to withdraw from contact with central authority and assert its own version of Malagasy rule, or local autonomy (see, for example, Condominas, 1960; Serre Ratsimandisa, 1978; de Gaudusson, 1978b).

Pre-monarchical Merina society was also divided into four endogamous castes: *andriana*, or nobles, *hova*, or commoners, and two slave castes, the *mainty* and the *andevo*. The creation of a centralized state both strengthened and complicated the existing system of stratification. Internal and external trade increased as the monarchy extended its control to the coast, and large fortunes developed, particularly among those who were able to use political power to secure monopolies of trade in various commodities. Many came from *andriana* families, but a class of wealthy *hova* emerged, and joined the *andriana* in sharing in—and fighting over—political power (Campbell, 1981; Ellis, 1980). A series of palace coups in the 1860s shifted actual control of the empire from the monarch to this group. Access to the resources created by increased trade and the growing powers of the state were not limited to the group at the top. A commercial class also developed, and middle-level state officials used booty from the perennial military campaigns, opportunities for bribery, and the retention of tax money and fines to ensure that public service, still formally unremunerated, at least did not impoverish them. One result was a growing corruption that was impossible for the rulers in Antananarivo to control, especially since they too engaged in it on a larger scale.

The latter half of the nineteenth century saw the intensification of an island-wide system of interaction, in which the Merina empire attempted to extend its boundaries, the other groups of the island either resisted or were absorbed, and foreign powers came to play an increasingly important role in the politics of the island. The Merina state had early developed a 'British connection' to counterbalance the more insistent pressures of the French, and since 1817 British officers had helped train the imperial army, members of the London Missionary Society had established an educational system, and a treaty with Britain had recognized the Merina claim to control the whole island. The most dramatic incident in the developing importance of foreign alliances was the 1869 baptism of Queen, Prime Minister, and much of the royal court into Protestant Christianity. This conversion was accompanied by a series of other changes that included the adoption of 'cabinet government' with formal ministries and the drafting of a written legal code. A major goal of the changes was to give the kingdom an aura of international respectability that would identify it with other nation-states protected by international law and distinguish it from colonizable 'savages'. The conversion to Christianity had internal advantages as well. The missionary school system was already closely linked to the monarchy and a major source of its bureaucrats; the adoption of Protestantism as a state religion made possible an even tighter control of the system. However, the strategy also had its costs. Internationally, it aligned the Merina empire with the British against the French and made the international survival of the state dependent on British goodwill. Internally the change deepened the division of the elite into those identified with the British connection, those who favoured ties with the French and those who rejected such a radical abandonment of the traditional bases of the monarchy. The change also alienated the Catholics in the population and weakened the monarchy's claim to legitimacy as the summit of a system of traditional ceremonies and the crucial link between the population and the sphere of the sacred (see Raison-Jourde, 1983).

The Merina empire never achieved its ambition of controlling the whole island. At its height it controlled, in addition to the central province of Imerina, Betsileo territory as far south as Ambalavao, and most of the territory between the plateaux and the east coast. It also controlled the port of Mahajanga and a corridor leading from Imerina to the port, and maintained garrisons at other west and south coast ports. It was never able to conquer the Sakalava to the west, or the diverse groups of the south. Under pressure from the Merina, the Sakalava and other coastal groups developed a countervailing 'French connection' that often involved trading recognition of a French protectorate for weapons and other supplies.

The French had claimed jurisdiction over all or part of the island since the beginning of the century, and these claims were pressed with growing insistence under the Third Republic in response to the development of imperialist competition in Europe. The activities of a disparate alliance of Marseilles-based commercial companies and deputies from Réunion, who saw Madagascar as a potential area of settlement, pressed successive French governments to 'do something' about Madagascar. A first Franco-Malagasy war in 1883–5 ended with important Malagasy concessions, including an agreement to pay the French government an indemnity of ten million francs, and after 1885, Merina internal and external politics were dominated by attempts to prevent total subjugation. The weakness and divisions of the Merina elite contributed to the demise of the Merina state, but to a large degree this state and the other states and societies of Madagascar were simply caught in the wave of late nineteenth-century imperialism. Reliance on British protection proved vain; in 1890 Britain and France signed a treaty exchanging French recognition of British control over Zanzibar for British acceptance of the French claim to Madagascar. In 1895 the French embarked on another war of conquest, occupied Antananarivo, and declared a protectorate. In 1896 the Merina monarchy was abolished, the Queen was exiled, and a formal law of annexation added Madagascar to France's African colonies.

The Period of French Occupation

The goals of the French colonizers included the destruction of the power of the 'Merina oligarchy', the development of a profitable economy, and the location or creation of a group of political intermediaries loyal to the colonial regime. The pursuit of these goals often involved conflicting policies and met with only partial success. The first priority was the dismantling of the Merina state and the destruction of the bases of its elites. The French took over the summit of the state, dissolved the army and reconstituted the administration under French direction. The economic bases of the oligarchy were undermined by the abolition of slavery and the distribution of land confiscated from opponents of the conquest to former slaves. Measures requiring the use of French in the schools reduced the importance of the Protestant education system, which used Malagasy and English, and led to a decline in the school population of Imerina. The corollary of the attack on the Merina state was to be an alliance with 'coastal' populations and the underclasses of the plateaux, to whom the French presented themselves as liberators from Merina despotism. However, pursuit of this goal conflicted with the desire to limit state expenditures and to draw a profit from the new colony. The economic goals of the colonial power led to the introduction of forced labour, and the seizure of land for distribution to settlers and commercial companies, policies that destroyed any favourable impression created by the abolition of slavery. The first Governor-General, Gallieni, attempted to redress the regional imbalance in education by establishing secondary schools in coastal cities, but his successor closed them as an economic measure. Subsequent institutions such as the medical school at Befelatanana and the Ecole Le Myre de Vilers, established to train Malagasy auxiliaries for the medical service and the administration, were located in Antananarivo. As a result, the state education system reinforced, rather than counteracted, the regional imbalance of the existing system.

Politically, the French at first attempted to follow what Gallieni called the *politique des races*, a policy of governing the territory through the traditional institutions of each group. This policy met with considerable resistance since local rulers often refused to be turned into subordinates in the French administration system (see, for example Feeley-Harnik, 1984). In the end, most local authorities were removed and either replaced with more malleable substitutes, or their positions were simply abolished and a policy of direct rule instituted with, at the lower levels of the administration, Merina and to a lesser degree Betsileo officials. These policies had the effect of exacerbating existing divisions without necessarily having the favourable results the French wanted. The colonizers warned the Malagasy of the dangers of Merina domination, but the concrete result of their policies was a perpetuation of the differences in access to education and state position that modernized the domination and extended it to the whole island. It was not until after the 1947 rebellion that the French were willing to invest significant resources in the development of regional elites.

Building a Colonial Economy

French economic policy was designed to make Madagascar a profitable colony for France overall but especially for the two groups most interested in the colonization of the island, the large commercial companies and prospective settlers, mainly from Réunion. A prohibitive tariff ended trade with former partners such as Britain and the United States and, at the time of independence in 1960, nearly 75 per cent of Madagascar's trade was with the franc zone (Gendarme, 1962). A system of monopolies and oligopolies, linked by formal ties of investment in each other and by informal social ties, took over the economy. The Havraise, which had a monopoly of shipping to and from the island, also had a dominant interest in the two major banks. Three commercial companies, the Marseillaise, the Lyonnaise, and the Société de l'Emyrne (a branch of the Rochfortaise) handled the wholesale end of the export–import trade. Their business practices were to earn them the title of 'the three crocodiles of the island'. Indo-Pakistani and Chinese middlemen formed the link between the producer and the companies. The profits of the system came from trade rather than production, and it was largely based on the control of credit facilities. The system survived independence, and was described in 1966 by a European Community report as

a strongly hierarchical structure, linked by credit. The commercial companies get credit on the best terms and at the beginning of the season (for collecting agricultural products). This enables them to organize the chains of debt that link them to the wholesalers, the wholesalers to the local merchant, and the merchant to the producer ... conditions of credit become increasingly onerous the closer one gets to the peasant. [EEC, 1966, p. 76.]

At the bottom of the system, the peasants were often permanently in debt.

In agricultural policy the French never decided whether the products whose export was to provide the basis of the system should be produced by large plantations, small- and medium-scale settlers, or by the Malagasy themselves (Desjeux, 1979). After the conquest large blocs of land, especially along the east and north coasts, were expropriated and granted as large concessions to the commercial companies and in smaller units to settlers. The concessions never did produce on the scale planned. Some were never exploited and others were abandoned when agricultural depressions led to losses for companies and wiped out settlers. Malagasy also began to enter production for the market, and in some areas were required by law to cultivate cash crops. This policy was hotly opposed by the settlers, and to a lesser degree by the companies, since their profits depended on a supply of cheap Malagasy labour, a supply that was contingent on restricting the opportunities to make money elsewhere.

In fact, the whole system depended on the ability of the colonial bureaucracy to get labour out of an unwilling population. The importance of the issue and the difficulties encountered meant that more ordinances regulating labour were passed in Madagascar than in any other French colony (Freeley-Harnick, 1984). The most direct method of dealing with the problem was forced labour, instituted in 1897 and retained until 1946. Technically the labour was to be used for 'works of general interest' but often, through various semi-legal or illegal arrangements, it was used to provide settlers and plantation managers with unpaid workers. A poll tax and taxes on houses and cattle were also imposed, in order to 'liberate' a work-force by creating a need for money. Famine in the south, and food deficits in areas of expropriation and cash crop production also drove people to seek employment outside their regions.

French economic policy not only created a classic, dominated and dependent colonial economy in Madagascar, it also created a variety of economic regions. The east and north coasts were regions of cash crop production with food deficits. The south was increasingly impoverished and served as a pool of unskilled labour that migrated all over the island, but particularly to the plantations of the north and the ports of Antseranana and Toamasina. By the 1950s between 25 per cent and 50 per cent of its active male population was outside the region, depending on the time of year and local circumstance (xxx, 1971b). The plateaux were also a labour reserve, but of educated labour for the lower levels of the colonial administration (Althabe, 1980). They furnished some rice for the food deficit areas, but in general neither agriculture nor industry received much attention. The plateaux's higher standard of living came from administrative salaries and services provided to the European community of Antananarivo. The west was the most isolated region, and was also undeveloped, but not as impoverished as the south.

Another result of the imposition of the colonial system was the introduction of new bases of division and the complication of old patterns of stratification. In rural areas, the French administration followed a variety of policies designed to identify and reward local intermediaries, usually grouped under the general term of *notable*. Their privileges were not always great, but even being appointed to organize rather than being obliged to participate in a forced labour group had its rewards. The significance of *notable* status became even greater after 1947 when the colonial administration began to expend more resources on this group. Agricultural 'development' policies singled them out, and educational opportunities and posts in the administration went to their children (Desjeux, 1979). In areas like the southeastern coast, a class of Malagasy planters developed as did a class of small-scale merchants.

The situation on the plateaux was more complicated. Merina *andriana* and *hova* had collectively lost power but maintained it on an individual basis as they continued in or moved into administrative and commercial opportunities. Wealthier families lost the part of their wealth that was in the form of slaves, but via the sharecropping system were able to maintain much of the essence of this source of wealth. Several maintained and added to their positions by moving into small-scale commerce and liberal professions such as pharmacy and medicine. Freed slaves were usually still economically dependent and the introduction of forced labour and heavy taxes only increased this dependency. Individual *mainty* and *andevo* did move up in the system as local authorities and agents at lower levels of the administration, but if anything the difference between freeman and former slave grew during the colonial period as members of free castes moved into cities and continued to benefit from the restricted educational opportunities (Bloch, 1971). The growth of cities during this period was steady but not explosive, and there was no development either of a large-scale permanent work-force or of a large group of urban unemployed. The main areas that developed anything even approaching a proletariat, however loosely defined, were the port of Toamasina, the rail line linking the port and Antananarivo, and the port and naval repair facilities at Antseranana.

From Resistance to Rebellion: Nationalist Movements to 1947

By the time of independence, Madagascar had gained the reputation of being a 'docile' colony. However, an examination of the political history of the colonial period shows a continuing resistance that culminated in the revolt of 1947, and a continued countervailing repression. It was this repression and in particular the trauma of 1947 that were responsible for the docility of 1958. Armed resistance to the imposition of colonial rule occurred throughout the island. The revolt of the *menalamba*, whose goal was the replacement of the new foreign rulers with a purified Merina monarchy, lasted from 1895 to 1897 (Ellis, 1985). The south was not 'pacified' until 1904, After attempts at primary resistance had been defeated, anti-colonial movements continued, but in what Munslow terms 'unequal but parallel' fashion, and with little contact with each other (Munslow, 1983). At the village level there was both tacit and overt resistance to intrusions of state power, while in the cities, and particularly among the educated, there were demands first for inclusion in the state and later for the return of state power to Malagasy hands. The two sets of activity did not connect in any real sense until 1947, when their interactions gave the revolt much of its force and complexity.

Peasant resistance to the colonial system took many forms, not all of them overt or even easily distinguishable. The colonial system itself introduced a multitude of new requirements, including taxes, forced labour, and a myriad of laws and regulations. It was easy to be in contravention of one or the other of them and the dividing line between inadvertent law breaking, unavoidable law breaking—taxes were collected in spite of famine and countervening family responsibilities—and deliberate refusal to obey was not always clear-cut. The role of inertia as passive resistance, the role of maintaining newly illegal traditional practices such as cattle-raiding and *tanety* culture, and the retreat into the cult of the ancestors all had an element of resistance to them (Feeley-Harnik, 1984). Certainly the French authorities were quick to see challenges to their authority in these practices. 'The nationalist movement has never completely disappeared,' a French governor wrote to his replacement, 'although it has never stirred the mass of the population, it appears from time to time in some areas . . . by systematic delays in the payment of taxes and by a more or less systematic use of the power of inertia' (Koerner, 1974, p. 438). The colonial period was also punctuated by sporadic peasant revolts and open resistance to specific laws and administrative acts: land surveys that were seen as preludes to expropriation, tax collection in times of famine, abusive individual administrators. These revolts occurred in isolation from each other and, given the balance of forces, were easily controlled.

The resistance of the educated elite was harder to control. A written national language freed them from the need to communicate in the language of the colonizer, the previously independent and internationally recognized status of the Merina monarchy served as a rallying point, and the already existing organizational network of Merina society in particular, including the Protestant parishes and school system, gave the movement a ready-made communications network. The French brought in a series of laws designed to deal with the problem: the *indigénat*, pre-publication censorship of newspapers in languages other than French that included a blanket interdiction of all discussion of local politics; and the banning of meetings other than family and traditional gatherings. In general, any activity likely to have a 'disturbing' effect on public opinion was forbidden.

These laws made the constitution of openly political organizations like parties or unions impossible, and gave the Malagasy nationalist movement several of its important characteristics. Much of its organization occurred underground, in the form of at least nominally secret societies. Secret societies formed for one purpose or another had been characteristic under the Merina monarchy, although given the closely knit character of upper class Merina society their existence and membership were generally not unknown (Archer, 1976, pp. 29–30). The movements also used non-political organizations as vehicles, and the French suspicion that the Protestant parishes were hotbeds of 'subversion' had considerable basis in fact. The nationalist movement also tended to be highly personalized, organized around a restricted number of leaders, based on the personal links they were able to exploit or create. These leaders could, sporadically, mobilize a mass following, but it was not until after 1945 that they were able or had an incentive to organize it.

The nationalist movement at this level went through several phases. Immediately after the occupation it was limited to members of *hova* and *andriana* families connected to the monarchy. They retreated into literary societies and parish organizations and dreamed of a restoration, a project that would have limited their own appeal had they sought adherents outside their own circles and that became increasingly unrealistic (Randrianja, 1983). An organization with a larger audience, and the declared purpose of expanding Malagasy participation in the existing system, was founded in 1913. Nominally a secret society, the VVS included members from the elite of the capital, but also from other regions, and was centred in the new medical school at Befelatanana. In 1915 it was accused of plotting an uprising and was dissolved, those accused of membership being sent to the prison island of Nosy Lava or to assigned residence outside the capital. The dissolution of the VVS and even more the end of the First World War broadened the social and geographic range of nationalist politics. The exile of the VVS leaders to outlying regions forced them to widen their perspective, while the development of a small urban work-force and the return of large numbers of *anciens combattants* gave them a new audience. The inter-war nationalist movement concentrated on trying to secure the abolition of the *indigénat*, claiming for Malagasies the rights of French citizenship. In the post-Bolshevik revolution atmosphere, the colonial regime was quick to identify any opposition as part of the red menace, an identification that was furthered by the involvement of French settlers who were members of the French communist party in support of the nationalist movement (Koerner, 1974, p. 452). The identification and alliance were curious, since the nationalists were still largely Merina of good and even aristocratic families. However, the equation of nationalist politics with communism made this group one of the main recruiting grounds for radical politicians, an anomaly that outlasted the colonial period. In the period between the wars they were simply one wing of a nationalist movement with leaders of diverse origins, opinions and tactics. Their activities increased during the brief liberalization that accompanied the period of the Popular Front, but the outbreak of war in 1939 led to a re-imposition of the colonial system and an intensification of its rigour. The end of the war saw another period of political activity that was once more cut short, this time by the rebellion of 1947 and the repression that followed it.

The rebellion had its immediate roots in the changes the war created in the colonial system and in the nature and goals of the nationalist movements. The war led to a major disruption in the French occupation. In 1940, after some initial hesitation, the local colonial administration aligned itself with the Vichy regime. In response the British invaded and occupied the island, but then handed it over to the Free French, to the disappointment of many nationalists who had hoped that they, rather than the 'unreliable' French, would profit from the British intervention. The Free French treated the island as a reservoir of men and raw materials for their war effort, drastically increasing the level of extraction practised by the system. To the disruptions created by these demands were added the hardships that resulted from the black market that developed around the system of rationing and official control of rice supplies.

The combination of disruption of the system and its re-imposition in an even more severe form created conditions for widespread unrest. To these were added hopes for change created by events in the last part of the war. The

United Nations Charter and the Brazzaville declaration were read and commented on. Echoes appear in a 1945 declaration of a nationalist leader:

The great powers have resolved to create a new order ... in which force will no longer dominate the world ... a new order in which the people will be sovereign and free to govern themselves. A new order that will respect the dignity and rights of human beings without distinction of race, color, or religion. [Tronchon, 1974, p. 134.]

In Madagascar forced labour was abolished and the laws forbidding political activity were relaxed. A restricted number of Malagasies were added to the electorate in a separate 'Second college' and parties formed to send delegates to Paris to the two Contituent Assemblies and later to the French legislature.

Under these circumstances, the nationalist movements radicalized their goals and extended their base. The elections to the first Constituent Assembly returned two well-known nationalist leaders from Antananarivo, Raseta and Ravoahangy. In Paris they recruited Jacques Rabemananjara, a Paris-based poet who had little personal following in Madagascar but who, as a Catholic from the east coast, provided useful religious and regional balance. The three founded a party, the MDRM (*Mouvement de la Rénovation Malgache*) and returned to Madagascar to organize. The resulting party was a composite of different movements with varying goals, differing views on strategy, and differing visions of the common goal, independence. Returned *anciens combattants* furnished much of the middle-level leadership between the top and the electorate. Also adhering to the party were two 'secret societies', PANAMA and JINA, formed during the war to resist the colonial system, with geographic centres on the east coast, but with adherents all over the island and in all of the groups that gravitated around the nationalist movement. *Anciens combattants* and secret societies in particular had other goals beyond simply re-electing the three deputies, and under their impetus the party pushed its organization beyond the still restricted electorate, establishing peasant cooperatives and organizing workers (Camacho, 1981). The party's organization covered the island, but it was strongest in three areas that, geographically, often coincided: traditional bases of nationalist activity including Antananarivo, Antseranana and Toamasina including the rail lines; areas that had been heavily hit by requisitions of manpower and to which many *anciens combattants* had returned, mainly the plateaux and the east coast; and areas that had been most heavily affected by the exactions of the colonial system itself, the plantation and settler areas of the east coast. The west coast and the south were areas of party weakness.

The French administration was quick to respond to the threat, and as early as 1946 many local MDRM organizers and most of the leaders of JINA and PANAMA were under arrest. In addition, the administration encouraged the formation of an anti-MDRM Malagasy party, PADESM (Parti des Déshérités de Madagascar), playing on fears of a return of the 'Merina oligarchy' (hence the 'disinherited' in the party name). The system of local rule by *notables*, revived in 1944, enabled the administration to locate and recruit 'reliable' Malagasies. The party sought an audience on the coast and among the former slave castes of Imerina, but in general was strongest in the west coast and its hinterland. However, it was not able to counter the MDRM in national level elections, and the three founders of the nationalist party returned to Paris as deputies to the Second Constituent Assembly where they continued their pursuit of Malagasy autonomy. They were not successful. The 'French Union' created by the new constitution of the Fourth Republic was a modernized version of the old empire, and Madagascar's status remained that of the other African colonies rather than the semi-autonomy granted to other French possessions like Vietnam or Syria. Attempts to have the 1896 annexation law repealed were no more successful.

The Rebellion

In the night of 29 March 1947 armed groups of Malagasies attacked French administrative centres, French-owned plantations and Malagasies considered to be collaborators of the French regime along the east coast and in parts of the eastern plateaux. It was December 1948 before the revolt was completely repressed, and by then over 50,000 people had died, either as a direct result of the fighting or from hunger and exposure as the inhabitants of whole villages fled into the eastern forest to escape the danger. Tronchon gives the figure of 550 non-Malagasy dead (350 soldiers, 200 civilians). Figures for the number of Malagasy dead vary widely. In 1948 the commander of the French forces stated that over 89,000 had died, in 1949 the High Commissioner put the figure at over 100,000. An official 'enquiry' held from 1950-2 arrived at a figure of 11,200, but all subsequent commentaries on the rebellion have taken the higher figures as being more accurate (Tronchon, 1974, pp. 73-4). The repression was severe, and in many parts of the coast the state of siege was not lifted until 1956. The colonial administration declared the rebellion an MDRM plot to restore Merina domination and arrested the three deputies along with hundreds of party members and people such as Protestant pastors who came from categories suspected of MDRM sympathies. Trials and executions continued until 1954. Two of the MDRM deputies were condemned to death and the third, Rabemananjara, to life imprisonment. The sentences were later commuted to exile, an exile that lasted until 1960.

There are several competing theories about the genesis and nature of the rebellion, including the colonial thesis of a Merina-led MDRM plot and a counter thesis of a provocation by the colonial authorities designed to give them an excuse to eliminate the nationalist party. In his study of the revolt, Jacques Tronchon rejects both theses. He argues that the rebellion was the work of the secret societies affiliated with the MDRM, recruiting leaders from the *anciens combattants*, and port and railroad workers, with followers recruited from villages throughout the region. Nearly forty years later it is extremely difficult to offer definitive proof of any theory, but Tronchon's arguments are plausible. The rebellion was too serious and too deeply rooted in Malagasy grievances and political beliefs to be a simple creation of the administration. The MDRM deputies did have a connection with the revolt. They knew that some sort of uprising was being planned (as did the colonial authorities), and on 29 March sent a telegram to various parts of Madagascar urging their followers to stay calm. The deputies had much to lose from a rebellion and the note of panic in their telegram suggests that they knew this. Although their attempts to bring about Malagasy independence by parliamentary means had failed, these had been only first attempts and MDRM strength in Madagascar gave the deputies a strong base from which to continue their efforts. Tronchon argues that the nature of the connection between the MDRM and the rebellion lies in the nature of the party itself. It was not a hierarchical structure, but rather a coalition of other organizations and personal networks, some of whose components were much more sceptical of the possibilities of peaceful independence and much readier to resort to violence than others. Tronchon also rejects the thesis of a Merina-led revolt. The leadership, and many of the fighters came from all over the island, and the fighting was fiercest, and lasted the longest, in the territory of the Tanala, noted for their previous successful resistance to the Merina empire. The revolt was centred in those areas of the east coast that had been most affected by the colonial system of land, labour, and rice expropriation, that were best suited to guerrilla warfare and where the organizational coverage of the secret societies was extensive (Tronchon, 1974, *Lumière*, 19 March, 1967).

Tronchon also poses, but does not fully answer, a final question: was the rebellion a war of independence or a popular revolt against state structures? It was probably both. In several areas the rebels attacked not only French and Malagasy colonial administrators, but also other symbols of alien *fanjakana* such as merchants and teachers. However, the goal of the leaders was an independent Malagasy nation with a Malagasy controlled state. This combination of elite attempts to conquer the state and popular rejection of state power in all its forms was to reappear in later African rebellions (Welch, 1980) and in the Malagasy revolution of 1972. The 1947 revolt left a mark on Malagasy political life. The demonstrators of 1972 portrayed themselves as the heirs of the martyrs of 1947, and an observer of this second revolt remarked that the involvement of many of the leaders of the First Republic in the 1947 repression was 'the original sin that damned it from the start.' (Leymarie, 1973).

3   The Construction and Collapse of the First Republic

A Successful Decolonization?

Supporters of the First Republic considered it a perfect example of successful decolonization, in that 'the accession of the Malagasy people to full independence took place calmly, without animosity to the former colonial power, and without sacrificing on the altar of triumphant xenophobia the legitimate interests of minorities living on the island' (Spacensky, 1970a, p. 79; sources on the First Republic include Thompson & Adloff, 1965; Cadoux, 1969; Spacensky, 1970b). The interests of these minorities were so well respected that the First Republic is also a classic example of a neo-colonial regime in which an elite, selected and prepared by the departing colonial power, moves into government positions, exchanging its protection of the interests of the former colonial power for that power's protection of its own position.

Although the French regime paid considerable attention to the cultivation of political support after 1947, it did not seriously consider the possibility of preparing a successor elite until the mid-1950s, and the party and regime that were the result of its efforts showed the marks of hasty improvisation (Covell, 1974). The task was complicated by the general disintegration of Malagasy political life after 1947: the continuing state of siege inhibited any attempts at organization as did heavy administrative surveillance. The MDRM had been dissolved, and PADESM simply disappeared. Elections continued to be held, but candidates concentrated on local issues and ran as *sans partis*. There were no national elections, and even in elections to the French National Assembly, for which the island was divided into three districts, candidates ran as individuals supported by their own personalistic election committees. In the period immediately after 1947, the colonial power concentrated on building up local support. Development funds were channelled increasingly to agriculture, and increasingly to Malagasy rather than French producers. A series of reorganizations of village level government reinforced the links between local administrators, village *notables* whose selection was ratified by the administrators and the use of development funds, whose allocation was determined by the two groups (Desjeux, 1979). The Malagasy levels of the administration were also the object of some attention. A post-1947 ordinance allowed Malagasy administrators to be fired for 'suspected bad moral character'. This provided the basis for a purge of administrators suspected of unreliability and their replacement by more certain supporters of the regime. Links with PADESM, and origins in the west, were among the guarantees of reliability. Finally, geographical quotas for scholarships to universities and training courses in France were introduced to show that the regime was attentive to the needs of coastal populations.

It was the impending passage of the 1956 *loi cadre* that forced the colonial administration to take more explicit actions to establish an acceptable Malagasy-led regime. The choice of the administration for party founder and national leader fell on the western electoral district's deputy, Philibert Tsiranana. Tsiranana had several qualifications for the role beyond his personal qualities of intelligence and energy. His reliability had been proven in Madagascar where, after a brief membership in a Groupe d'Etudes Communistes, he had been one of the founders of PADESM, and in France where he had rejected the existing Malagasy students' organization as too nationalist and too Merina, and had started a rival organization 'where the *côtiers* would feel more at home'. He had been in France in 1947, so he could not be accused of personal involvement in the repression and therefore would not be totally unacceptable to nationalist elements. He had joined the French Socialist party during his stay in France, and by a fortunate coincidence the Governor-General of Madagascar was also a socialist. The fact that Tsiranana was opposed to immediate independence as contrary to the interests of the coastal populations and had proposed a twenty- to thirty-year transition period was taken as further evidence of his willingness to maintain a close connection with France should independence come more rapidly (see Tsiranana's reminiscences—*RFEPA*, April, 1970). In 1952 Tsiranana was elected to the Mahajanga provincial assembly and was later chosen as one of the assembly's delegates to the territorial assembly. In January 1956 he became a deputy in the French National Assembly, and in December of that year he called together a group with similar views to found the Social Democratic Party, or PSD.

The party was formed just in time for the March 1957 provincial elections. There was not to be another national election until after the granting of full independence in 1960, and the PSD's growth at the local level occurred *after* it was firmly entrenched as a governing party. (The party had 45 sections in 1958, the year Madagascar gained autonomy within the French Union; 816 sections in 1960, the year of independence; and 2,784 sections in 1963 (*Nouvelles Malgaches*, 1963). In the period between 1957 and 1960 the party grew largely by incorporating important local leaders who had already registered their own electoral successes and by using the Malagachization of the territorial administration both to reward its followers and to forge alliances with local *notables*. One result of this strategy was an explosion in the size of the administration, which grew from 32,476 in 1958 to 50,344 in 1960 (Maestre, 1968). Another was the nature of the party itself: a loose collection of regional barons at the top and local *notables* at the bottom, firmly identified with state power: the party of the *fanjakana*.

The PSD also benefited from the failure of its opposition to unite. In part this was the result of PSD control of the only nation-wide organizational network, the administration, and its liberal use of this control to discourage opponents, but the fault also lay with the opposition which was divided along personal, religious, regional and ideological lines. Thirty-seven parties contested the 1957 provincial assembly elections, many of them destined to be absorbed by the PSD. Only two parties survived this process, the AKFM and Monima, and only the AKFM was the result of an attempt to unite the diverse opposition movements.

The AKFM (Ankoton 'ny Kongresi 'ni Fahaleovantenan Madagasikara or Independence Congress Party of Madagascar) was the result of a congress held in Toamasina in 1958 to unite parties opposed to a 'yes' vote in the referendum on the French Fifth Republic constitution. (Rejection of the constitution would mean immediate independence.) After the referendum, in which, not surprisingly, the 'yes' vote supported by the PSD and the administration won, several of the parties united to form the AKFM. The party recruited from non-Catholic nationalist groups throughout the island, with its areas of greatest strength being Antseranana and the plateaux from Antananarivo to Fianarantsoa. The party's top leadership was Antananarivo based, and divided into 'pure nationalist' and 'scientific socialist' wings with the President, Richard Andriamanjato, playing a mediating role between them. He was himself from a noble Merina family and pastor of one of the capital's most fashionable churches, but had also been responsible for creating links between the AEOM and the World Youth Movement when he was a student in France. Andriamanjato was representative of the ambiguity of the party, which recruited from the conservative bourgeois and petit-bourgeois circles of Antananarivo with revolutionary rhetoric that attacked imperialism and advocated state socialism (Leymarie, 1979; for a portrait by one of the party's Marxists see Rabesahala, 1972). Throughout the First Republic the AKFM led an eventful existence as a tolerated opposition. It controlled the town of Antananarivo, where Andriamanjato became mayor in 1959 and one of three AKFM deputies in the Malagasy National Assembly after 1960, but the PSD used its powers to push the party out of the countryside and to challenge it in other cities. However, it did continue to exist and contest elections. In part this was because Tsiranana enjoyed pointing to the contrast between his 'multi-party democracy' and the one-party states of continental Africa. It is also true that although the First Republic was an oppressive regime it was not, and until 1971 did not aspire to be, a violently repressive one. Moreover the existence of the AKFM and especially of its leader served to keep the PSD on its toes. A brilliant orator in both French and Malagasy, born of a noble Antananarivo family, and surrounded by well-known local communists, Andriamanjato was precisely the embodiment of the dominating aristocratic communistic Merina the PSD liked to warn its adherents about.

Monima (Mouvement National pour l'Indépendance de Madagascar), the only other opposition party to survive through the First Republic, had a contrasting set of strengths and weaknesses (Althabe, 1972). A regional party, it never had the national coverage of the AKFM, but it was the one party the PSD was never able to oust from the provinces. Its leader, Monja Jaona, was also a contrast to Andriamanjato. He had begun as an itinerant evangelical preacher in Toliara, Madagascar's poorest province. An outstanding orator, although in a quite different style from that of Andriamanjato, Monja Jaona was more known for political activism than education, and for irrascibility and bluntness than elegance. This activism found expression in his member-ship in JINA and in his arrest in 1946 in one of the first roundups of MDRM militants. Monima itself was as much a movement of peasant solidarity as an electoral organization, a fact that allowed it to survive when PSD pressure denied it electoral victories after 1960.

In the short run, the Tsiranana regime began with a considerable foundation of goodwill. Autonomy within the French community came in 1958 and full independence in 1960. Tsiranana enjoyed the prestige of being 'the father of his country', the man who had succeeded where more strident nationalists had failed. This prestige was increased in 1960 when the three exiled deputies returned from Paris and two, Ravoahangy and Rabemanan-jara, joined his government. The regime continued to entrench itself both politically and administratively. The PSD's Secretary General, André Resampa, became Minister of the Interior, a post that he used to move PSD militants into the administration, and to control the organization (and the results) of elections.

There were, however, several flaws in the regime that did not seem important in the early 1960s, but which interacted with developments of the late 1960s to produce its downfall. The basic flaw was the result of the fundamental political purpose of the regime, the creation of a formally independent state in which the essentials of French presence would be maintained. The concrete expression of this goal was the series of cooperation agreements signed by France and Madagascar in April 1960 (Delcourt, 1969; Leymarie, 1972; Randrianarison, 1974). There were over a dozen such agreements, covering a diverse range of topics, but the four most important dealt with defence, foreign policy, economic policy and education. The defence agreement provided for close integration between Malagasy and French armed forces. The new Malagasy army, to be formed on the base provided by Malagasies serving in the French army would continue to be trained and equipped by France and would be subsidized by the French budget. France would have the right to station troops in Madagascar and to maintain its base at Antseranana. French forces could use Malagasy territory, territorial waters and air space, as necessary. In the agreement covering foreign policy, the two countries promised exchanges of information and consultation. Citizens of each country were to enjoy most of the rights of nationals in the other country, and the French Ambassador was to be the permanent doyen of the Antananarivo diplomatic community. Madagascar would remain in the franc zone. Similarly close links prevailed in education, particularly at the post-secondary level which was to be financed by France and whose professors would have the status of French university personnel. The rector of the University of Madagascar would be named by the French Minister of National Education. This agreement also provided for identity of Malagasy diplomas from the baccalaureate on up with the corresponding French diplomas, the French Ministry of Education setting the standards and qualifying examinations.

These arrangements had rather obvious advantages for France and the French in Madagascar. The defence agreements allowed France to maintain its military presence on the island as if independence had never occurred, while the foreign policy agreements ensured that the diplomatic activity of the new nation would be acceptable to France. The monetary and 'assimi-lated nationality' accords allowed both large French companies and small settlers to operate as they had before independence, while the education agreements were designed to perpetuate the whole system by ensuring that future elites would be Francophone and imbued with French culture and values. However, the agreements were not forced on the Malagasy nego-tiators (Leymarie, 1972). Tsiranana and his supporters found several advantages in the continuation of French influence in Madagascar. Their political hold on the island was still far from consolidated in 1960, and administration, in spite of regional recruitment quotas, was still dominated by Merina, particularly in the technical branches but also in the territorial section. Continuing regional disparities in education made a short-run change in the situation unlikely. The French provided a useful counter-weight. Internationally, Tsiranana and his colleagues were obsessed with fears of communist subversion and Chinese expansionism and considered French military and diplomatic protection essential to Madagascar's survival. Finally, as Spacensky pointed out, the PSD leadership was the result of French policy in Madagascar, and 'the current cotier leaders will not forget that they owe [France] their introduction to politics and their accession to power' (Spacensky, 1970b, p. 80). Sober calculation of the requirements of survival, a real Francophilia and personal links between Tsiranana and de Gaulle all lay behind the accords. Continued dependence on France in economic affairs and external policy were traded for the rewards of local political office in what was seen by Malagasy nationalists as a phoney decolonization and a betrayal of the martyrs of 1947. The cooperation agreements were one of the main targets of the demonstrators of 1972 and a 'Second Independence', one of their major slogans.

Under the circumstances, the Tsiranana regime had neither the means nor the incentive to undertake policies for economic development. The three commercial companies continued to monopolize shipping and the import-export business, to dominate private banking and insurance and, via associated plantations, to grow many of the export crops. Indian and Chinese middlemen continued their domination of local distribution systems. Agricultural policy served mainly as a source of patronage for the PSD's local barons and their followers. As a result, production, both of rice and of cash crops, stagnated and large-scale importation of rice necessary to feed the population began in 1965. Industrial policy had some successes, mainly in the development of import substitution industries, but the growth was not enough to absorb the increases in the active population. A 1960 survey estimated wage employment in industry at 26,500: in 1972 it was estimated at 32,000. The whole of the modern sector including administration grew from 205,000 to about 350,000, enough to absorb about 20 per cent of the increase in the urban work force. Real income of both rural and urban populations declined by as much as 30 per cent during the First Republic (see Bastian, 1967; Atlan and Magnard, 1972; Hugon, 1977; Rakoto, 1969).

Malagasies did get rich under the system, but mainly through their role in the civil service or political sphere. The upper levels of the Malagasy bureaucracy were able to enjoy a life-style modelled on that of the wealthy Europeans of the island. Studies of the Malagasy economy estimated that 10 per cent of the population, a category that included both Europeans and Malagasies, consumed 80 per cent of the total income of the island. Political leaders benefited in several ways. Most cabinet members added directorships in companies such as Bata, CIMELTA, and even the three commercial companies (Archer, 1976). Corruption was not *the* major issue in the 1972 revolt, but the fact that Resampa could become the largest landowner in Madagascar while preserving a reputation for incorruptibility is perhaps a comment on the activities of his fellow ministers.

The politico-economic system of the First Republic provided the basis for the formation of a privileged Malagasy class that cut across the Merina–*côtier* division in the elite without, however, lessening the importance of the division. New wealth allowed politicians and the increasing numbers of administrators drawn from regions other than the plateaux to acquire the consumption patterns of the capital and to secure for their children the educational advantages formerly associated with Merina status. However, the capital–hinterland distinction was maintained. Opportunities to get and spend the money were limited to Antananarivo and to a handful of top officials in each provincial capital, who usually spent most of their time in Antananarivo maintaining their political connections. The division also cut the top PSD leaders off from their original clientele of local *notables* as the key to entry into the system became less a local power base than access to the education and 'culture' that would allow one to operate in the Antananarivo political and economic systems. Moreover, the absorptive capacity of the system was limited by the stagnation of the economy and foreign domination of both economic and political posts. To those outside the system, foreign domination and the construction of an edifice of privilege from which they were excluded were two faces of the same process. The 1972 revolt took place at the centre of the formation process, Antananarivo, and focused on the twin issues of educational opportunity and nationalism.

1972: Issues and Actors

The events of 1972 that led to the demise of the First Republic were an amalgam of regime collapse, popular uprising and military coup, and involved coalitions among groups as disparate as the urban lumpenproletariat and conservative generals, small shopkeepers and Maoist intellectuals. The revolt demanded the reassertion of Malagasy nationhood, but many of its participants were deeply influenced by the ideas that had fuelled the May 1968 events in France. Different groups with different agendas were able to unite to overthrow the First Republic, but were not able to agree about whether they were staging a political revolution that ended with Tsiranana's departure or a social revolution that began with that departure. The central goal of the May 1972 movements, Malagasy rule, had both the virtues and defects of its ambiguity: it was vague enough to serve as a basis for the original coalition, but disputes over its exact meaning led to the collapse of the coalition when the time came to implement it.

The ambiguity can be seen in the issue that provided the main body of actors in the 1972 uprising, the reform of the education system. The system was attacked for its role in perpetuating a structure of privilege, but by some for perpetuating privilege and by others for excluding them from it. If education was the key to positions in the political and economic elite, the main role of the education system was that of rejecting aspirants to these positions. The regime had been unable to resist pressures from its clientele to increase education at the primary and secondary levels and was only able to keep from being inundated by applicants to the civil service posts, for which a secondary school certificate qualified its holder, by operating a series of drastic cut-off points. The most crucial cut-off points were the entry examination to secondary school, the examination between the first and second levels of secondary education and the baccalaureate, which gave access to the summit of the university (see Table 3.1). The level to be reached in the system before economic security was achieved also increased. By 1970 four-fifths of those who had passed were without a job one year later (Rakoto, 1971, xxx, 1970b).

The system was further stratified according to type of school. The state system charged some fees, which were onerous for poorer families but which were still less than those charged by the religious or secular private systems. Most of the private system consisted of profit-making establishments that specialized in recruiting students who had failed examinations for the state schools, raising their hopes and keeping the fees coming in through high grades, and then re-exposing them to the examinations they had failed—and

Table 3.1 Numbers of students in education

Level	1960	1970
Primary	450,000	882,000
Secondary	26,000	100,000
University	1,100	7,000

Source: Rakoto, 1971, p. 56

which they usually failed again. Access to the state system was further limited by the fact that 75 per cent of places in the second section of the *lycées*—the only schools that prepared for the baccalaureate—were reserved for students from the first section. Students from the private system and from the state Collèges d'Enseignement Général competed for the remaining 25 per cent of places. In 1971, in the final year of the first level there were approximately 3,000 students in the *lycées*, a further 3,000 in the CEGs, and 14,000 in private schools (**xxx**, 1972). Secondary education and examinations were, of course, entirely in French. Because of differential success rates in the examinations, and often because of direct parental intervention, it was the children of the political and economic elite who went to the *lycées* and the poorer children whose families paid the fees in the private system. Access to the *lycées* was further limited by location. There were only twelve, seven in Antanarivo, and the others in provincial capitals. The *lycées*, particularly in the capital, formed a kind of 'gilded youth' whose golden days were darkened by the shadow of the baccalaureate, which only 25 per cent of them would pass.

At the summit were the institutions of higher education, grouped in the Fondation Charles de Gaulle, under the direction of a rector named by the French Ministry of Higher Education. Of the institutions of higher education, the University of Madagascar, whose campus was located some five kilometres from the city, played the most significant part in the events of 1972. At the university the Draconian selection process of primary and secondary schooling continued, at a pace that was only slightly more relaxed. The university had a further significance as an essential component in the perpetuation of the neo-colonial basis of the Tsiranana regime and as a place where French domination of the regime was demonstrated and even exaggerated. Although 80 per cent of the 1,000 students were Malagasy, 200 of 250 professors were French. The authoritarian style of professor-student relationship against which French students had revolted in 1968 had survived in Madagascar. When the professor was French and the student Malagasy the relationship reproduced the colonial era; when the professor was Malagasy the relationship underlined the point that only Malagasies who became like the French could command other Malagasies. Degrees given by the university were French degrees and the research and teaching of the university reproduced that of a French establishment. The regional geography course used the Paris basin for its illustrations and the journal of the Faculty of Literature, *Lettres Malgaches*, published articles on Provençal poetry (**xxx**, 1970). Again, the point was clear: it was through learning about France, not Madagascar, that one had to pass to aspire to even the subordinate position in the system for which Malagasies were destined.

Technical Assistants

One of the reasons for the extreme selectivity of the system lay in the fact that the absorptive capacity of the higher levels of the system was almost saturated. This was true not just because of the limitations imposed by a stagnating economy, or by French domination of that economy, but also because of the presence of French personnel in political and administrative posts. Here, too, issues of opportunity and nationalism coalesced. Not only were the technical assistants, as they were known, occupying posts that might otherwise have gone to Malagasies, their numbers and presence in important posts underlined the neo-colonial nature of the Tsiranana regime. There were two major areas where the assistants were found. The first was in teaching, where they constituted 80 per cent of the state secondary teaching staff and also served in the religious system. The second was the administration and armed forces, where technical assistants filled over half the senior level positions and dominated the President's office. The President's *Chef d'état major* and the head of the Deuxième bureau, also attached to the President's Office, were French as were the President's closest advisers, including the director and secretary-general of the presidential cabinet (xxx, 1970). The assistants were seen both as the means by which French domination over the Malagasy economic and political system was maintained, and as the means by which Tsiranana maintained himself in power, by cultivating the support of foreign rather than Malagasy interests.

The Antananarivo Crowd

These problems were posed with particular acuteness in Antananarivo, where the majority of the actors of 1972 were located. It was here that the French presence was strongest. The French embassy, located in the old Governor-General's residence was in Antananarivo, and only twelve kilometers away were 4,000 French paratroopers, a visible sign of the regime's lack of trust in the local population. To this were added the problems of the capital itself, where the contrast between those who profited from the system and those who did not was sharpest. The capital had nearly doubled in size between 1960 and 1970, mainly as a result of immigration from the overcrowded rural areas of Imerina. The migrants were usually from poor *andevo* and *mainty* families and/or young people whose families could not provide them with fields and who faced a future as a rural proletariat working on the fields of others. Families and youths came to Antananarivo where they lived in slums like Isotry in average densities of five per room (Donque, 1971). Over 60 per cent of the people living there were under twenty-five years of age. The slums also housed many of the urban employed poor. The structure of the education system was of importance to both employed and unemployed, since it was their children who were being rejected. The youth of the city gathered in bands that lived by petty thievery and small-scale extortion in the main market place and elsewhere. The most colourful were the Zwam, or Zatovo Western Andevo Malagasy—young cowboys of Madagascar. *Andevo* refers to the slave origin of most of them, and cowboy to their fascination with the 'spaghetti westerns' of the period. Those who could afford it affected the flat-topped hat and thin cigar of their hero, Clint Eastwood, while all affected the slouch, the narrowed eyes and the role of the outlaw who is yet more the champion of real justice than are the venal guardians of formal law (see Althabe, 1980; Leymarie, 1973).

The Radical Opposition

As the First Republic moved from decay to crisis after 1969, the generalized discontents of the population were given a focus, not by the existing opposition parties, Monima and the AKFM, but by a group of radical intellectuals based in the university and the research institutes of the capital. Led by a sociologist, Manadafy Rakotinirina, they developed a critique of the system that was heavily influenced by ideas current in international student milieux of the period, and emphasized themes of class struggle, generational conflict, opposition to imperialism and Third World solidarity. In the Malagasy context they argued that the perpetuation of authoritarian state-society relations in the countryside, the inequalities and irrelevant content of higher education, and continuing French economic and political influence were part of the same system. Their arguments, published in a semi-clandestine journal *Ny Andry* (The Pillar) and their attempts to give a political content to the activities of groups like the Zwam, were a crucial element in the creation of the coalition that made the May 1972 uprising (Althabe, 1972; Bouillon, 1973).

One of the main targets of the radical opposition's attacks was the AKFM, which maintained a cautious position throughout the period. The party had become accustomed to its role of 'official opposition' and to the privileges in the system that position guaranteed it. Its leaders continued to nourish participationist dreams of a coalition with the PSD in which, in cooperation with the Resampist wing of the party, they would move the regime into a state capitalist phase that would be the necessary prelude to 'scientific socialism'. As early as 1967 Adriamanjato declared that the AKFM and the PSD were '80 per cent in agreement', and proposed a coalition government. The PSD never agreed to these proposals, but never decisively rejected them either. Moreover, the themes of the radical opposition were unacceptable to the AKFM leadership, which had no interest in dismantling the authority of the state, seen as the main actor in the transition to socialism. The radical opposition's emphasis on direct democracy was too peasant-centred and, in the context of the late 1960s, too 'Maoist' for a party whose international ties were with the ultra-orthodox PCF and the Soviet Union (Leymarie, 1979).

The radical opposition did attempt to establish links with Monima, whose continued opposition to the Tsiranana regime and whose rejection of imposed state authority structures suited the opposition's vision of a radically decentralized state. This interest was not always well received by Monja Jaona and his associates. The newcomers seemed alien to the leaders of a party most of whose followers and mid-level cadres were illiterate, and whose reasons for rejecting state dominance did not include an enthusiasm for the theories of Marcuse. Moreover, Rakotinirina and his followers argued that decentralization had to be preceded by class and generational struggles in the villages, an idea that was not likely to charm Monima leaders who were drawn from an older generation of 'notables, small merchants, lower level bureaucrats and pastors' (Althabe, 1972) of southern villages. They came from an oppressed region, but they were the elite of their small worlds. The arguments of the radical opposition had more appeal for the younger generation of the party, and under pressure from the two groups the leadership did make some attempt at rejuvenation. In 1967 the party changed its name to Madagasikara Otronin'ny Malagasy (Madagascar for the Malagasies), attempted to develop youth sections and held a congress in which it condemned both the continuing French presence and the local manifestations of the regime: taxes, police, military service and cooperatives. A 1969 Monima youth congress showed how far apart the two generations were by calling for the application of class analysis to Madagascar's problems and demanding preparation for an armed liberation struggle (Althabe, 1972; *Lumière* October 1969).

The Armed Forces

The Malagasy armed forces were the final, and essential, component of the coalition that brought about the downfall of the Tsiranana regime (see Leymarie, 1977; Escaro, 1983; Serre-Ratsimandisa and Rasoarahona, 1981). Although issues internal to the military were an important influence on their participation and later political activity, their situation also made them responsive to the twin issues of nationalism and opportunity that moved the civilian participants in the May movement. The armed forces were grouped in two categories. The first, composed of the army, navy, air force and gendarmerie was covered by the military cooperation accords and governed along fairly classical lines. The second was made up of the Service Civique, to which most conscripts were sent, and the paramilitary Force Républicaine de Sécurité (FRS). The regular armed forces had been created after independence by the transfer of officers and men 'of Malagasy origin' from the French army. By 1972 the army had grown to approximately 4,000, with an air force and navy of approximately 500 each. The gendarmerie had about 4,500 men, and a level of armament equal to that of the army. It was directly attached to the presidency and had the general task of maintaining peace in the countryside and helping the local police control cattle rustling and collect taxes. Together the two components had a Malagasy officer corps of approximately 200, including two generals and three colonels. After independence the new state continued to send officers for training to France. The most promising, or those from the most influential families, went to Saint-Cyr; others to a secondary level of schools. In 1965 a Military Academy was created at Antsirabe, and a gendarmerie officers' training school at Moramanga, but a 'finishing' in France was still an important stage in an ambitious officer's career. Before independence a career in the army was not very prestigious, and officers were recruited from younger sons and less promising members of the better-off families of the plateaux. After independence the chances of rapid promotion made the career more attractive, while government policy broadened the regional basis of recruitment.

The political issues of the larger society were replicated in the organization and operation of the armed forces. The gendarmerie had been created and given the type of armament it had because of the regime's feeling that the army was 'too Merina'. Like the other institutions of the state, the army and gendarmerie were dominated by French technical assistants and Francophile Malagasies (see Table 3.2).

Table 3.2: Officer corps, 1966, 1968

	1966	1968
Technical Assistants	318	260
Malagasy		
Army	124 (3,382)*	126 (3,457)
Gendarmerie	39 (3,884)	47 (4,036)
In training		
Antsirabe (army)	51	71
Moromanga (gendarmerie)	—	21
France (army and gendarmerie)	69	70

* Figures in brackets refer to total number of men in the force.
Source: République de Madagascar. *Rapport sur les activités gouvernementales*, 1966, 1968.

The army was commanded by General Gabriel Romanantsoa who was distantly connected to the Merina royal family, but whose distinguished performance in the French army's campaigns in Indo-China and Algeria freed him from suspicions of Francophobia. The gendarmerie was commanded by a French colonel until 1969, when the command was transferred to Colonel Richard Ratsimandrava, a Tsiranana protégé whose father had been one of the founding members of the Antananarivo section of PADESM. Ratsimandrava's combination of elite training and slave ancestry made him a crucial linkage figure in the military. Tsiranana's personal *état-major* was made up of six French officers and most of the posts at the military schools of Antsirabe and Moramanga were held by French officers. In addition, the presence of 4,000 French troops at Ivato airport (doubled from 2,000 after the 1966 wave of African coups) served, among other things, as an insurance policy against ambitious officers.

If the status of the armed forces was ambiguous, so was their function. The army was squeezed between the gendarmerie and the French forces, and in daily reality its role was primarily decorative, as a symbol of Madagascar's independent status—and an ambiguous one at that since 85 per cent of its budget came from French aid. The gendarmerie had a clearer role: to defend the PSD regime against its enemies, but again, the daily reality of the role, that of rural police, was galling. By the late 1960s both Monima and the AKFM had established secret sections in the armed forces. The radical opposition made little attempt to cultivate military support although some contact existed at the individual level.

The officer corps itself was divided by generation, regional and social origin, and military career. Pre-independence officers, those who had begun their careers in 1960–5 and who by 1972 occupied the ranks from captain to lieutenant-colonel, and those who had joined after 1965 formed distinct generations (Serre and Rasoarahona, 1981, p. 19) often paralleled by differences in career between those trained entirely in Madagascar, those trained in France and among the latter between those who had been educated at Saint-Cyr and those who had attended 'lesser' schools. These differences had not crystallized into visible factions before 1972, but were to become important with the rapid politicization of the armed forces after their intervention in the May uprising.

The armed forces were completed by two other corps. The Service Civique was composed of conscripts (universal military service was enacted in 1960, but only a small proportion of each promotion actually served). Mainly stationed in the countryside, it played little role in the 1972 events. More important was the FRS, to a large degree André Resampa's private army. It had been created in 1966 and by 1972 had 2,000 members. Recruited almost exclusively from the southern coastal areas, it was attached to the Ministry of the Interior. Resampa took a personal interest in both recruitment and promotion of its members. Loyalty and brutality were of more importance than intelligence in its recruitment and activities (Althabe, 1980; Archer, 1976).

The Fall of The First Republic

By 1970, the Tsiranana regime had moved into crisis. The economy was suffering from events such as the 1967 closure of the Suez Canal, the French strikes of 1968 and a series of cyclones in 1969. The regime's attempts to solve its economic problems by developing closer links with South Africa only added to the opposition it had already created by maintaining links with states like Taiwan, Israel, South Korea and South Vietnam. However, the event that definitively began the end of the First Republic was not economic or political, but medical. In February 1970, while he was attending an OCAM heads of state meeting at Yaoundé, Tsiranana had a stroke. Paralysed and unable to speak he was transported to the Hôpital de la Salpetrière in Paris, where doctors held out little hope of improvement. In fact it was two months before he could speak and seven months before he returned to Madagascar.

The supposedly hopeless illness, and subsequent miraculous recovery had the effect of opening the competition to succeed Tsiranana while forcing the participants to pretend it was not happening. The main contender for the succession was André Resampa, who made no secret of his belief that he should have the presidency. During Tsiranana's illness Resampa began to consolidate his position with a reorganization of the PSD. His efforts aroused considerable opposition, since his role as the 'strong man' of the regime had made enemies, and his character was not conciliatory. The group most opposed to a Resampist succession was the wing of the PSD connected with Tsiranana and his group of personal advisers, a group that would inevitably lose power and position in a new regime. Tsiranana's illness put them in a dilemma. Their preferred successor, Rabemananjara, had by 1970 been discredited by his connection with a series of scandals and his involvement as a foreign minister in the negotiations with South Africa. The only possible strategy for this group was to try to perpetuate Tsiranana's rule as long as possible, undermine Resampa as much as possible, and hope for the appearance of a potential successor (Leymarie, 1973; Archer, 1976).

Their task was both helped and hindered by the state in which Tsiranana returned (see Maynard, 1972). The illness had affected his mental balance to a degree that made it difficult for him to conduct the business of government, but it had also made him obsessed with fears (partly justified of course) that the rest of his government was plotting to overthrow him. In this mood, he was easily persuaded to begin the task of destroying Resampa's power. In December 1970 Resampa's control over the police and territorial administration were given to a newly appointed adjunct minister of the interior, a close adviser of the President known for his personal and political quarrels with Resampa.

As the regime began to disintegrate from the inside, it also came under attack from the outside. In March 1971 a series of student strikes involving both secondary schools and the university led first to the closing of the establishments, but later to government concessions. A commission was established to examine the problems of the university, and the government promised a nation-wide examination for entry into the second cycle of education, with no reserved places for *lycéens*. At the beginning of April, while the strikes were still going on, the peasants of the south staged a demonstration of force in which they occupied villages and towns in the region, seizing administrative offices and gendarmerie posts, and withdrawing the next day. Always governed more or less as occupied territory, the south had been suffering since the late 1960s from drought, and since 1969 from an outbreak of cattle anthrax. Government measures to combat the outbreak, which included quarantine and slaughter of affected animals, only exacerbated relations with the population as did the regime's insistence on basing the collection of cattle taxes on pre-outbreak estimates of herd sizes. The rebellion was not a spontaneous anomic outburst, but rather a planned demonstration, largely coordinated by Monima, of what the peasants could do if aroused. The major error the organizers of the demonstration made was in underestimating the fury of the government response, and if the term anomic outburst is to be used, it should apply to this reaction. The original demonstration had left one gendarme and six peasants dead. By 15 April, government sources gave an official total of 45 dead in the repression while unofficial sources argued that the total was more like 1,000. Over 1,500 were arrested, and 523 deported to Nosy Lava. The government also used the occasion to try to destroy Monima as a political force. The party was dissolved and many of its adherents arrested, along with Monja Jaona. Significantly, the army refused to participate in the repression, although it did provide some logistical assistance and back-up in areas where the gendarmerie had been sent south (Allen, 1975; Althabe, 1972; xxx (*RFEPA*) 1971; xxx, 1971a).

Reaction in Antananarivo was slow to form. Periodic outbursts in the south were not uncommon, and it was only slowly that the full extent of the repression became known. The AKFM denounced the uprising as leftist adventurism and pledged its support to the government in the restoration of order. The immediate result of the revolt was the hastening of the fall of André Resampa, who was from the southwest. The end came in June, when Tsiranana accused him of a leftist plot to overthrow the regime in collusion with Monima and the American embassy. Resampa was arrested and deported to the Ile-Sainte-Marie. To reaffirm Tsiranana's hold on the party and country, a presidential election was called for January 1972. No other candidates were allowed to run, and the campaign was used to celebrate Tsiranana as the man destined by God to govern Madagascar. Administration and party officials exerted themselves to prove their loyalty, with the result that Tsiranana was re-elected with 99.7 per cent of the vote. He was inaugurated on 1 May, less than two weeks before the beginning of the revolt that brought the whole regime down.

The May Revolution

The uprising that overthrew the Tsiranana regime brought together the issues of education policy, government performance, and the legitimacy of the regime itself. The slogan of the uprising, 'Malgachization' had originally been a demand for an education in the national language reflecting the national culture, but in the course of the uprising its meaning widened to include the ouster of the French technical assistants, and then the real departure of the French and the regime they had installed: a second independence and the vindication of the sacrifices of the martyrs of 1947. As the slogan acquired new meanings, new groups joined the movement: urban workers, middle-class elements and finally the armed forces. The catalytic work of expanding the significance of Malgachization and of contacting new groups was done by the radical opposition but the decisive acts that solidified the coalition and convinced the reluctant were the work of the government itself. It was this characteristic of the May Revolution that was one of the limits on the ability of the radical opposition to push the uprising beyond an attack on the Tsiranana regime to an attack on the state system itself. Many groups only joined the uprising when the government began to be the main source of instability, and their goal, once an oppressive regime had been overthrown, was not a continuing revolution, but a return to stability (see Althabe, 1980; Gimoi, 1972; Archer, 1976).

The uprising began in the lower levels of the education system. In January 1972 the medical students of Befelatanana went on strike to protest against the subordination of their degrees to those of the Faculty of Medicine. (Befelatanana, known for the role of its students in nationalist movements such as the VVS, had been founded to train 'native medical assistants'. When the university medical faculty was created the hospital kept this function, leading to a two-tier medical system in which a French degree granted professional status and a Malagasy degree trained people to be the subordinates of the holders of the French degree.) In February, the regime reneged on its promise to hold a nation-wide examination for entry into the upper level of secondary education. This had an impact beyond disappointing students in the CEGs and private schools. Their parents, particularly in the provinces, had formed a crucial section of the PSD's support before its leaders went on to become ministers. Abolishing the examination 'united in a common opposition the petit bourgeoisie of Tananarive and that of the provincial cities, which until then had been the clientele of the regime' (Althabe, 1980, p. 424).

By late March the CEGs and private schools in Antananarivo and provincial cities were on strike. The *lycées* and the university were resentful of the slow progress of the negotiations for Malgachization of their curriculum and organization that had been going on since July 1971, and by the end of April had joined the strike, demanding more rapid progress on Malgachization, the revision of the cooperation agreements, and the departure of the technical assistants. The university campus became the headquarters of the strike movement as its students were joined by the others, by the CGT, an organization of employed and semi-employed workers of the capital who were dissatisfied with both governmental and opposition wings of the existing trade-union movement, and by groups of Zwam, rebaptized Zoam, or young unemployed of Madagascar. The licensed unions and the AKFM refused to join the movement or support the strikers' call for a general strike to be held on 13 May. Once more it was an act of the regime that gave plausibility to the arguments of its critics and sent more groups over to their side. On the night of 12 May the FRS raided the university campus, Zoam strongholds in Isotry, and the homes of other opposition figures such as the editor of the capital's major Catholic newspaper. In all 375 were arrested and deported to Nosy Lava.

By dawn on 13 May crowds had begun to gather in front of the Hôtel de Ville. The FRS took up positions in front of the building, with the gendarmerie in reserve. At noon, the crowd, now several thousand, attacked the building. The FRS fired, causing the first deaths. After this clash both FRS and gendarmes withdrew, and when the FRS returned in the afternoon they were alone. After that, while the gendarmerie and army protected the presidential palace and other central government buildings they did not disperse the crowd, or intervene in the battles between the FRS and groups led by the 'suicide squads of Isotry'. By the evening, several more on both sides were dead.

The government's response was a confused mixture of concession and threats. On the evening of 13 May Tsiranana gave a radio address in which he accused the demonstrators of being 'potheads' and threatened the capital with more deaths if order were not restored (Althabe, 1980, p. 427). The next day a procession of 100,000 marched to his palace, demanding the return of the deportees, and the dissolution of the FRS. Turned back by the army and gendarmerie, they returned to the Hôtel de Ville, which was now rather casually guarded by the gendarmerie, entered without much opposition and started a fire that burned it to the ground. By the time the crowd reassembled on 15 May, the movement had been joined by representatives of the established organizations of the capital: the AKFM, the unions, and the churches. The next day saw the continuation of the government's policy of concession and threat. The deportees returned from Nosy Lava and were presented to the crowd in front of the ruins of the Hôtel de Ville, and the FRS withdrew to its camps. That evening, however, Tsiranana made a speech in which he called for an end to the crisis now that the prisoners had been returned. If not, he said, the FRS would return and there would be more deaths. He ended the threat with an imitation of machine gun fire—Ack—Ack—Ack! (*Africa Confidential*, 1972). Neither concessions nor threats worked. At dawn on 17 May the crowd was back in front of the Hôtel de Ville, with placards demanding the end of the Tsiranana regime and calling on the army to take power. The scene was repeated the next day, and in the afternoon General Ramanantsoa appeared before the demonstrators to announce that Tsiranana had given him full powers. Accompanied by an enthusiastic crowd, he went to the radio station to announce the news to the country. Antananarivo began celebrating the fall of Tsiranana and the coming of 'the second independence'.

The Reasons Why

Tsiranana's fall resulted when his usual sources of support moved into neutrality, and when those who had been neutral towards him moved into opposition. When the government began exploring sources of support at the beginning of the crisis, it found almost no one willing to stand up for it. Ironically, the only public declaration of support came from the AKFM and even this support was withdrawn as the size of the movement against the regime grew. As news of events in Antananarivo reached provincial capitals, similar demonstrations occurred there, indicating that the PSD could not count on its historic clientele of provincial elites. Neither side made any attempt to enlist the support of the rural areas: the groups involved in the uprising were entirely urban, and the PSD base in the countryside too much an artefact of the administration to serve as a line of defence for the regime. Tsiranana did seek assistance from the French, but without success. The French command at Ivato refused to send troops to guard government buildings, and on 17 May the French embassy announced that French forces would intervene only to protect French lives and property. It was at this point that Tsiranana's French advisers began to urge him to step down. By mid-May it was clear that the choice facing the French government was not between Tsiranana and an anti-French government but between continued chaos under Tsiranana that might lead to a serious revolution, and a more nationalistic but still 'reasonable' military government. The proposed head of the government, Ramanantsoa, was well known to French officials in both Tananarive and Paris, and was considered 'safe'.

It was, however, the refusal of the armed forces to support the regime that was the direct cause of Tsiranana's downfall. The army had already demonstrated its reservations about the regime by its refusal to play any major role in the repression of the 1971 revolt in the south, while the gendarmerie had become increasingly resentful of the blame it had incurred for its role in that repression. The slogan of the May uprising, 'Malgachiza-tion', had obvious relevance for armed forces still largely dominated by French officers, and while the radical opposition to the regime had few connections with the officer corps, Monima did. Aside from general reasons for alienation from the regime, and the possible ambitions of some officers, there were several immediate precipitants of the armed forces' refusal to defend the regime. One was the withdrawal of French support. On 11 May, when the FRS raids were being planned, the Malagasy army sent its own delegations to French headquarters at Ivato and asked for a loan of additional weapons. They were turned down (Gimoi, 1972, pp.47–8). This meant not only that if the Malagasy armed forces chose to defend Tsiranana they would have to do so alone, but also, of course, that should they choose to overthrow him, they would not have to face French military opposition. The decisive precipitant was the use of the FRS against the population of Antanarivo. The FRS were recruited from such a narrow regional and political base that this act was not really equivalent to the declaration of the Merina–*côtier* civil war, but rather revealed that the regime could only depend on the support of what was very nearly a group of mercenaries. It was the gendarmerie that was the alternate force to the FRS, and it was their refusal to defend the regime that was crucial. When the commander of the gendarmerie Colonel Ratsiman-drava, himself once a Tsiranana protégé, announced to the President the armed forces' refusal to disperse the crowd, the regime was over.

Whose Revolution?

The 'May movement', as it came to be known, was a mixture of different groups whose various goals were not always compatible. The catalytic groups, led by Manadafy Rakotinirina, saw the overthrow of Tsiranana as part of an overall revolution in the Malagasy political and social system. Their vision of a radically egalitarian society that would be self-governing at every level found an echo in the aspirations of the Zoam and some of the students and workers involved in the May movement, but was not widely shared. The original demand of the students, for an expansion of the education system that would make it easier for them to acquire the degrees that were their passports to administrative posts, and the eviction of the French from those posts presupposed the maintenance of state power and social hierarchy. The Zoam themselves alternated between rejecting the system of privilege and protesting their exclusion from that system while the mobilizing forces for the other participants were also the combination of nationalism and opportunism that the 'Malgachization' slogan captured so well. For many, the decision was the result of Tsiranana's two May broadcasts, which showed just how unstable he was, and which made him seem even more frightening than revolution. The result was a loose alliance, united by demands for Tsiranana's overthrow and the final departure of the French. These demands represented a minimum programme for some and a maximum for others. Calling on the army to take power represented a crucial step in cementing the alliance since the military forces represented a reassuring guarantee that order rather than chaos would follow Tsiranana's departure. The radical section of the May movement had the ability to provide the catalyst for an explosion in the making but it had neither the numbers nor the organization to create a social revolution (see Bouillon, 1973; Archer, 1976; Althabe, 1980).

For the rest, what had happened in May 1972 was revolution enough: the end of the Tsiranana regime and the prospect of the removal of the remains of the colonial period. The martyrs of 1947 were at last vindicated (if only their urban wing). It was this attitude that allowed the new regime to resist the attempts of the radical element of the May movement to pursue the process of revolution. The organized groups of the nation declared their support for Ramanantsoa, and the regime moved to construct its own basis of support. The minimum salary was raised, the poll and cattle taxes abolished, and a referendum held in October that gave the regime a source of popular legitimacy distinct from that conferred by the Antananarivo crowd.

4 The Democratic Republic of Madagascar

The Ramanantsoa Interval

The regime established by the referendum was intended to last until 1977, using the time to lay the basis for a new civilian political system. Ramanantsoa himself saw the period as a sort of rest cure, in which he would 'put the political life of the country to sleep for a while' (Archer, 1976). In fact, the period lasted only until 1975, and was one of intense political activity as old and new political forces competed to secure a favorable position in the forthcoming civilian regime. Although the PSD's political base had been seriously damaged before and by the events of 1972, much of it remained intact. Tsiranana himself continued to claim that he was still the real President, and Resampa, released from the Ile-Sainte-Marie by the new regime but not in the least grateful, worked towards a reconciliation with Tsiranana and a coordination of their efforts to restore the old regime and undermine the new. Opposition groups from the old regime, in particular the AKFM and Monima, considered that they had a special claim to direct the policy of the new government, while the elite groups of Antananarivo believed that Ramanantsoa, who was after all 'one of them', should give special consideration to their interests. The radical opposition, after the failure of its attempts to take control of the revolution, regrouped under the name Mpitolona ho amin'ny Fanjakana ny Madinika (MFM—the Party for Proletarian Power) a partly overt, partly clandestine movement that considered the military regime at best a stage on the road to revolution and at worst an obstacle. In addition the 'crowd' of Antananarivo and to a lesser degree of the provincial capitals had discovered the use of riots as a political strategy with the result that Ramanantsoa's time in office was marked by several outbursts, some encouraged by PSD figures, others by the MFM (see Althabe, 1980; Archer, 1976; Bouillon, 1973; Serre and Rasoarahona, 1981).

All these groups sought allies in the military, although the PSD elements concentrated on maintaining their contacts with the FRS, which had been renamed the Groupe Mobile de Police and left to rot in its barracks, but not disbanded or even purged. The other groups pursued their contacts with the officer corps of the army and gendarmerie where the divisions of civilian society interacted with the military's institutional divisions to produce factional alliances that cut across the civil–military boundary. This symbiosis of civilian and military factions is not unusual in African military regimes, particularly those of a populist or 'left' character (Bienen, 1985; Decalo, 1979), but several characteristics appear to distinguish the process of faction creation under Ramanantsoa's regime from similar patterns elsewhere. First, until the very end of the period, no attempt was made to appeal to the common soldiers for support. While the factions cut across ranks at the officer level, the officers–other ranks distinction was preserved, and even those officers who were former non-commissioned officers were largely excluded from alliances. When populist appeals were made, they were directed at civilian groups like the Zoam and the peasantry. Moreover, the civil–military combinations of the factions were matched and furthered by the official character of the regime itself. It included a number of civilians, holding important posts like the Ministry of Finance. A series of elections in 1973 not only renewed local officials, but also chose a National People's Development Council (CNPD). Although the Council itself met rarely, it had a Permanent Committee that, as the name suggests, was a permanent official source of civilian commentary.

Ramanantsoa's suspicion of political intrigue and his refusal to develop a personal power base made it impossible for him to impose his views on his government. (Observers of his regime also doubted that he had any firm political views to impose. See Archer, 1976; Andriamirado, 1977b.) The politics of the regime increasingly came to centre on the factional struggle between Ramanantsoa's three strongest ministers and most likely successors. Each used the policy area for which he was responsible to construct a political base, and each pursued his policy choices and faction building with minimal supervision by Ramanantsoa or consultation with the rest of the government.

Didier Ratsiraka, the Foreign Minister, was the one exception to the Ramanantsoa regime's adherence to the principle of military hierarchy. A naval lieutenant serving as military attaché in the Paris embassy, he had been promoted to captain when he was named minister. His father had been a colonial administrator in Toamasina province, one of the earliest members of PADESM, and a close friend of Tsiranana. This background, solidified by marriage to the daughter of another PADESM founder, had not prevented him from establishing connections with Monima, a sign of a radicalization that he himself attributed to his service at the French naval base of Antseranana. His prestige in Ramanantsoa's government was based on his renegotiation of the cooperation agreements with France. The new agreements included the departure of Madagascar from the franc zone, the departure of French forces from Madagascar, and the ending of the other signs of the 'special' France–Malagasy relationship, and were presented by Ratsiraka as 'the consecration of what the martyrs of 29 March 1947 had always demanded' (Leymarie, 1973, p. 34). Ratsiraka developed a more radical Malagasy image in foreign policy, establishing relations both with the 'African socialist' countries that the previous regime had shunned and with the Soviet Union and other socialist regimes, adhering to the non-aligned movement and reversing Malagasy positions in the United Nations. These activities brought him considerable prestige and the support not only of the AKFM, which had been urging these policies for years, but also of the other groups on the left normally more critical of the government. (For the AKFM's attitude, see Rabesahala, 1974.) Ratsiraka's major handicap in the competition to succeed Ramanantsoa was the weakness of his base in the armed forces. He was still a junior officer and his service, the navy, was both small and logistically unsuited for either a peaceful or violent power struggle.

Although Ratsiraka was considered by many to be Ramanantsoa's own choice for his successor, the general's closest associate in power was the head of his private cabinet, Colonel Roland Rabetafika, who came from the same type of protestant upper-class family, and who was a Ramanantsoa rather than a Tsiranana protégé. Rabetafika was entrusted not only with general oversight of the economy, but also with the direction of the Deuxième Bureau and with decisions about the management of the armed forces, including promotions. 'Malgachization' of the economy had been one of the vague goals of the May 1972 movements, given a variety of different meanings by the different participants. As interpreted by Rabetafika and his assistants it included moving Malagasies into positions occupied by foreigners, and attempting to assert national control over the levers of the economy. In general the regime's economic policy followed the pattern of creating state enterprises to drive out local non-Malagasy entrepreneurs in areas like the commercialization of rice, and participation in and indigeniza-tion of French-owned enterprises. The three commercial companies were not touched directly, although some of their affiliates were affected. These policies allowed Rabetafika to strengthen his base in Antananarivo but not elsewhere. His critics claimed that they benefited only the business interests and middle-class job seekers of the capital, and both Monima and the MFM argued that they did not improve either the economic position of the bulk of the population or the real control of the country over its economy.

By 1974, the economy had become a liability rather than an asset in Rabetafika's pursuit of his political ambitions. Peasants complained that the new state marketing boards cheated them just as much as the traditional collectors and rural stores, and did not at least provide credit facilities in return. Supplies disappeared and soon a thriving black market came into existence alongside the companies, providing rice and other essentials that they often lacked, precisely because their stocks had been diverted to the black market. As well as cheating peasants and diverting supplies to the black market, those running the societies often simply diverted the money directly from the budget to their own pockets (see Andriamirado, 1977a). Corruption reached higher levels as well. French companies fearful of further national-izations began cultivating the new ministers and their assistants. By late 1974, rumours accused Rabetafika and at least the wife of Ramanantsoa if not the chief himself of involvement in illegal activities. Economic problems and corruption sapped the government's prestige, and divided the government itself.

Within the government, Rabetafika's main opponent was the Minister of the Interior, Colonel Richard Ratsimandrava. The two men came from opposite ends of the traditional Antananarivo social hierarchy, and their political antagonism was reinforced by personal contempt and. social resentments. Ratsimandrava had made an interesting personal journey since his participation in the repression of the 1971 revolt in the south. Ramanantsoa had appointed him to the Ministry of the Interior in the hope that he would be a strong 'law and order' man, and his early performance in controlling the Zoam and putting down both the PSD and MFM inspired riots seemed to bear this out. By 1974, however, he was in the process of putting together a coalition that included the urban *sous-proletariat* and the peasantry and many radical intellectuals not affiliated with the MFM. The programme that attracted this support was the reform of the *fokonolona*, a project that came under the control of the Ministry of the Interior. Under Ratsimandrava's direction, the reform developed into a radical vision of rural autonomy and urban populism aimed at the destruction of the state apparatus and the creation of 'popular control of development' (see Andriamirado, 1977b (Andriamirado was a member of the committee Ratsimandrava charged with drawing up the reform); and Leymarie, 1975a; and the articles cited in the section on the *fokonolona* reform).

The project itself was riddled with ambiguities. Ratsimandrava was a very authoritarian populist, and by 1974, the opposition the reform aroused inside and outside the government and the lack of enthusiasm of the territorial administration, charged with implementing a policy whose goal was its own elimination, had united to prevent the reform from reaching its stated goals. Ratsimandrava responded to the stalling of the reform by undertaking a cross-country campaign to revive and radicalize it, a performance that included speeches and question and answer sessions with peasants that were later broadcast on national radio. The failures of the reform, ironically, aided him in the process of attracting a national following since hopes aroused and then disappointed were refocused on his person. 'Playing on his humble origins and his knowledge of the country, travelling extensively to speak to the peasants he developed a form of populism centered on himself. He presented himself as a man of integrity and determination, ready to attack the advantages of the bourgeoisie and to struggle against all forms of corruption'. (Serre and Rasoarahona, 1981, p. 187). The alarm created by Ratsimandrava's charismatic appeal and evident ambition was increased when he used the Minister of the Interior's police powers to begin an investigation into corruption that he vowed to pursue to the highest levels. His popularity in the countryside and among the urban poor was matched by his support in the officer corps of his service, the gendarmerie and by the support he was attracting in some quarters of the army.

By mid-1974 the government was almost totally paralysed by its quarrels over personalities and policies. In general Ratsiraka and Ratsimandrava supported each other's stands in the government, although often without much enthusiasm. Ratsimandrava was not greatly interested in foreign policy, and Ratsiraka had his reservations about the development possibilities of radical decentralization. Moreover, as the sinking economy took Rabetafika down with it, they were the obvious choices to succeed Ramanantsoa, and then one, in self-preservation, would be forced to destroy the other (Serre and Rasoarahona, 1981, p. 203; Archer, 1976 also has a section on relations between the two).

The incident that precipitated Ramanantsoa's fall came not directly from the three rivals, but from those who considered that they had been excluded from the power and privileges the armed forces had acquired since 1972. In late December 1974, Rabetafika's Deuxième Bureau discovered a coup plot organized by Brechard Rajaonarison, the only one of the country's three colonels to be excluded from real power under the regime, an exclusion that he blamed on his *côtier* origins and status as a former non-commissioned officer. Several of those suspected of involvement in the coup were arrested, but Rajaonarison himself escaped to Antanaimoro, a GMP camp on the outskirts of Antananarivo, and issued a communiqué accusing the government of corruption, disgracing the armed forces, and preferring Merina to *côtier* officers in promotions. He claimed to have assembled a coalition of *côtiers* of all ranks and branches of the armed forces at the camp.

Ramanantsoa's attempts to preserve his position merely demonstrated how totally the support of 1972 had disappeared. Not only did figures from the old regime, like Tsiranana and Resampa declare their support for the rebels at Antanaimoro, so did critical supporters of the new regime like Monja Jaona. People even more closely connected to the regime, like Ratsiraka's brother, visited the camp. Ramanantsoa and his supporters were simply too unsure of their position to order an armed attack on the camp. In the end, even the AKFM called for Ramanantsoa's resignation, and Ratsiraka and Ratsimandrava joined forces to refuse to serve in any new government that included either Ramanantsoa or Rabetafika. However, their alliance fell apart when Ramanantsoa proposed that he be replaced by a government led by Ratsiraka with the support of Ratsimandrava. Ratsiraka agreed, on the stipulation that the colonel give up the Ministry of the Interior, command of the gendarmerie and any personal involvement in the reform of the *fokonolona*, a set of conditions that Ratsimandrava naturally refused. He was able to use his stronger base in both military and civilian constituencies to block this proposal and on 5 February Ramanantsoa resigned, naming Ratsimandrava as his sole successor, a position that the colonel occupied for less than a week. On the evening of 11 February, as he was being driven home, he was ambushed by a group of gunmen. Ratsimandrava, two of his bodyguards and two of the attackers died. (For a discussion of the question of who killed Colonel Ratsimandrava, see the Appendix; see also Archer, 1976; the series of articles in *Jeune Afrique* (by Andriamirado) in January and February, 1975; Leymarie, 1975b; Molet, 1977; and Serre and Rasoarahona, 1981.)

The Military Directorate

Other officers arrived on the scene almost immediately and arrested the surviving members of the assassination squad, all GMP from the Antanaimoro camp. They also called an assembly of officers of the army and gendarmerie that met later that night at the Palace of Andafiavaratra. Old divisions and new fears made the meeting a tense and noisy confrontation as the officers tried to agree on a collective leadership and avoid intra-force warfare. Rabetafika tried to be named to the new 'Military Directorate' but was voted down; some Ratsimandravists tried to keep Ratsiraka off too, but he was able to assemble enough support to gain a place for himself and two brothers-in-law. By the morning of 12 February the assembly had agreed on an eighteen man Directorate under the leadership of the ranking officer, army general Andriamahazo, which declared martial law and finally cleaned out both the Antanaimoro camp and the ex-PSD headquarters where they discovered and arrested André Resampa and more GMP officers. Led by groups of Zoam, the Antananarivo crowd levelled the building.

The real task of the Directorate was not to govern the country, but to hold the ring while factions and personalities struggled for power. Maintaining this façade of collective rule was simplified by the fact that public attention was focused on the trial of Ratsimandrava's accused assassins, the 'trial of the century' with 297 defendants including Rajaon-arison and his co-conspirators: Resampa and Tsiranana and, eventually, Roland Rabetafika. 'Terrible and fascinating', widely reported on radio and television, the trial turned into an examination of the wrongs committed by a section of the political elite against Madagascar itself, as well as a trial for murder (Archer, 1976, p. 119). After three months of testimony, the defendants were dismissed for 'lack of evidence'; only the actual members of the assassination squad received sentences. On 15 June just after the end of the trial, the Directorate named Didier Ratsiraka President of the Republic and dissolved itself (Archer, 1976; *Jeune Afrique*, 6 June 1975; *Le Monde*, 17 June 1975).

In the months between Ratsimandrava's death and his own selection, Ratsiraka had succeeded in putting together a coalition that held a middle ground between those who wanted to return to the state capitalism of the Ramanantsoa period and those who wanted to pursue Ratsimandrava's vision of radical change in economic and political structures. Given the existing balance of political forces, it was necessary for him to appeal to the left without totally alienating the right which, while discredited by the revelations of the 'trial of the century' and neutralized by the threat of the continuing investigations into corruption still, through personal ties and strategic position, remained a group that had to be reassured rather than directly attacked. The variety of Ratsiraka's civilian contacts helped in the coalition-building process, and his position in the military was strengthened when the bulk of the Ratsimanadravists decided to support him. Other forces also had to be consulted. Between the 18 and 27 of May, Ratsiraka dis-appeared; later it was learned that he had spent the time in Algiers and Paris (Archer, 1976). Exactly what he was doing there is not known, but he was probably reassuring and being reassured in both cases, since Algerian support and French neutrality would help establish his regime both internally and internationally.

When Ratsiraka took office, he promised to implement 'a general policy whose principles and methods will be based notably on the socialist revolution by means of an improved and updated fokonolona'. This statement was the first use of the term 'socialist revolution' to describe the intended course of future government policy. To what degree did the arrival of Ratsiraka and his supporters to power represent a decisive redirection of the Malagasy regime? Evaluations at the time varied. Ratsiraka had come to power by convincing both the left and right that he was 'really' one of them, but each side had corresponding doubts about his degree of commitment. The group responsible for Archer's book on the period, generally drawn from the left, concluded by recording its suspicions that his proposed reforms would simply multiply the number of posts available to the Antananarivo and provincial bourgeoisie, whose creature he could easily become if he was not already (Archer, 1976). From the other side, Escaro presented the argument that 'his success was due, in part, to the support he received from the Soviet camp, whose interests he had always wanted to favour, and of powerful French pressure groups whom he has artfully deceived for several years, convincing them of his supposed conservative and Gaullist sentiments.' (Escaro, 1983, p. 53; Moine, 1975; Molet, 1977).

If Ratsiraka's commitment to socialist revolution was ambiguous, that of the regime taken as a whole was even more so. The coalition was divided into left and right with a large middle group whose reasons for joining the coalition ranged from personal loyalty to Ratsiraka to personal loyalty to themselves and their own interests. If Ratsiraka could not count on the whole hearted allegiance of his closest supporters, the instruments of rule including the bulk of the army and administration and, of course the population in general, all of whom had been left out of the process by which he came to power, were even less to be relied on. After power had been gained, it was necessary to consolidate it, and under difficult circumstances. The administration was paralysed, the economy in crisis, and the military itself had come close to internal war. In another sense, however, the atmosphere of crisis worked to Ratsiraka's advantage, allowing him to appear as the 'providential man' (*Le Monde*, 17 June 1975).

Consolidating Power

Ratsiraka accompanied his accession to power with a series of measures designed to reinforce his assertion that he represented a new, radical direction in Malagasy politics. Further nationalizations, including the take-over of the French-owned banks and the CMM, and the closure of the American satellite tracking station at Imerintotsika were all measures that had been on the programmes of the parties of the civilian left, and the announcement of their enactment earned him a declaration of their support or, in the case of the MFM (which considered his regime 'a stage in the proletarian revolution') of 'non-opposition'. However, it was not in Ratsiraka's interest to remain permanently dependent on the approval of these parties, and the rest of 1975 was devoted to establishing an independent political and legal basis for his regime. The steps he took included the publishing and publicizing of the Charter of the Malagasy Revolution, and the drafting and adoption via a December referendum of the Constitution of the Democratic Republic of Madagascar.

The Charter, based on a series of broadcasts Ratsiraka made in August 1975, is not only a revolutionary document but also an electoral platform, whose purpose was in part to establish Ratsiraka in the public's view as a national leader and to serve as a basis for the referendum campaign. As well as a general analysis of Malagasy society and a description of the proposed revolution (to be discussed later), it contains some quite specific promises to specific interest groups, reassurances to the 'bourgeoisie' and a general commitment to the *épanouissement* [flowering], collective and individual, of the Malagasy soul. With a new constitution, the Charter formed the basis of a referendum held on 21 December 1975. The question, as is usual in such cases, did not encourage a 'no' answer: 'For a new society, and to bring about the reign of justice and social equality, do you accept the Charter of the Socialist Revolution, and the Constitution that will apply it, and Captain Didier Ratsiraka as President of the Republic?' Given the intensity of the campaign, and the efforts made to mobilize the voters, the results were not surprising, and indeed, the promise of stability and coherence after a year of chaos preceded by nearly three years of drift makes them plausible as well. Of those eligible to vote, 92.6 per cent did and 94.7 per cent of those voted 'yes', with significant negative votes only in Antseranana (25 per cent) whose prosperity had been greatly harmed by the departure of French forces from its naval base, and Antananarivo (13.2 per cent) although whether these votes represent hesitations about the revolutionary direction of the Charter or disappointment at its substitution of scientific socialism for the 'republic of the humble' is not clear (Andriamirado, 1977a; Calvet, 1976; *Afrique-Asie*, 1976; *Afrique Contemporaine*, 1975, 1976). With the passage of the referendum, the process of installing the new regime began. Ratsiraka took his oath as President on 4 January 1976, and moved into the palace recently vacated by the French Embassy. The new constitution provided an eighteen month transition period for the establishment of its new institutions. During this period, government policy, including the detailed frameworks for the institutions themselves would be enacted by presidential decree. In spite of his centralization of policy making, there were considerable delays in setting up the institutions, and elections to the new National Popular Assembly did not take place until 1977.

There were several reasons for the delay, including disagreements among presidential advisers and between Ratsiraka's group and the other parties of the revolutionary coalition. Crises and challenges to its authority including riots in Antananarivo and Mahajanga distracted the regime's attention throughout the period. However, the major reason for the delay in setting up the legal institutions for the new republic lay elsewhere: the regime had no intention of putting them into operation until it had created its own political foundation. The lessons of the *fokonolona* elections of 1973, in which there was no clear regime party and which saw the return of many local PSD figures for lack of an organized alternative, were clear. There would be no elected institutions until the party structure of the new republic had been established.

Arema: The Vanguard of the Malagasy Revolution

There were several possible strategies for creating this political base. The regime could adopt one of the existing parties as its own, it could attempt to fuse the existing parties into a single party, it could establish its own party and bar the rest, or it could add a new party to the existing spectrum. Ratsiraka himself preferred the creation of a single party (see *Le Monde*, 28 December 1977; *Afrique-Asie*, January 1978; Calvet, 1976), whether by fusion of the existing ones or by the creation of a new one and dissolution of the others. These possibilities were blocked by the opposition of the parties themselves. Negotiations to form a single party broke down over quarrels among the parties and over their united refusal to give Ratsiraka and his followers the leading role in any new party. The alternative, elimination of the existing parties, would simply have taken more power than Ratsiraka's regime possessed at the time. Moreover, he owed his rise to power in part to the support of the parties at crucial moments in the armed forces' political manoeuvers, and eliminating them meant eliminating this possibly useful source of future support. The only remaining alternative was a new regime party in some sort of multi-party framework. The constitution had provided for the creation of a National Front for the Defence of the Revolution, to 'motivate and guide the spirit of the Revolution toward the establishment of Socialism' (article 9) but had left its exact form and functions unspecified. The Front could either provide the basis for a single party or serve as a forum for multi-party cooperation. When it became clear that the creation of a single party regime would not be possible, the establishment of the Front was delayed until the regime's own party was created.

The creation of the party, Arema (Vanguard of the Malagasy Revolution) was announced in March 1976. Unlike the other Malagasy parties, Arema leaders declared, the new regime party would be 'non political'. This declaration was not enough to distinguish Arema on the crowded party landscape, or to reassure a public considerably fatigued with politics, and party growth was slow. Finally, the territorial administration was given the task of setting up local party cells, with the result that recruitment increased and by the end of the year, Arema claimed to have over 90,000 members, more than any other Malagasy party (Calvet, 1976, p. 365). The party had a range of auxiliary organizations, and, in Antananarivo, a body of shock troops in the form of the TTS. Organized by the Minister of Youth and Population, these were a semi-paramilitary organization recruited from the Zoam, one of whose functions appeared to be to direct a flow of money to this volatile group and counter the other parties' troops. (*Afrique-Asie*, June 1976).

In May, the new party was admitted to the FNDR as its charter member. An earlier ordinance had laid out the conditions for membership in the Front, including adherence to the Charter of the Malagasy Revolution and to the principles of democratic centralism. Most important, a candidate for membership had to be approved by the Front's president, Didier Ratsiraka. This approval was delayed for other parties for several months, and two parties in particular, Monima and the MFM, refused to apply for membership, claiming that their revolutionary credentials hardly needed ratification by a group of newcomers whose own commitment was open to question. It was not until after the Antananarivo riots of September that the regime moved to open the Front to the other parties. In October the AKFM and a new party, Vonjy joined, as did Monima in December, although the latter refused to submit its party statutes for Ratsiraka's approval. The statutes of the FNDR were published at the end of December. Although these added little further illumination on what the Front would actually do, they did make one thing clear: only parties who were members of the Front could present cadidates in the elections planned for 1977. This excluded the MFM, the only party of the left to remain outside the Front, from participation in the round of elections to be held in 1977.

The end of 1976 marked the beginning of the electoral campaigns of 1977 with a flurry of nationalizations and 'charters' including a new statute for the university, a 'Charter for Socialist Enterprises', and a 'Statute for decentralized collectivities', the new version of the reform of the *fokonolona*. The statute extended the reform to urban areas, where the *fokonolona* generally corresponded to a neighbourhood or *quartier* (Antananarivo, for example, had 198 *fokonolona*: Calvet 1978, p. 308). Direct elections occurred at the *fokonolona* level and for the National Popular Assembly: councils at other levels were elected by the council of the lower level. The publication of the statute was followed rapidly by a series of elections, which served not only to staff the new institutions, but also to demonstrate the territorial reach of Arema. The first election, on 20 March was for the members of the Councils of the *fokonolona*, in all some 75,000 places. The sheer number of places to fill gave the party an advantage beyond that it had as the party of the government, since none of the other parties had the national organization necessary to run candidates in all areas; in fact, in many rural *fokonolona* the Arema list of candidates was the only list. Not surprisingly, the party received an overwhelming majority of the seats: 88.2 per cent in all, with some regional variations. Its lowest score was in Antananarivo province, especially in the capital where it received less than half the votes. The succeeding indirect elections simply magnified the results of the *fokonolona* elections. After this demonstration of strength it was not difficult for Arema to convince the other members of the FNDR to present a single common list of candidates for the national legislative elections. The only exception was Monima whose leader, discontented with the party's existing electoral results and prospective share of ANP seats withdrew the party from the FNDR and government.

   Given the fact that there was only one list, and that there had already been two general elections that year, the participation rate of 88.9 per cent was another demonstration of the regime's capacity for mobilization, particularly since both the MFM and Monima had urged abstention. If the elections indicated a seeming increase in the security of the government, so did the events surrounding the naming of the new CSR, where the departure of Monima was compensated for by the adhesion of the MFM, in the person of its leader, Manandafy Rakotinirina, who stated that while he would prefer a more thorough change he had decided to accept the existing 'revolution by ordinance' as the best available alternative (see the interviews in *Le Monde*, 28 December 1977). One month after the adhesion of the MFM, the regime's base was further solidified when a split in the Monima Central Committee led to the formation of the VSM (*Vondrona Socialista Monima*). The new party denounced Monja Jaona's 'dictatorial' leadership and asked to rejoin the FNDR. The request was quickly granted.

Towards the Crisis: Outrageous Investment and Omnidirectional Debt

Although Arema's electoral victories, and the consolidation of the FNDR seemed to indicate a stabilization of the regime, they did nothing to help those in charge coordinate their own activities. The breadth of Ratsiraka's coalition, so necessary for the acquisition of power, was a handicap in its exercise. By 1977, the regime was seriously divided by quarrels over economic policy, particularly between those who saw nationalization as a way of constructing a state-run economy, and those who saw it as a transitional phase that would end when the nationalized industries were turned over to the Malagasy entrepreneurs (de Gaudusson, 1979, p. 217). These quarrels were reflected in the drafting and application of the regime's economic policy documents, the Charter of Socialist Enterprises, 'Options for Socialist Planning', and 'Plan for the Year 2000'. The Charter was withdrawn for further revision immediately after its publication, and the 'Options' and 'Plan' were vague and general except for the timetable that predicted the establishment of the basic structures for socialist economic development by 1984, and the achievement of 'multi-faceted and balanced development' by the year 2000. The actual plan for 1978–80 was both more specific and less encouraging. It projected an average growth of 5.75 per cent in GNP and sufficient growth in personal income to bring consumption back to the 1970 level, itself already a decline from the 1960 level. The plan admitted that even this growth would not create enough new jobs to absorb the projected increase in the work-force, and spoke longingly of overall industrialization (see RDM, 1977, 1978).

Both the overall plan for the year 2000 and the 1978–80 plan are perhaps best treated as 'wish lists'. In any event, neither could have predicted the direction government policy took in 1978. In that year, it was announced that a policy of all out investment would be adopted, to be financed by borrowing *tous azimuts* [omnidirectional]. The results of this policy were to have such a devastating effect on the economy that by 1980 Madagascar had to apply for financial aid from the IMF, a regime under which it is still existing. The political consequences of the crisis included a series of revolts in some of the most essential sectors of society in 1981–2 and a split in the governing group itself, that in conjunction, threatened the existence of the regime.

Madagascar was, of course, not the only Third World (or other) country to embark on a policy of 'omnidirectional borrowing' in the late 1970s, and the ways in which this pattern alleviated problems of the First World international economic system have been well-documented and described. In the case of the Malagasy Republic the international pressures to undertake a policy of greater borrowing can be seen in a World Bank country study published in 1979, the result of a mission undertaken in the summer of 1978. After criticizing both the Plan for the Year 2000 and the 1978–80 plan for paying 'insufficient attention to the immediacy of the need to stimulate output growth and employment' the report presented a 'different planning strategy' that was 'not likely to be feasible without substantially greater recourse to external resources than is presently considered necessary'. It argued that by following this strategy, 'the Malagasy economy could sustain an annual growth rate of 4–5 per cent until the end of the next decade and lay the foundations for more rapid and self reliant development in the period beyond.' (see the Introduction to the World Bank Report, especially p. iii). In the conclusion the report pointed out that Madagascar's external debt— 10 per cent of GNP in 1976—was half that of the average for low income countries and once more urged 'a departure from traditional attitudes towards external finance' (World Bank Report, 53).

By the time the Bank's report was published, the policy of 'outrageous investment' had begun. Adoption of the policy was not simply the result of outside pressure, but also met several of the internal needs of the regime. Like many disastrous undertakings, it 'seemed like a good idea at the time' given the strengths and weaknesses of Ratsiraka's position. Politically, the regime's attention was no longer monopolized by considerations of survival, and the economic conjuncture seemed favourable: the price of coffee, Madagascar's major export, was at a historic high point, and the balance of payments, for once, was positive. State expenditure had grown, but income had increased, too, with the nationalization of such profit-making enterprises as banks, insurance companies and import-export establishments. The regime seemed to have a strong basis from which to gamble (see Cadoux and de Gaudusson, 1980, also *Afrique-Asie*, Special Madagascar, 1980, Latrémolière, 1980; Ramaro, 1980; Roux, 1980).

On the other hand, its political and economic weaknesses provided reasons for seeking large sums of money to inject into the society. Public and private investment, already low under the Tsiranana regime, had virtually stopped after 1972, and the economy not only was in no shape to provide the basis for the socialist economic development foreseen by the Plan for the Year 2000, it was in a process of accelerating degeneration (see World Bank Report for figures). Production of both subsistence and cash crops had stagnated or declined, leaving the regime with the necessity of importing ever increasing amounts of rice with a declining income. Only the high price of coffee made it possible to continue the imports. Industrial production had also stagnated and the transportation and communications infrastructure deteriorated. It was not hard to argue that massive investments were required simply to prevent further decay of the economy.

The infusion of large amounts of money into the system also seemed to be a way of solving several political problems, since those groups with the capacity to threaten the regime all had demands that implied increased government expenditure. The most important were the education system, the administration, the armed forces, and Arema itself. In its efforts to placate potential and actual students and their parents, the regime had expanded the education system until, in 1978, it absorbed 26 per cent of the national budget (Hugon, 1978, p. 125). The primary and secondary level had expanded to such a degree that the existing expansion of the University could not meet the demand for places. Further expansion of the university would simply create another problem, that of finding places for the graduates. The increase in the number of graduates that had occurred between 1972 and 1978 had been absorbed by increasing the number of state employees to nearly double the pre-1972 level (D. in *Sudestasie*, 1985, p. 35), a solution that the regime did not have the means to apply indefinitely. Educational policy itself was a source of controversy, and the willingness of students to take to the streets in demonstrations that often turned into riots combined with the memories of 1972 to make their demands on the regime a continuing source of concern.

The administration itself was another group with which the regime had difficult relations. Unsettled by the political upheavals of the last several years, it met the political initiatives of the government with a 'wait-and-see' attitude that was as damaging as direct opposition would have been (Andriamirado, 1977a, p. 3). Administrator's salaries had been falling behind inflation since before the revolution and shortages of imported goods, limited by quota since 1975 but available on the black market at the usual exhorbitant mark-up, made it difficult for them to maintain their expected consumption patterns. At the lower levels it was difficult for bureaucrats to keep above poverty, and the open and lavish expenditures of the new elite brought to power by the revolution served to increase hostility to the regime.

Another critical, and expensive, pressure group was the armed forces, which had expanded to at least 30,000 since 1972. While they had been more directly involved in the creation of the regime than the administration, and might therefore be expected to be more supportive of it, large numbers of officers belonged to factions that had lost out in the power struggle and were hostile to the 'revolutionary' orientation of the winners. Occasions for resentment increased as an army was reorganized to strengthen the position of those considered most loyal to the regime and as French advisers and weapons and training in France were replaced by Soviet and North Korean advisers and weapons and training in Moscow and Pyonyang. Promotions and salary increases helped calm the discontented, but combined with the expansion of the forces and the acquisition of new weapons they raised 'essential' expenditures on the armed forces to at least 25 per cent of the national budget (see Hugon, 1978).

Finally, there were the divisions in Arema itself. By 1978 these had crystallized to the point that observers spoke of a 'left' or 'presidential' Arema led by Ratsiraka and a 'right' or 'oppositional' Arema dominated by the Minister of Finance, Rakotovao-Razakaboana, and centred on the Antananarivo federation of the party, which he led (see for example Cadoux and de Gaudusson, 1980; Chaigneau, 1983a; Langellier, 1982; Leymarie, 1982; Moine, 1981). The federation was small, but its strategic position in the capital, the personal ties its members had in the administration, in the army, and in circles outside Madagascar, particularly in France, made up for its minority position in the party. In fact, given the mildness of the revolutionary commitment of many regime figures and Arema supporters, real support for its arguments was probably close to a majority. Since many of the day-to-day disputes between the Arema factions, and among the parties of the FNDR were over places in the administration, fellowships and in general over the division of government expenditure, increasing the amount of money available could be expected to improve relations within the regime and reduce the bitterness of quarrels over policy. Moreover, the fact that the money would be channelled through the part of the regime apparatus controlled by Ratsiraka and his supporters would have the added benefit of reinforcing their own position. In short, if the long-term goal of the 'outrageous investment' policy was some type of economic development, its adoption also reflected the immediate need of the regime for money to meet the demands of both supporters and potential or actual opponents (see Cadoux and de Gaudusson, 1980, p. 343; D. in *Sudestasie*, 1982, p. 39).

So the policy of outrageous investment and omnidirectional borrowing began. The education system was a major beneficiary, particularly at the secondary and university levels. Regional university centres were created in all provincial capitals (including Antananarivo) and by 1981 the number of university students had doubled to 30,000 (Cadoux and de Gaudusson, 1980, p. 373). The armed forces received planes, artillery and tanks. The transportation and communication sectors improved, and a dam at Andekaleka, capable of producing enough electricity to fuel a major industrial plant, itself still to be built, was completed. Industry and agriculture were not neglected: one of Africa's largest textile factories was built at Morondava, and another one at Toliara, and a project for growing and processing soya beans in quantities that would make Madagascar a major exporter was started at Antsirabe. Fertilizer factories, shrimp processing plants, plans to exploit deposits of oil-bearing shale were among the multiple projects undertaken. 'Never since the time of Queen Ranovalona have there been so many realizations' Ratsiraka declared (*Afrique-Asie*, 16 March 1981; for more about the 'outrageous investment' policy see *Afrique-Asie*, Special Madagascar, June 1980; Cadoux and de Gaudusson, 1980; Leymarie, 1982; Ramaro, 1980).

Money for investments came from a variety of sources, the largest public contributors being the World Bank and its family. However, most loans were raised from commercial banks at commercial rates: for example, the Boeing 747 that Air Madagascar bought as part of its plan to develop an international network was financed by loans from Chase Manhattan and Citibank (LOI 14 April 1984). What the final result of the 'outrageous investment' policy would have been had all the projects operated as planned is open to debate, as are the reasons for the economic collapse that occurred instead (for further discussion, see the section on economic policy). The seriousness of the crisis, however, is not debatable. By 1981 the country's external debt had increased from US$293.5 million in 1978 to US$1,372.0 million and debt servicing took over one-third of export earnings (Cadoux and de Gaudusson, 1980, p. 372). The government's deficit had increased from 1.5 per cent of GNP in 1977 to 19.2 per cent (see *Afrique-Asie*, Special Madagascar, October 1982). Rice imports tripled between 1980 and 1982 and with the increased bill for imports of petroleum put further strain on export earnings and led to the virtual cessation of imports of other commodities including replacement parts for machinery and fertilizer for agriculture. By 1982 the industrial plant was working at 30 per cent of capacity, GNP per capita had declined by 10 per cent from the previous year, and inflation, even by official figures, was reaching 30 to 50 per cent (see *Afrique-Asie*, Special Madagascar, October 1982, p. 37; Chaigneau, 1983a, p. 17). The shortages of imports and rice further entrenched the black market and continued the vicious circle of shortages creating the market and the market absorbing goods to create further shortages.

The first signs of the crisis had driven the government to seek the assistance of the IMF as early as 1980. The regime did look for other sources of aid notably in Libya and the Soviet Union, but although Libya gave some immediate short-term assistance and the Soviet Union agreed to furnish some petroleum, neither was willing to bankroll Madagascar to the extent necessary to meet its debts and, of course, neither had the influence with Western lenders necessary to arrange the alternative solution, a rescheduling of the debts. This left only an approach to the IMF, and a *rapprochement* with Western countries, most notably France, the United States and Great Britain. Between 1980 and the present a series of agreements have been negotiated, always with great difficulty, since the IMF has insisted on its usual package of devaluation and reductions of government expenditure via decreases in the size of the administration and the ending of subsidies for items like rice. Individual countries refused to take on Madagascar's burdens without the participation of the IMF, and private lenders doubted that any attempts to rescue the country would succeed (in 1984 Chase Manhattan and Citibank tried to repossess the Boeing). The Malagasy government followed a strategy of using the influence of those countries or organizations with which it had reached temporary agreement to persuade the recalcitrant, developing closer ties to the Western countries without totally abandoning its relationship with the Soviet Union and other socialist countries. This latter relationship, crucial to regime survival in other, non-economic ways, was also a useful bargaining counter in the economic negotiations. Economic conditions continued to deteriorate during the period, and political crises resulting from economic hardship caused both by the crisis and by the application of IMF austerity measures left the government with little choice in later negotiations. In the end it accepted, at least in appearance, almost all the conditions for assistance, including a reorientation of economic policy symbolized by a new invest-ment code published in 1985 and designed to attract rather than control foreign public investment (see *Le Monde*, 23 June 1985). By mid-1985, the IMF was pointing to Madagascar as one of its success stories (for an evaluation, see the section on economic policy).

The success, if success it was, had its price: what a World Bank Report of the same period called the 'unacceptable social costs' of austerity and economic decline (see *Afrique-Asie*, Special Madagascar, July 1985; *LOI*, 15 December 1984; De Barrin, 1985). The turmoil created by these costs combined with other weaknesses of the regime to create a series of internal crises that culminated in serious uprisings in Antananarivo in 1984 and 1985 and that threatened Ratsiraka's control of his most important base, the armed forces. Demonstrations and riots continued to be a regular feature of life in the capital throughout the period. Whether they involved university students (the university was on strike again from November 1980 to June 1981), or uprisings in popular quarters like Isotry, the riots followed what had become a classic pattern:

the scenario is always the same: first the circulation of unbased rumors, incidents, in general at a football game, followed by looting and arson in town, massive intervention by the army and declaration of a curfew . . . At the origin of this series of events are always the same groups of unemployed youths . . . Now that the government has taken charge of them called the TTS . . . [*LOI*, 14 November 1981]

As an example of the type of rumour involved, a series of incidents occurred in Isotry in October 1980, when several people were lynched by crowds who accused them of killing Malagasies to sell their breasts and testicles to North Korean military and technical assistants for use in some obscene ritual. The regime accused the MFM of being behind most riots, although the party had in part lost, in part abandoned, its contacts with the groups the TTS sprang from. The MFM, and others, in turn accused the regime of using the TTS as provocateurs, to create incidents justifying armed intervention to break up strikes and demonstrations. They pointed to the general immunity the TTS seemed to enjoy for their more illegal activities and to the promotion of the Minister in charge of relations with them, Remi Tiandraza to the Arema political bureau in 1982.

Uprisings also occurred elsewhere in the country. In Antseranana crowds protesting against corruption in the marketing of vanilla forced the resignation of several local officials. Government attempts to reimpose the officials led to riots whose suppression took at least nine lives. (The regime did eventually arrest some of those accused of corruption, including the director of the provincial ministry of the economy and several Arema elected officials. See *LOI* for 6, 13 and 20 March 1982.) In Toliara in May a clash between gendarmes and a band of 2,000 peasants left several dozen dead. The gendarmes claimed to have mistaken the peasants for a band of outlaws while the peasants—through Monima—claimed that they had been pursuing the outlaws and that the gendarmes were acting on the orders of a local rancher, an Arema official who was the head of the cattle stealing operation (see *LOI*, 29 May 1982; Langellier, 1982).

The riots in Antananarivo and elsewhere were merely an overt expression of a more general political *malaise* that affected the coalition supporting the regime. Among the first groups to begin open criticism were the churches. In mid-1980 the cardinal of Antananarivo published an episcopal letter in which he attacked the regime for disappointing the hopes it had created by its espousal of socialism (Cadoux and de Gaudusson, 1980). Criticism continued and by late 1984 relations had reached the point where the churches were suspected of contemplating an armed uprising and the regime suspected of arranging, with the TTS as its agents, the murders of several priests. A bishops' letter, published in January 1985, discussed in abstract terms the characteristics of a dictatorship:

Dictators say that the people rule, even as they confiscate their power ... It is no longer competence that determines the attribution of responsibility, but ideological affinities ... the regime proclaims urbi et orbi that national independence is not negotiable ... But what is the reality? On one side are the great powers from whom it borrows its ideology and on the other side those to whom it goes for economic and financial assistance. [The letter is reprinted in *Jeune Afrique*, 2 March 1985, and *Etudes*, May 1985.]

In case anyone had missed the point, a second letter, published in March, directly criticized the regime for the disintegration of Malagasy society.

Other signs of opposition also appeared. Former PSD politicians organized openly for the first time since 1976, and secret societies were rumoured to be forming in the capital and to be recruiting members in the armed forces and right Arema. A new type of organization, self-defence societies, also began to appear in Antananarivo and the provincial capitals. Usually based on the principles of Kung Fu, and vowing a cult to the films of Bruce Lee, they had an ominously wide base of recruitment: not only youth from the middle and lower middle sectors that had been particularly hard hit by the economic crisis, but also the same type of unemployed uneducated that had formerly joined the Zoams. The Kung Fu clubs had open links with the churches, with non-Arema parties in the FNDR, (one club president was a member of the MFM's bureau politique) and rumoured links with the newly revived secret societies. In general they portrayed themselves as a counterweight to the 'corrupt' TTS (*LOI*, 15 December 1984).

More directly threatening to the regime than general popular discontent was opposition in its own bases of support: the FNDR, Arema, and the armed forces. These had never been cohesive entities, but rather arenas for disputes over policy and the distribution of benefits, and the economic crisis exacerbated both types of disagreement. Since Ratsiraka's position depended in part on being able to keep the factions at least minimally satisfied, the simultaneous increase in conflict and decline in resources made the maintenance of support more difficult at the same time that external negotiations and internal uprisings made it more necessary. The conflicts became visible in a series of plots, and other incidents that demonstrated the degree to which oppostion existed within the regime as well as among excluded groups. In response to a particularly serious crisis in 1981-2 the regime undertook a series of measures designed to reinforce its position. It was successful in overcoming the specific crises and in reducing the power of some of the groups involved in them, but many of the internal and external sources of opposition remained in place, and reappeared at the end of 1984.

The lack of cohesiveness of the FNDR was increased in March 1981 when Monja Jaona brought his branch of Monima back into the Front and was rewarded with an appointment to the CSR, where his age made him the *doyen* and formal second in the regime. This 'reconciliation' did not stop him from continuing to criticize the regime for corruption, economic failures and lack of zeal in pursuing the revolution, and given his irrascible nature, relations in the FNDR and CSR were, if anything, worse after his return than before (*Afrique-Asie*, 20 March 1981; Cadoux and de Gaudusson, 1980). Like the leaders of the other parties in the Front, he developed contacts with opposition groups outside the Front and seemed to be contemplating, if not preparing, the possibility of a change of regime. In Arema, divisions were so bad that Ratsiraka had included members of the party and his own entourage in the list of enemies of the revolution cited in his 1981 New Year's speech, castigating them as Judases and Simon Peters. More concretely, the Minister of Finance and leader of the 'right' Arema, Rakotovao-Razakaboana (generally considered to be the person Ratsiraka saw as Judas) was using his position to dominate negotiations with the IMF. The negotiations had too many political consequences for Ratsiraka to allow this to happen, but the Minister's official position and the fact that he enjoyed the confidence of the IMF negotiators as a reasonable rather than a revolutionary Malagasy made it difficult to evict him (Cadoux and de Gaudusson, 1980, 379; Leymarie, 1982; *LOI*, 9 January 1982).

The real danger to the regime, of course, would come from an opposition coalition that included the armed forces. In January 1982, Ratsiraka announced the discovery of just such a coalition and the arrest of eighty-two people, including priests, bureaucrats, some Arema members, and five colonels from various branches of the armed forces. This was one of several plots the regime had 'discovered' since its founding, but it seemed to have more foundation than some of the others (*Le Monde* characterized it as 'apparently real this time') and rumours claimed that Ratsiraka and his entourage had felt threatened enough to leave the capital temporarily and take refuge at the Soviet-run air base near Antseranana (*Le Monde*, 24 February 1982; Cadoux and de Gaudusson, 1980; *LOI*, 30 January 1982). Among those questioned, but later released were some leaders of 'right Arema'. The existence of the plot, the breadth of its recruitment, and the fact that the plotters included people from the regime itself, all indicate the seriousness of the general crisis the regime found itself in.

The 1982 presidential elections announced in January and to be held in

November provided the occasion for Ratsiraka to begin to reassert his control of the situation (local and legislative elections were postponed until 1983). The presidential elections were, of course, expected to provide confirmation of his leadership of the party, the Front, and the country, and any weaknesses they revealed in the Arema position could be corrected before the other elections. Within Arema, Ratsiraka began to follow a strategy that consisted of undermining the power of the members of 'right Arema' even as he was adopting their policies and trying to prove to the IMF that he was 'reasonable' as well as 'revolutionary'. A government shuffle that preceded the election removed Rakotovao-Razakaboana from the Ministry of Finance, and 'promoted' him to a seat on the CSR. Again the election was useful. As head of the Antananarivo section of Arema, the minister had a choice between openly opposing Ratsiraka or campaigning on his behalf. Any sign of disloyalty would provide an excuse for further attacks on his position.

The elections also provided an occasion to test the loyalties of other participants in the Front and elsewhere in the system. Ratsiraka had not asked for the investiture of the Front as a whole, which left the way open for the other parties of the Front to present candidates. In the end, most did endorse Ratsiraka, all after extensive internal debate. The AKFM was the only party not to add a long list of conditions to its support. There was, however, to be one other candidate. In September Monja Jaona announced his candidacy in a speech that attacked the regime for economic failure, corruption and the collapse of law and order. He was supported in the campaign by a curious coalition of his own section of Monima, some members of the VSM, some radical members of the MFM dissatisfied with their party's decision to support the regime and, on the other hand some dissidents from the right-wing parties of the Front, (quietly) by some right Arema, and even by some former PSD figures.

Although the campaign was saluted by *Le Monde* as 'a political debate in a climate of relative liberty rare enough in Africa to be a credit to the regime' (*Le Monde*, 10 November 1982) the results were, of course, predictable. It is probable that Monja Jaona would not have won under any circumstances given the lack of real organization of his party. Ratsiraka won 80.17 per cent of the votes, with, however, only 50 per cent in Antananarivo, and that only after a recount (early published results had given Monja Jaona the victory, *LOI*, 20 November; *Le Monde*, 10 November 1982). Its failure to 'deliver' the capital further undermined the position of right Arema. Ratsiraka summoned Rakotovao-Razakaboana to his office and attacked him for *maladresse* (the presidential campaign had been run out of a bank, hardly an attactive venue in a city whose population was poor, and increasingly so, or a logical choice for the vanguard of a revolution), for excessively visible irregularities, but above all for the meagre results. Ratsiraka's fellow candidate was no more pleased with the results of the election. Monja Jaona declared that by his count he had received 68.17 per cent of the vote and called for a general strike to bring down the regime. Although there were supporting demonstrations in Antananarivo and the provincial capitals, there was no general uprising, and Monja Jaona was once more put under house arrest. (He was released for the 1983 legislative elections, in which he won a seat in the ANP in Antananarivo; *Afrique-Asie*, 3 January 1983; *LOI*, 3 September 1983.)

In 1983, a series of trials began, in which the regime dealt with real and symbolic enemies, both civilian and military. A trial of the officers involved in the 1982 plot ended with surprisingly light sentences, a surprise that Ratsiraka called the result of a Merina plot. However, the regime made its point in a second trial, of three officers who had been held since 1977 on accusations of spying for South Africa. They received sentences of deportation (in effect, permanent house arrest) and ten years of hard labour. These trials demonstrated the regime's intention to control the armed forces, but not necessarily its ability to do so. Ratsiraka resumed his commission (he had resigned it in 1979 as part of the civilianization of the regime, itself part of the policy of outrageous investments) and was appointed Admiral by the ANP, thereby becoming the ranking officer in the forces. However, rivalries continued, particularly between the regular forces, and the DGID and the regiments directly associated with the presidency. The gendarmerie, which had taken second place to the regular armed forces after Ratsiraka's accession to power, was particularly disaffected. In May 1984, the body of the head of the presidential guard, a key witness in the second trial, was found near the gendarmerie officers' mess at Antsirabe, and there were rumours of other clashes between the President's guard and the gendarmerie (*LOI*, 9 June 1984).

The military's loyalty became especially crucial in late 1984 as popular resentment at economic conditions grew. In Antananarivo these tensions centred around the Kung Fu groups, who by then claimed over 10,000 members in the capital and elsewhere, and who had provided Monja Jaona's bodyguards in 1982. There were said to be secret Kung Fu sections in the armed forces. In September, the regime was sufficiently alarmed that the Minister of Sport (also the minister 'responsible' for the TTS) banned the practice of the martial arts. The clubs retaliated by burning the Youth Palace. However, their real show of force came in the first week of December when they invaded the main camp of the TTS, a no-go area even for the police.

With the enthusiastic cooperation of the local population they killed as many as they could, anywhere between 100 and 250. The killing went on for three days, while the police and gendarmerie encircled the area but did not move in (*LOI* 8 December 1984, 15 December 1984; *Le Monde* 10 December 1985).

It has never been established whether Ratsiraka gave an order to intervene that was refused or whether he acquiesced in the violence, either to get rid of the TTS, who had become an increasing embarassment to the regime and/or out of fear of the reaction of the Antananarivo crowd at being denied the opportunity to take revenge on the group. The failure of the armed forces to intervene was followed by several changes designed to improve the regime's control over them. The Minister of Sport, already in trouble because of his bad relations with Celine Ratsiraka, was removed. The head of the army, rumoured to have connections with both the MFM and the Kung Fu movement was 'promoted' to the presidency of the Military Council and replaced by one of Ratsiraka's closest collaborators. The gendarmerie, which had been without a direct commander following the death of its commanding general (it had been nominally under the direction of the Prime Minister in December) also received a new head known for his loyalty to the President.

In spite of these changes, Ratsiraka did not attack the Kung Fu movement directly, and the question of what to do about them divided the regime. Groups like the DGID argued that they should be eliminated as quickly as possible, while others argued that given their level of support both in the general population and among important groups an attack on the Kung Fu movement might lead to resistance and the end of the regime. Ratsiraka sided with the latter group, and spent the early part of 1985 cultivating opposition groups, particularly the churches, and foreign powers. His 1985 New Year's speech declared that the Malagasy revolution was open to other currents of thought, and urged Malagasies to read Pythagoras, Descartes and the Bible as well as Marx. At the ceremony celebrating the 150th anniversary of the translation of the Bible into Malagasy, he declared that while he accepted Marxism as an economic doctrine, 'I also believe firmly in God, even at the price of my life', and proceeded to demonstrate his knowledge of the Bible with an exegesis of the ten commandments and several parables (*Le Monde*, 21 March 1985). The churches were not immediately impressed: the head of the island's protestant churches suggested that the first to take the President's advice to read the Bible more often should be his own ministers (*Madagascar Matin*, 21 March 1985), but they drew back from further confrontation. In mid-July *Lakroa* published an article criticizing foreign reports that characterized the churches as an 'opposition to the regime'. Individual Christians should recognize the accomplishments as well as the shortcomings of the regime, and the church itself would never aspire to the role of opposition in the sense of furnishing the basis for alternation in power (*Lakroa*, 15 July 1985). Continued liberalization of the economy and cabinet changes that brought post-revolutionary 'technocrats' into office reassured foreign powers, and completed the process of destroying the power of right Arema.

By July the regime felt strong enough to move against the Kung Fu organization, and on 31 July the army and gendarmerie destroyed their establishments in Antananarivo and other cities, killing their leader and several hundred of his followers. Within a few months TTS were appearing again on the streets of Antananarivo. Ratsiraka stated that the armed forces had acted to prevent a coup designed to overthrow his regime and establish a state dedicated to religion and the principles of Kung Fu. He had been reproached for weakness in December, now he was acting to show the strength of the regime. In effect, ten years after the establishment of his regime, the incident showed both its strength and weakness. Perpetually under challenge, not always sure of his control of his own instruments of rule, but able to balance oppositions, and extract support when absolutely necessary, Ratsiraka has achieved a kind of stability in instability.

5 Social Structure and Political System

The most important characteristic of Malagasy society is the number and diversity of structures that serve as arenas for political interaction and as the bases for political action in other arenas. Another important characteristic is the degree to which the operative units of political interaction are not formal organizations but networks of personal relationships, what Archer (1976, p. 34) calls 'alliance groups' without structured organization or precise boundaries. This is to be expected in the face-to-face environment of local politics, but it is also true at the national level, in spite of the existence of formal organizations and institutions. The diversity of these groups, their diffuse organization, and the fact that very few have nation wide coverage, means that Malagasy society offers few levers for political elites seeking wide spread change or even a broad base of support; as Calvet and de Gaudusson argue (1980, p. 387), it is a society that resists monolithism and that offers an inauspicious environment for an aspiring revolutionary power (see also Camacho, 1981, p. 30; D. in *Sudestasie*, 1982, p. 39).

The number and variety of structures is the result, not only of pre-existing diversity, but also of the impact of state polity since the nineteenth century, as successive regimes introduced different reward systems, each modifying the groups and relationships created by its predecessors without eradicating them. The interaction of pre-colonial, colonial, post-independence and now post-revolutionary reward systems varies from region to region and even from village to village as does the original point of departure (See Althabe, 1969; Bloch, 1971; Feeley-Harnik, 1982; Kottak, 1980 for descriptions of the process on the east coast, in Imerina, on the west coast, and in Betsileo territory). Another reason for the diversity lies in the fact that the central state has never had a monopoly of control over the sources of individual or group prestige or prosperity. Many of Madagascar's different types of group have one or more of the following characteristics: their own status system, independent access to sources of income, including external income, an independent network of contacts within and outside the country. The churches are an example of a set of groups enjoying all three sources of autonomy. This is not a new situation. The colonial state also had to deal with competing arenas for the allocation of values and resources, and even added to the complexity of the situation by relying politically on elites from the least developed and least populated regions, the west and southwest, without destroying the economic and social advantages of the groups it was excluding from political power. By relying as extensively as it did on outside support, the Tsiranana regime perpetuated the division between political and other types of power, although it did distribute enough advantages to its supporters to give them their own powers of resistance when the First Republic was displaced. As a result, while control of state office and power is useful to all groups in Madagascar and essential to those without the bases of autonomy, it is not crucial to group survival and individual enrichment to the degree considered characteristic of other African countries. Rather, as Chazan argues for Ghana (1983, p. 7), the state in Madagascar has been an important but by no means exclusive focus of group activity.

If Malagasy society is diverse, its units are also diffuse and its political actors not always well delineated. Formal organizations like trade unions exist, but they are not necessarily more structured, coherent or cohesive than an extended family network or a group based on old school ties; often they are less so. Many of the 'groups' discussed in this section are obviously only categories, some of whose members can be mobilized for action by some type of 'leadership' some of the time: youth, and students are examples of this type of group. However, formally constituted organizations, including both weak ones like the trade unions, and stronger ones like the churches or the armed forces, often have a similar lack of structure. Their membership is not always in regular communication with the leaders, nor are all parts of the organization always in regular communication with each other. The groups rather provide a potential base of supporters, opportunities for the making of contacts, and often the material resources that aid in the construction and maintenance of the alliance groups that are the real units of political action (see Archer, 1976; Camacho, 1981; Serre, 1975). These alliance groups can be structured in two different ways, either as patron–client networks with a hierarchical organization based on mutual exchange of goods and services or as horizontal cliques organized around the pursuit of common advantage. Groups based on ethnicity or family often take the form of a patron–client network centred on one or more members in high position, while Archer's 'Club des 48' is an example of a clique. Both types of group are usually reinforced by social links, and when these do not exist they are often created via mechanisms like marriage or fictive kinship (for example, Ratsiraka's own marriage to the daughter of a close political associate of his father). At the national level especially, groups overlap since most individuals participate in more than one network. While the 1972 revolution and the 1975 introduction of a Marxist regime have led to changes in Madagascar's social structure they have not reduced the importance of these groups; on the contrary, much of the structure and many of the activities of the current regime can be explained by the fact that it is itself organized along the same principles.

Class

Among the important changes in Malagasy society have been the linked processes of consolidation of elites at the national level, their increasing separation from the rest of the population, an increase in the importance of access to state power in the process of self-enrichment, and a corresponding increase in the proportion of state based elites in the total. (See Roux, 1980; Hugon, 1977; Rabemora, 1985; Archer, 1976 and Serre, 1975 predict much the same outcome for the revolution.) In part these changes are the result of trends that began during the Tsiranana regime, in part they are the result of external economic conditions that have little to do with government policy, but to a large degree they are the intended and unintended result of the policies of the two post-1972 regimes. Most observers agree that while distinctions between traditional and new, private and state based, Merina and non-Merina elites are still important, the old opposition between a traditional Merina elite based on private enterprise and the liberal professions and a new state based *côtier* elite is becoming blurred (see also Bezy, 1979; Leymarie, 1982; Rabemora, 1985). President Tsiranana may have started life as a barefoot peasant boy guarding the family herd, but coastal families of the type represented by Ratsiraka and his associates are now into at least their third generation of people accustomed to wealth, education, and Western consumption patterns. They have used their wealth to move into private business (both the President's brother and one of his brothers-in-law have made the transition from state employment to private business) while Merina of both traditional and non-traditional status have moved into state positions, particularly in the nationalized enterprises (it was his connections with both state and private economic elites that made Rakotomavo-Razakaboana such a threat to Ratsiraka). The post-1972 increase in the state's role in the economy has meant that both legitimate businesses, like those requiring imports, and illegitimate ones like the black market cannot function without cooperation between state-based and private based elites. Finally, the increasing gap between this group and the rest of the population reinforces perceptions of common interest.

Increasing the number of Malagasies who benefited from state employment and economic activity was one of the goals of the participants in the May 1972 events, and it is clear that since that time the number of people drawing benefits from the state has grown. The size of the bureaucracy has doubled, numbers in armed forces have tripled, and the Malgachization of economic activity and the creation of new state enterprises have added an unknown but substantial number of posts. Not all of these people are getting rich from their positions since, according to most observers, the real incomes of lower and even middle level state employees have declined in the last five years: but many are, and quite visibly. However, this increase in the number of state posts has not absorbed, and could not possibly absorb the new job-seekers who arrive on the market each year. (The World Bank estimates their numbers at 100,000. Even assuming no rural–urban immigration, this would mean 16,000 urban job-seekers a year (1979, p. 15). Hugon puts the yearly number of new job-seekers at 250,000, with 40,000 seeking urban jobs (1982, p. 294). Increasing the number of secondary schools and university places has taken some pressure off the bottom of the system, but at the cost of increasing it at the top, particularly since the growth of the administration has stopped with the arrival of the economic crisis.

The growth in the number of people drawing incomes from the state has therefore not prevented, and to a degree has even accelerated, the impoverishment of the rest of the population. Ending the long-term decline in general income was another of the goals of 1972 and 1975, and it is probable that immediately after 1972, when the minimum wage was increased and the poll and cattle taxes abolished, most people's real income increased (see Hugon, 1977; Roux, 1980). However, this was just a temporary reversal of a long term trend to lower per capita incomes. Added to the trend were the activities undertaken by the privileged to maintain their position in an economy that shrank even as their numbers increased. The money to do this has come from two sources: external borrowing and assistance and increased extraction from the general population. This extraction, under-taken by both state-based and private elites, takes place through 'official' channels such as the differentials between the price paid to producers of cash crops and the price at which state agencies sell the crops, as well as through 'parallel' channels like corruption and black marketeering. This 'redistribu-tion' has increased the poverty of the general population even more than the per capita income figures suggest. As poverty spreads, social and economic differences that were once important, like those between workers and small businessmen, and even caste differences, have become less important. (See Bouillon, 1973 for an early discussion of the phenomenon, which pre-dates both the Ramanantsoa and Ratsiraka regimes, but which appears to have accelerated under them. See also Andriamirado, 1977a; Cadoux and de Gaudusson, 1980; D. in *Sudestasie*, 1982; De Barrin, 1985; Gintzburger, 1983;

Hugon, 1977 and 1982; Langellier, 1982; Leymarie, 1982; Rabemora, 1985; Ravaloson, 1983-4. Not all of these writers are sympathetic to the current regime, but sympathizers and critics agree in their descriptions of general impoverishment and widespread corruption.) There has been some popular resistance to this process, seen most dramatically in the attacks on official profiteers in Antseranana in 1982 and in the appeal of groups like the Kung Fu. The regime itself has made some attempt to mitigate the effects of impoverishment by subsidizing essential products like rice, but most of these subsidies have been ended or reduced as a condition of IMF assistance.

As a result of these changes, diversity based on economic position is declining in Madagascar. Elites are becoming more unified at the top, and economic gradations among the other strata are fading. Can we call this a process of class formation, a term increasingly used by both Marxists and non-Marxists to describe similar processes in other African countries? (For descriptions of the debate, see Tordoff, 1984, pp. 87-96; Young, 1982a.) Many observers of Malagasy politics do argue that one of the outcomes of the 'revolution' is the constitution of a new bourgeoisie, with a dual basis in the state and private entrepreneurial activities (see, for example, Rabemora, 1985, and for a counter-argument based on a critique of Archer's discussion of the issue, Molet, 1977) and it is a common criticism of socialist regimes, whether 'scientific' or not that their ideology serves only to cloak the perpetuation of old class relationships or the creation of a new class, as exploitive of the general population as the one it displaced.

While it is clear that a considerable amount of individual, and individualistic, accumulation is going on in Madagascar, it seems premature to argue either that the elites in place constitute a crystallized class or that one will come into existence as a result of their activities. First, the consolidation of elites described above is only partial: economic and non-economic differences remain important. While non-economic divisions, such as ethnicity, rarely form the basis for united action on the part of elite and non elite, they often prevent united action by elites. Second, the activities of the elites have been destructive of the country's economic base, on which their own enrichment depends, and of their political base both internally and among the external groups on whose continued confidence their survival as a group rests. Finally, the rural areas of Madagascar are not yet totally drawn into the system, and at this level local sources of wealth and status remain important.

Localisms: Ethnicity, Family, Region

Another organizing principle of Malagasy society and politics is that provided by the non-class solidary ties of ethnicity, extended family, and locality. These lines of division are not unrelated to economic differences, and, indeed, much of the social and political importance of these groups comes from the use made of them as bases for individual and group protection and advancement. To a degree this cohesion rests on the belief that 'in unity there is strength', but the groups also form useful bases for the phenomenon Schatzberg refers to as social closure. This is 'the process by which social collectivities seek to maximize rewards by restricting access to a limited number of eligibles. This entails the singling out of certain identifiable social or physical attributes as the justificatory basis of exclusion' (1980, p. 28). Similarly, Bates argues that the persistence of ethnic groups does not rest on the attachment of their members to 'traditional' values, but that 'Ethnic groups persist largely because of their capacity to extract goods and services from the modern sector' (1974, p. 471). However, these solidary links serve other purposes as well. In Madagascar, at the national level, 'ethnic group' is too large a unit for effective social closure, and the extended family is the most important unit, but individuals still preserve ethnicity as a part of their identity with a value of its own. At the local level the links, usually of family, village, and group of villages, are used less for the purposes of advancement than for the purposes of defence against the exactions of the modern state, not only in the form of taxes and other material types of extraction, but also in the form of attempts to impose an outside set of values that denigrates the values and accomplishments of local society. Adherence to these 'traditional' groups is a way of asserting a united front against a state that individuals could not oppose on their own (see Chazan, 1983, 28; also Althabe, 1972; Feeley-Harnik, 1984). The possibility of strengthening this line of defence was one of the attractions of the reform of the *fokonolona* in its original form.

One of the reasons for the relatively low salience of ethnicity in Malagasy politics, particularly at the local level, lies in the lack of extreme differentiation between the country's 'ethnic groups'. In general migrants to a region do not stand out unless they are from very distant parts of the island. New immigrants will suffer some exclusion because they lack the networks of relationships through which the local inhabitants operate, but not because of religious beliefs or style of life. Most of the numerous rules and taboos (*fady*) that characterize Malagasy society are specific to families or villages rather than ethnic groups. A 'stranger' will stand out because of dialect, possibly by clothing or occupation, and by the stereotype characteristics sometimes attributed to his group—the Antandroy are supposed to be quarrelsome and the Betsileo dour—but not by a whole way of life. Families who have lived in an area for more than one generation often move their family tomb and consider themselves *originaires* of the region if not precisely members of the local ethnic group (Covell, 1974).

Although family and locality are, on a day-to-day basis, the more important components of an individual's identity in Madagascar, there are times when ethnic identity has important political consequences. The division with the greatest potential for leading to political action is the overarching 'Merina versus others' distinction, based both on historical relationships and on still existing differences in access to education, wage employment and other aspects of 'modernity'. These advantages are not only distributed unevenly by region (see Table 5.1), they are also concentrated in the cities, where the Merina make up a disproportionate number of the population (71 per cent according to a survey conducted in 1960, when they were approximately 25 per cent of the population. The proportion has almost certainly diminished since then, but probably not to the point of parity (République malgache, n.d., p. 15).

The division continues to have political importance at the elite level, as Ratsiraka's outburst against the 'Merina plot' in which Merina judges handed out light sentences to the predominantly Merina defendants in the 1983 treason trial indicates. That this resentment also exists in the general population is shown by the anti-Merina riots that took place in the other provinces in 1973 when the proposed Malgachization of the education system appeared likely to involve the introduction of the Merina dialect of Malagasy in place of French as the language of instruction in secondary schools. The riots led to an exodus of Merina from the provinces and frightened national politicians of all groups. (See Leymarie, 1974. Archer, 1976, argues that the riots were organized by the PSD as part of its campaign against the Ramanantsoa regime, while Ratsiraka later characterized them as 'class warfare in an ethnic guise' (Malley, 1978a).

In education, the results of this conflict have included delays in Malgachization and the creation of a (slow-working) commission to establish a 'common Malagasy' based on all dialects (Bemananjara, 1986; Turcotte, 1981). 'Decentralization', a code word for increased allocation of facilities and opportunities to regions and groups outside the plateaux is enshrined in the Revolutionary Charter, and governments since 1975 have been scrupulously proportional in the allocation of formal and visible posts. The current regime has the advantage of being based on the most numerous groups of the island,

Table 5.1 Distribution of population, industrial production and social infrastructure by province (% of total)

	Antananarivo	Fianarantsoa	Toamasina	Toliary	Mahajanga	Antseranana
Population	28.5	23.6	15.5	13.9	10.6	7.7
Industrial production	45.7	6.5	14.3	9.3	13.8	10.0
Hospital beds	30.2	21.8	13.9	13.1	11.5	9.2
School population	37.7	22.7	13.9	7.9	7.9	7.7
Teachers	47.0	21.6	9.5	8.0	7.9	5.7
Teacher:student ratio	1:28.7	1:37.8	1:52.2	1:35.6	1:43.9	1:48.5

Source: Options Fondamentales pour la Planification Socialiste, 1975, 32. Industrial production figures are for 1972.

the Betsimisaraka and Betsileo with, despite Ratsiraka's outburst and the Antananarivo basis of right, or opposition Arema, considerable Merina participation. In this it differs from both the Tsiranana regime, based on the less populated coastal regions, and the Ramanantsoa regime, which had a clear tilt to the plateaux.

Regionalism is important in its own right. It divides the large ethnic groups (significantly, the core political groups in the regime, the 'Tamatave mafia' and the 'Fianarantsoa clique' are named after their provincial bases), while disputes between rich and poor regions divide the country into opposing multi-ethnic blocs. The cash crop regions of the country, particularly Antseranana and Toamasina, have demanded more local control of money raised in their areas, while Antseranana, isolated from the rest of the country by a mountain ridge, has even threatened separation.

More visible and more important are the differences between the Malagasy and non-Malagasy groups of the island. There are four major non-Malagasy ethnic groups: the French, the Indo-Pakistanis, the Chinese and the Comorians. Each has a distinct role in Madagascar's society and economy. Their numbers are difficult to estimate. As Andriamirado wrote (1977a, p. 2): 'How many foreigners are there in Madagascar? No statistic tells the whole story ... the Indo-Pakistanis are often listed as French or stateless, many Comorians chose to remain French in 1972, and a good number of Chinese have taken Malagasy citizenship.' Even these imperfect statistics are lacking for the current period, since the numbers of foreign residents are among the unpublished parts of the 1975 census. It would appear that the number of French residents has declined by about half since 1972, from 36,000 to less than 20,000 (Calvet, 1978, p. 354. See also *Le Monde*, 23 February 1974). Approximately 1,000 technical assistants remain, mainly in teaching positions, while the rest are still to be found running businesses and serving as consultants to the nationalized enterprises. A larger proportion of the Indo-Pakistanis and Chinese (about 10,000 each (Thompson, 1987, p. 530)) have remained, in part because, as Andriamirado states, many of them either held Malagasy citizenship or were stateless. Although they have been among the main targets of nationalization, and although the Indians in particular have been the targets of actions ranging from boycotts to riots, the two groups have generally maintained their economic position. There are several reasons for their survival. First, much of their wealth was in the form not of nationalizable commerce or industry, but of property, which has not been nationalized, or bank deposits held outside the country. Second, like the French, many stayed on as consultants once their firms were nationalized. Finally, much of the work of organizing the black market has been done by them. Both groups have been able to come to terms with successive governments, and neither persisted in its attachment to the Tsiranana regime once it was clear that regime would not return to power. The new investment code, which defines foreign capital held by foreigners rather than capital coming from outside the island, gives a certain advantage to the members of the group who have not taken Malagasy citizenship (*LOI*, 1986, p. 3).

The Comorians were concentrated at the lower end of the economic scale, in more direct competition with Malagasies. About 60,000 in 1970, most had chosen French citizenship at independence, and when the 1972 renegotiation of the cooperation agreements deprived French citizens of their special status, many began to return home. In 1977 a series of anti-Comorian riots broke out in Mahajanga, where Comorians made up half the population, leaving over 1,000 dead. Most of the remaining Comorians were repatriated, and it is now estimated that only about 15,000 to 20,000 remain, largely in Antananarivo (Delval, 1978, p. 11; Robert, 1979).

Rural Society

Although the major actors in the events of 1972 and 1975 were urban based, many of the participants also aspired to change the structure of Malagasy rural society. The authoritarian nature of state–society relationships in the countryside, characteristic of the colonial period and unchanged by the 'false decolonization' of 1960, was one of the main objects of attack in 1972, one of the main targets of the reform of the *fokonolona*, and one of the new areas where change was promised in the Revolutionary Charter. Carrying the revolution to the 86 per cent of the population living in rural areas, a goal expressed in the slogan 'popular control of development', seemed an important part of its success. For the radical participants of 1972 and 1975 ending authoritarian relationships *within* villages was seen as an essential step in the process of ending the hierarchical relationships between villages and the state and the key to ensuring that decentralization would lead to democratization (de Gaudusson, 1978b, p. 6; Leymarie, 1975a; Serre-Ratsimandisa, 1978). These internal hierarchies, based on traditional position, property in the form of land and/or animals, age and sex are to be found in all Malagasy villages, whatever the variations in specific structures. Successive regimes' use of the *notable* system of rule led to perpetuation of, rather than changes in, positions in the hierarchy: it was quite common to find the same family serving in this position under the Merina monarchy, the colonial government, and the Tsiranana regime (Covell, 1974; Desjeux, 1979). Most analyses of state power in the villages argue that although it was successful in maintaining its own position of power and that of its local agents, it was in general unable to bring about much in the way of positive change. The policies introduced after 1972 and 1975 attempted to turn Madagascar's villages into 'dynamic motors of development'.

Just as there is variation in the specific structures and situation of Malagasy villages, there is also variation in the impact of post-revolutionary change. A village in the undeveloped south, located far from transportation networks, is less likely to be affected by events and policies emanating from Antananarivo than, for example, a village in the east that is engaged in cash crop agriculture and tied into a variety of communication networks. However, the generalization of the transistor radio during the Tsiranana regime did reduce some of these differences, and the events of May 1972 and the achievement of a 'second independence' appear to have been much discussed. The possibility of changes in village structure and in village–state relationships was introduced even more explicitly during the first attempt at *fokonolona* reform, from 1972 to 1975. Ratsimandrava's speeches and discussions with peasants were broadcast almost daily and the colonel toured the country extensively, using a helicopter to reach villages that were not accessible by road. The post-1975 establishment of Arema, the extension of MFM activities to the countryside, and the implementation of the final version of the *fokonolona* reform all increased the level of political activity in the villages.

The results have been mixed. Observers agree that there has been considerable displacement of pre-1972 incumbents and some change in the type of person occupying political posts at the village level, but less change in village structures and still less in the relationship between village and state. Claims for an increased share of power at the village level were put forth by those who had formerly been excluded, and particularly between 1972 and 1977, the oldest of the *notables* and those most identified with the PSD either left office or were pushed out. However, many of the established leaders who had been PSD 'ex officio' rather than owing their position to their party affiliation simply switched their allegiance to the new party of the *fanjakana*. Where new types of *notables* did emerge they appear to have been drawn from middle generation holders of middle-sized properties rather than the young, landless, and even less from the female aspirants to a share in power. (For the nature of allegiance to the PSD see Covell, 1974; for a survey of changes in several regions see Camacho, 1981; see also Andriamirado, 1977a; *Afrique-Asie*, 1976.) Serre argues (1975, p. 258) that a place has been made for some of the formerly excluded 'curiously, among the landless peasants the young, and particularly those with some education, have increased their numbers in the intermediate elected institutions . . . it was less disruptive to give them the power they demanded in institutions removed from the immediate village community'.

Moderate rather than revolutionary change appears to have been the goal of the post-1975 regime's rural policies, and where even moderate change clashed with the requirements of building and maintaining a rural political base, it was the latter goal that won out. The effects of this choice can be seen in the revised version of the *fokonolona* reform, the regime's treatment of the territorial administration, and the manner in which Arema was introduced at the village level. The Ratsiraka version of the reform of the *fokonolona*, published in 1976 as the 'Charter of the Decentralized Collectivities', departed considerably from the original version of 'popular control of development', and revisions to the policy in the course of implementation removed the institution still further from the conception of policy formation occurring as the result of a political will emerging from the base of society. The charter indicated this change in orientation by referring to its basic units as *fokontany* the geographical village rather than *fokonolona*, the village as community. It preserved the hierarchy of levels of government and the practice of indirect election to the intermediate levels, but added the new principle of democratic centralism interpreted as the responsibility of the lower levels of government to carry out the instructions of the upper levels and of the central ministries of Antananarivo. This principle reflects the reservations Ratsiraka himself had expressed about the political reliability of rural populations and the degree of economic dynamism that could be expected from autonomous *fokonolona* (see Archer, 1976; Serre, 1975). The decentralized collectivities are required not only to respect the Revolutionary Charter in their conduct of local affairs, but also to carry out a whole range of more specific responsibilities, and they must report to the territorial administration, the councils at the next highest level, and the agents of the functional ministries. As Calvet noted (1977, p. 308), 'for all that it is decentralized and socialist, the fokonolona is nevertheless highly regulated' (see also the sources cited in the preceding paragraph and Andriamirado, 1977b; de Gaudusson, 1978a, 1978b; for a more favourable evaluation Givelet, 1978; Rajaona, 1980; Serre-Ratsimandisa, 1978).

The territorial administration extends to the level of the *fokonolona* in the person of the Secretary of the executive committee. Although successive post-1972 regimes have purged administrators, particularly at the top, most closely connected with previous regimes, the administration as a whole has been largely untouched. In the post-1975 reorganization most *prefects*, *sousprefects*, and *chefs de canton* were simply given new assignments after 'consciousness-raising' seminars on the content of the Revolutionary Charter (Camacho, 1981; de Gaudusson, 1978; Andriamirado, 1977a). Since it was the territorial administration that was largely responsible for setting up the rural branches of Arema, it is not surprising that the party has played an ambiguous role in intra-village power struggles. Particularly when the party was first introduced some did try to use it to challenge the established local authorities. The general reaction to their efforts is suggested by the comment of an Arema organizer about the party youth movement: 'we tell them to assume their responsibilities in the organization of rice collection and rural credit ... we can talk about the cultural revolution later' (*Afrique-Asie*, 1976, p. XV). This ambiguous attitude to village power structures is not limited to Arema. Monima followed much the same practice in its southern base, and the MFM, which did, in its early years, organize attacks on village hierarchies, has been much less active in recent years. Its current organizational strategy attempts to work through rather than without or against people in local positions of power.

Although it can plausibly be argued that one result of post-1972 events has been a lessening of village isolation and regional particularities, and the creation of a more national system, there has also been an opposing tendency to increased isolation and attempts to insulate villages from the state. The use of village solidarity as a defence against rather than a linkage with the outside world has a long history in Madagascar, but the period since 1972 has seen an increase in the trend as well as a decrease in state capacity to intervene in rural areas. The political upheavals of the early 1970s both weakened instruments of intervention, like the administration, and increased the incentive to avoid entanglements. To a degree the reasons for the loosening of state-village ties are physical: especially since 1980 the collapse of the road system and the near disappearance of transistors have made communication of all types difficult. The increase in state economic exactions has made withdrawal activities like hoarding tempting, while 'parallel' institutions like the black market offer alternative outlets for produce. Uncertainty has also led to a simple reduction in planting. In addition, corruption means that the state itself strains its resources and increases the incentive to village self-reliance. Like earlier Malagasy governments, the Ratsiraka regime has reacted ambivalently. On the one hand extensive presidential tours attempt to maintain contact while on the other hand the decentralized collectivities are increasingly told to rely on their own resources. The dream of a self-taxing self-policing community—that is one that would combine maximum responsiveness to state needs with minimum demands on its resources—is an old one in Madagascar and elsewhere.

Urban Society

The rural areas of Madagascar have a general importance based on the proportion of the population they contain and the fact that the rice that feeds the country and the cash crops that provide most of its foreign earnings are grown there. However, the groups on which the government is most directly dependent and those by which it can be most directly threatened live in the cities. The numbers of city dwellers are increasing by about 5 per cent a year, both from natural increase and because of immigration from the countryside (World Bank, 1979, p. 68; D. in *Sudestasie*, 1982, p. 38 estimates that rural immigration accounts for about 15 per cent of the total increase in urban population). Antananarivo is clearly dominant, at approximately 800,000 larger than the five provincial capitals combined and growing faster than the other cities. It is also clearly dominant in economic terms, with 60 per cent of the country's wage employment (Hugon, 1982, p. 293). The government has attempted to counteract this imbalance, and the political dominance that goes with it through policies like the establishment of regional university centres, the increase in the number of *lycées* and other types of secondary school, and the regional distribution of the 'outrageous investment' projects. Not surprisingly the president's home town, Toamasina has benefited most from these 'decentralization' policies, and there are periodic threats to move the seat of government there. As in many countries, the relationship between the regime and its capital is an uneasy one. Not only is Ratsiraka an outsider in a city that is still predominantly Merina, but the most politicized groups and those most adversely affected by the post-1980 economic crisis live in the capital. 'I love Antananarivo, but it doesn't love me,' Ratsiraka has said (Calvet, 1978, p. 432; Malley, 1982b, p. 17).

Given their role in bringing about the regime changes of 1972 and 1975, and their continued political importance, it is not surprising that urban dwellers have drawn the greatest benefit from those changes. The French presence that aroused so much resentment was most visible in the cities and the 'Second Independence' that saw their departure corresponded most closely to the urban conception of 'Malagasy rule'. Increased access to the higher levels of education and to government employment were also most directly beneficial to urban groups. However, the post-1980 economic collapse has hit the cities harder since it has been most severe in the 'modern sector' on which urban residents are more dependent than rural inhabitants. Hugon demonstrates that the number of salaried jobs has been declining even as the number of those looking for employment has been increasing. Although he argues that the 'informal sector' of small-scale enterprises like market stalls, metal work and dressmaking 'has played an essential role both in absorbing migrants and former employees of the modern sector and in producing goods and services that were formerly produced in the modern sector,' he points out that the informal sector does not have the capacity either to make up the shortages or absorb all the unemployed (Hugon, 1982, p. 295). In addition, the standard of living of the employed has declined, slowly but steadily over the last twenty years, and dramatically since 1980 under the impact of inflation, tax increases, import shortages and the removal of subsidies on 'essential products'. (For example, the price of rice went from 15 malagasy francs per kilo to 140 in May 1982. See *Le Monde Diplomatique*, 1982.) As early as 1971 Donque could write (1971, p. 32) 'the standard of living of this population [of Antananarivo] has stagnated. Fortunes have been made, others are being made; there is a middle class, numerically small, whose resources permit a decent life, but no more, but the immense majority is poor'. By the late 1970s, the 'decent life' of this middle class was threatened, and by the mid-1980s many had lost it (Andriamirado, 1977a; De Barrin, 1985).

Reactions to the decline and subsequent collapse have been diverse and, of course, mitigated by the fact that some urbanites continue to derive psychological and practical benefits from the revolution. Earlier poverty gave rise to groups like the Zoam, and the ability of the Kung Fu to recruit from a wider range of groups shows the impact of the spread of poverty, as does the continued volatility of the Antananarivo crowd. Even in the cities, where government presence is strongest and most visible, there are signs of a withdrawal from integration in the state system, less thoroughgoing than the withdrawal in rural areas, but still there. There are reports that urban *fokonolona* now try to settle not only disputes but also criminal cases by internal processes, a practice that can occasionally take the form of vigilante action as the 1984 Kung Fu led attacks on the TTS demonstrate. Even more common are actions in which the government and its policies are simply ignored. For example, Hugon estimates that while 500 'authorized' houses are built in Antananarivo every year, over 5,000 unauthorized and illegal ones are constructed (Hugon, 1982. This disjunction between government and population is not a new phenomenon. See Covell, 1974).

Youth

If only by their numbers young Malagasies constitute an important social category: most sources estimate that 45 per cent of the population is less than 15 years old and 60 per cent under 30 (World Bank, 1979, p. 1). The proportion is probably even higher in the cities, particularly in Antananarivo, where hopes for education and employment attract immigrants from rural areas. As in other African countries urban youth is highly politicized and has already demonstrated its ability to bring down governments. The combination of marginal situation, politicization and past experience makes youth an extremely volatile category capable of moving rapidly from protest to demonstration to full-scale riot (see Cadoux and de Gaudusson, 1980, p. 373). The urban youth milieu is characterized by a variety of organizations: sports clubs, gangs, secret societies as well as party youth movements and the unions of students in various types of education. The party youth movements and student unions have a periodic press, while word of mouth and when necessary graffiti and wall pamphlets serve the others. Although educational issues alone are often enough to form a basis for mobilization, disputes over education policy are also the vehicle for the expression of social tensions and political opposition (see Calvet, 1977, p. 346). However, in spite of their ability to disrupt, youth, even in the capital, cannot claim even the ambiguous power that Decalo attributes (1979, p. 251) to the youth of Congo-Brazzaville which 'has to a considerable degree dictated the pace of radicalization of all regimes to date ... yet even while official rhetoric has been radicalized to meet this challenge from the left, all regimes have acted to subordinate and control the youthful elements'. Characteristics of Malagasy youth as a social category as well as government policy have made subordination and control easier for the government.

First, both traditional and modern social cleavages divide the group. The alliance of privileged and unprivileged youth that made the 1972 revolution was only temporary, and attempts to perpetuate or revive it have been unsuccessful (see Althabe, 1980). Second, the regime has used a combined policy of concessions and divisive tactics that has been, at least until the economic crisis, relatively effective. The education policies of both the Ramanantsoa and Ratsiraka governments attempted to meet the 1972 slogan of decentralization, democratization and Malgachization. Numbers in education were increased at all levels, standards, especially for acquisition of the baccalaureate, were relaxed, and both the number and value of university scholarships were increased (see Cadoux and de Gaudusson, 1980, p. 373;

Calvet, 1977) (Scholarships for study abroad are scarcer and their allocation such an important political issue both to the students concerned and to their connections that awards are determined by the top institutions of the system, the CSR and, where necessary, the President's office.) For those excluded from secondary and university education, government-funded groups like the TTS represent an attempt to reward and control.

There are, however, several limitations on the government's ability to control Malagasy youth. The first is simply one of resources. As Althabe notes, in 1972 the Ramanantsoa regime attempted to dampen the radicalism of the Zoam by providing jobs to the most vocal, but this strategy had to be abandoned when it was no longer possible to create enough jobs to absorb all potential claimants (Althabe, 1980). Resources, and the nature of the system itself limit the ability of the regime to use the educational system to minimize opposition. Malagasy education has retained the hierarchical French system crowned by the baccalaureate at the secondary level and a series of diplomas at the university level. The national budget already devotes 33 per cent of its expenditures to education (health care, in contrast, receives 6 per cent), probably the maximum possible amount given the competing demands of other groups like the military (*Etudes*, 1985, p. 588). Much of this expenditure has gone, in the name of decentralization and democratization, to the expansion and territorial diffusion of the primary school system. This policy meets, at least quantitatively, the promise to reduce regional and rural–urban inequities in access to primary education but at the cost of preserving the sharply pyramidal shape of the whole system, since there is simply not enough money available to the regime to expand the more expensive secondary and university systems to accommodate the numbers coming out of the primary system. The problem of jobs for those who are excluded at various levels, and even for those who survive and graduate remains as well.

Democratization and Malgachization have created other problems that make education policy a source of dissent as well as a means of control for the regime. The rapid expansion of education has led to shortages of teachers. The policy of Malgachization at the lower levels creates problems of transition at the university level, where Malagasy has not totally replaced French as a language of instruction (Turcotte, 1981; Bemananjara, 1986). Parents who can afford it, or who have the necessary connections send their children to the Lycée française in Antananarivo or abroad. As in other areas there has been a certain degree of reversal in policy since 1980, including an increase in the teaching of French and in the numbers of French secondary school teachers. However, the re-introduction of French has been criticized as a re-introduction of the old inequities of the First Republic. The close connection between education policy and issues of nationalism, class position and ethnicity makes education one of the most dangerous areas of policy for the regime, in which movement in any direction arouses some kind of opposition, and very often leads to violent protest. So far the regime has been able to maintain its control over education and the larger youth constituency, but the relationship is a difficult one.

Workers and Unions

In other African countries where the immediate post-independence regime was overthrown by popular uprisings urban labour and the union movement were important elements in the revolutionary movement. This did not happen in Madagascar. Rather, the coalition of 1972 grouped students, unemployed youth, and later unemployed and non unionized adults, with the unions joining the demonstrators only at the end of the May events. The 'left front' of 1975 included politicians and urban intellectuals, but not union leaders. The failure of the unions to participate in either the overthrow of Tsiranana or the establishment of Ratsiraka's regime reflects the weaknesses of the movement and, with those weaknesses, explains the marginality of unions and labour to the regime and its policies.

The weakness of the union movement can be partially explained by the nature of its audience. Only a small number of Malagasies are in permanent wage employment of the type conducive to unionization (see Table 5.2) and most of them work in small plants with fewer than 50 employees (Hugon,

Table 5.2 Employment (1975 estimates, per cent)

Traditional agriculture	83.0
Administration	2.8
Industry	1.4
Other 'modern'	3.0
Intermediate and casual	3.9
Unemployed	1.3

Source: World Bank Report, 1979. Many of those in the 'intermediate and casual' category should be considered as unemployed.

1982). Even the larger firms do not always have the structure of a 'modern' enterprise with management clearly separated from labour. As Camacho notes (1981, p. 420) for the large Toamasina factory she studied 'the managers, who are in a precarious situation largely due to their lack of training, tend to set up solidarity networks, often lineage based, that include employees'. Another reason for the lack of appeal and weakness of the unions lies in the highly politicized and divided nature of the movement itself. Under the Tsiranana regime unions were divided into three competing sectors, one attached to the PSD, one connected to the Catholic family of associations and the largest, FISEMA, affiliated with the AKFM (the reserved attitude of the AKFM to the 1972 revolution was one reason for the lack of union involvement). Events since 1972 and even more the installation of the Ratsiraka regime have changed this framework without simplifying it. FISEMA split from the AKFM in 1976 over the general issue of union autonomy and the specific issue of direct participation in the FNDR. The party created a new union, while the bulk of FISEMA leaders joined the new, Arema connected union, SENREMA (now the largest union federation; see Calvet, 1978, p. 339; Leymarie, 1979, p. 47). The Catholic union movement has continued to exist in various forms, and other parties have their own labour organizations. For many workers then, joining a union is seen not as a way of furthering their interests but as a dangerous excursion into the uncertain world of party politics. Only 30 per cent of Malagasy workers take this step. Most workers prefer to use informal channels of influence or the official, non-union, workers' delegate system. There are strikes in Malagasy factories, but they are usually either the result of disputes among unions or wildcat strikes that include non-union as well as union workers without the participation of union leadership. The only unions that do play an important role in politics are not, strictly speaking, labour unions. They include the unions of university teachers and researchers, and of administrators. Each has staged strikes in Antananarivo that were broken up by the regime using the army and TTS.

The regime has not, as might be expected given its Marxist-Leninist orientation, singled out 'the workers' or 'proletariat' for a special role in its revolution. The Revolutionary Charter lists them in conjunction with 'the peasants' as only one of the five pillars of the revolution. A 'Charter of Socialist Enterprises' published in 1976 provides an elaborate structure of worker consultation but the Charter is one of the most amended and least applied of the regime's policies. There has been some attempt to develop policies that reflect a more 'popular' orientation. Caps have been placed on the salaries of heads of state enterprises and top bureaucrats, and official wage differentials are less than they were under the First Republic (see Calvet, 1976, p. 370). Since the beginning of the economic crisis official permission, almost never given, is required before firms can fire employees. On the other hand, the regime has not hesistated to fire striking workers in its own factories (Racine, 1982, p. 266).

Churches

If the weakness of regime links with workers in general and unions in particular is one paradox of Malagasy style Marxism–Leninism, the far more important role played by Protestant and Catholic churches in the politics of the present regime is another. The present role of the churches is a continuation of their political importance under previous regimes and is based on several characteristics. The Christian Churches of Madagascar claim an estimated four million 'adherents'; a term that obviously covers a wide range of commitment. Both Catholic and Protestant churches have their largest number of adherents in central Madagascar, and one of the common physical features of plateaux villages is the presence of two spired churches, usually confronting each other from the opposite ends of the village. The Catholic church has a geographical centre of gravity in the southern plateaux, in Betsileo territory, and a sociological centre of gravity among the more humble. The Protestant church is divided among the long established churches of the plateaux, traditionally connected with Antananarivo based social and political power, and the churches of the south which are both more recent and more dependent on missionaries for their organization and activities (xxx, 1971c). Relationships among the churches have a considerable element of competition, but there have also been attempts to create coordinating organizations. The oldest, the FJKM, was founded in 1970 and linked the Protestant churches of the plateaux, formerly separated by their historical links with the London Missionary Society, the French Protestant Mission and the Quakers. Later a general federation of protestant churches linked the FJKM with the protestant churches of the south, and in 1980 a federation of Malagasy Christian Churches that included the Catholic church was established. However, the FJKM is the most active of these organizations, and the only one with any real decision-making authority (see Cadoux and de Gaudusson, 1980; *Année politique*, 1981).

Church membership appears to have declined after independence (Raison, 1970) and since, under the impact of general secularization, but the influence of the churches is only partly dependent on the numbers and commitment of their 'adherents'. Callaghy attributes (1984, p. 279) the position of the Catholic churches in Zaïre not only to the numbers of 'the faithful' but also to 'good organization, an established hierarchy, control of much health, welfare, educational and publication activities, and strong external ties' and in the same way Malagasy churches have the advantages of relative institutional coherence and visibility in an otherwise organizationally diffuse environment. While their membership is geographically concentrated, the churches have one of the few organizational networks with any pretensions to national, rural as well as urban, coverage. The churches also have a parallel organizational structure of laymen's association, women's groups, and organizations of children and youth, as well as associations of former students of their school systems. The church educational network has declined in relative importance with the expansion of the state system, but especially on the plateaux village church schools are numerous, and the system still has its 'prestige' secondary schools like the Catholic College St. Michel, attended by most of Tsiranana's cabinet as well as by Ratsiraka and many of his close associates. The Protestant secondary schools of Antananarivo are closely identified with the Merina social elite and the AKFM. At the village level, the persistence of the religious educational network means that the churches continue to dispense a scarce and valued commodity, while the more restricted secondary school systems serve as one of the bases of the personal networks that are the organizing principle of Malagasy political life. Professors and principals often play a continuing role as mentors to the networks and their members. The churches also control their own sources of money and foreign patronage. This control makes the pastor and the priest important village notables and at the national level gives the churches the means to withstand government pressure (see Lejamble, 1963; Raison, 1970).

The churches also have a tradition of involvement on the radical rather than conservative side of Malagasy political alignments at the national level. The Protestant churches have a long history of identification with Malagasy nationalism and, through the AKFM, more than a passing acquaintance with Marxism, while the Catholic church separated itself, at least verbally, from the colonial regime in the early 1950s (see Desjeux, 1979; Spacensky, 1970a). After some hesitation the churches became one of the major actors in the events of 1972, helping to arrange the return of the deportees, and giving important support to Ramanantsoa. They furnished, on an individual basis, several members of the left front that formed around Ratsiraka in 1975. Ratsiraka's visits to the pope and injunctions to read the Bible may be exceptions to expected Marxist practice, but can be explained by the power of the churches and by their contribution to the political and ideological origins of his regime. There are points of friction. The very strength of the churches makes them a potential danger and any attempt to increase the regime's control of the country necessarily involves an attempt to reduce their influence. Although the regime has not directly attacked religious schools or the church networks of charities it has regulated them and set up competing state-run institutions, while its censorship policies have devastated the church press. The churches nearly moved into open opposition to the regime in the late 1970s and early 1980s but neither side was willing to risk a direct confrontation and the current relationship is one of surface respect if not cordiality (see *Etudes*, May 1985; *Jeune Afrique*, 6 March 1985; *Année politique*, 1981; Cadoux and de Gaudusson, 1980; *LOI*, 30 June 1984; *LOI*, 6 July 1985).

Political System: Ideology, Institutions, Dynamics

The current Malagasy regime has been prolific in its ideological pronouncements. In addition to the Revolutionary Charter itself, other documents like the Charter of Socialist Enterprises and the Charter of Decentralized Collectivities contain ideological discussions. Ratsiraka's annual New Year's address and other speeches are often as much philosophical as political, while other regime figures also join in the ideological discussion. This emphasis on an explicit ideology reflects the role played by intellectuals of various types both in the 1972 revolution and in Ratsiraka's 1975 'left front'. The regime's ideological discourse is varied, but shows little sign of evolution until the 1980 economic crisis, when it went through a re-evaluation and revision, or at least a change in emphasis encapsulated in Ratsiraka's 1985 New Year's address and his speech at the celebration of the 150th anniversary of the translation of the Bible into Malagasy.

The Revolutionary Charter is the formal basis of the Malagasy system: adherence to its principles is the precondition for legal political participation, and it is taught in the schools, army and administration. Its critics have been severe. Archer (1976, p. 159) calls it 'general and inflamed', while Chaigneau describes it (1982, p. 110) as 'an ideological *melting pot* [in English in the original] whose only originality is to juxtapose the traditional principles of Marxism-Leninism, borrowings from Chinese doctrines of agricultural development, and echoes of Kimilsunisme, notably the theory of the three revolutions, the whole with an eye to adaptive references to the national society'. This is rather unfair to a revolution that is explicitly eclectic: as one of Ratsiraka's collaborators declared in 1977, 'the experiment we are living through will satisfy everyone, whether the Soviet Union, the People's Republic of China, economists, all kinds of technocrats, Catholics and so forth' (*Le Monde*, 28 December 1977). The Charter shows the signs of its origins, reflecting the diversity of the 1975 left front whose members were responsible for many of its provisions. It is as much an electoral platform, designed to generate broad support, as a revolutionary charter. As a result the Charter includes diverse points of view rather than following a single line of argument. The loose class analysis common to all Malagasy parties of the left in 1975, the state centred scientific socialism of the AKFM, and the popular participationism of the MFM and other radical groups of the May movement can all be found there as can specific promises to specific interest groups and reassurances to groups like 'the bourgeoisie' who might be tempted to oppose the revolution.

The Charter begins by exalting the Malagasy nation (pp. 12–13) and identifying the revolution not as a part of national or international class struggle but as the culmination of a long line of Malagasy nationalist movements. 'Even before the colonial period Madagascar was already a nation, with imperfections that were the result of her historical experience, perhaps, but a nation nonetheless, united in its diversity'. The revolution of 1975 is the heir of the *menalamba*, the VVS, and the martyrs of 1947. The Charter does recognize the existence of internal class conflict, a favourite theme of the radicals of 1972, but it follows the AKFM lead in arguing that the internal class struggles must be situated in the context of a more fundamental contradiction, between imperialist neo-colonialism and the Malagasy people. The real enemy is not an internal class but global imperialism. In these circumstances the Malagasy bourgeoisie has a role to play in the revolution, and the Charter distinguishes between the '*comprador* bourgeoisie' which is to be attacked, and the 'national bourgeoisie' which suffered under colonial domination like the rest of the Malagasy people and which is 'therefore capable of nationalism, and to a certain point, of revolutionary spirit' (p. 71).

The bourgeoisie is not the only sector of non-Marxist Malagasy opinion that the Charter seeks to reassure. The revolution is declared to be compatible with religion, small-scale private property, inheritance rights, and even with rule by social elites if they have the right attitudes. Its goals include the elimination of hunger, ignorance, inequality and injustice, and the achievement of balanced and autonomous development, goals that are hardly threatening to any particular group. The Charter does name some specific groups as 'pillars of the revolution', and they are as diverse as the Charter is eclectic: oppressed workers and peasants, progressives, young intellectuals, women 'as such', and the military. In addition, specific promises are made, with specific groups clearly in mind. The coasts are promised decentralization of economic benefits and political power. The youth constituency is promised increased access to education and Malgachization 'in moderation'. The section on international relations promises a continued assertion of national independence, and the pursuit of cooperation with 'progressive countries', a policy agreeable to groups like the AKFM.

The diversity of points of view makes it difficult to categorize the ideology of the Charter. Attempts to understand the ideological direction of recent African socialist regimes often distinguish between regimes that are genuinely 'scientific socialist' and 'populist' regimes, which may use Marxist rhetoric, but in less orthodox ways. Jowitt argues (1979, pp. 152–3) that populist regimes emphasize internal unity in the face of an external enemy rather than class struggle, and national particularities rather than the universal principles of socialism. Bienen (1985, pp. 357–8) identifies populist military regimes as those in which 'leaders try to have direct contact with followers ... couching their appeals to civilians in terms of equity issues'. Neither the Charter, nor the current Malagasy regime, can be considered populist in either sense. The Charter does emphasize the importance both of imperialism and of the internal class struggle but in giving greater importance to the struggle against imperialism it follows the line of the AKFM, the only Malagasy party with any claim to the 'scientific socialist' label. The adaptation of general Marxist–Leninist principles to particular national situations has been a distinguishing characteristic of most Marxist regimes, especially in the Third World (see Ottaway and Ottaway, 1981; Gonidec, 1981, p. 137). If populism is defined as an attempt to mobilize 'the people' against the structures of power, even if only rhetorically, the Charter and regime, with their emphasis on democratic centralism and the importance of ideological training before participation, do not qualify for the label. This is clear when the ideological position of the current regime is contrasted with that of Ratsiraka's predecessor, Colonel Ratsimandrava. Instead of attacking the State, the Charter proposes to strengthen it. In practical terms, with the exceptions of Monja Jaona and the MFM in its early days, none of the participants in present-day Malagasy politics has attempted to recruit supporters among the landless peasantry, the urban lumpen-proletariat, or the lower ranks of the army.

The most distinguishing characteristic of the Charter is the degree to which it selects those elements of Marxist theory that fit the authors' understanding of Malagasy realities and their own immediate and long-term political needs. The tolerance shown to 'bourgeois' elements, and the embracing of concepts like democratic centralism show this selectivity, as does the minimal role given to workers and peasants. Regimes that claim the title of scientific socialism have been criticized for not grounding themselves in these groups, but it was the judgement of Ratsiraka and his supporters, a judgement born out by the experience of the radicals of 1972, that those groups, as they existed in Madagascar, were not revolutionary. The argument of the AKFM that the road to revolution in Madagascar was through control of the state and the use of its power to change both population and economy was accepted by the new leadership. The attraction of the ideology lay in part in the way it fitted and justified both their experience and goals (for a comparison, see Markakis, 1978, p. 190).

The Charter of the Revolution was followed by a series of Charters dealing with specific areas of activity, including the 'decentralized collectivities', socialist enterprises, cooperatives and socialist planning. Like the original charter, these pronouncements contain a mixture of ideological extremism and pragmatic caution. For example, the 'Fundamental Options for Socialist Planning' declares boldly that 'the revolutionary socialist state must control the key sectors of the economy', but adds that 'during a transitional period, because of our lack of technical preparation, the state may decide to work with national and foreign capitalists' (*Les Options Fondamentales pour la planification socialiste*, p. 19). If the Charters were already cautious, their application has been even more hesitating. This hesitation is the result of several factors including individual or collective ambivalence about the goals proclaimed, and very often a lack of the resources or coercive capacity necessary to achieve those goals (see Callaghy, 1979, pp. 112–13; de Gaudusson, 1978a, p. 272). In any event the high ideological output of the early years eventually faded into routine and the economic crisis has brought about a reversal or at least a change in emphasis, of which Ratsiraka's 'read the Bible' speech is the most startling example (see also Cadoux and de Gaudusson, 1980, p. 357). Even more than the original choice of direction, this reversal quite clearly meets the requirements for cultivating internal and external bases of support. However, it also reflects a certain fatigue, or realism, born of experience. As Rakotonirina, the leader of the 1972 radicals and now an important figure in the regime told a reporter, the extreme policies of the early years 'were a dream of our youth. We thought we would attain real independence by taking over the economy for our own people' (*International Herald Tribune*, 6 May 1985).

Institutions

'They've given up drawing organizational charts at the Prime Minister's Office....Everyone in town knows that the real centres of power shift easily and can be charted with reference to yearbooks and alumni lists from St. Francis Xavier University and the law school at Laval university, Prime Minister Brian Mulroney's alma maters' (*Globe and Mail*, 2 September 1986). Informal lines of power and function are generally considered to be even more characteristic of countries like Madagascar than of countries like Canada. However, in the case of Madagascar at least, the argument, while valid, should not be exaggerated. Although personal networks based on a variety of ties are a major organizing principle of Malagasy life, institutions do have a real existence and importance of their own. Many actually perform, among other functions, their assigned roles. Most of the important figures in the regime have an official position and usually the things they do are related to that position. For example, when L. M. X. Andrianarahinjaka was given the task of keeping the legislature in order he was moved from a ministerial position to that of president of the ANP. Institutions that are empty façades or cloaks for totally different types of activity are rare in Madagascar. As a result, while an examination of the institutions of the second Malagasy Republic gives only an incomplete understanding of the country's politics, it is a necessary starting point.

Constitution and Presidency

The 1975 Malagasy constitution creates seven major national institutions (see Figure 5.1 and Table 5.4). Formally as well as informally, the President is the centre of the system: he is the head of most of the major institutions and to a large degree controls their composition. Comparing the Malagasy constitution to those passed in Algeria in 1975 and the Soviet Union in 1977, Chaigneau argues (1982, p. 110) that 'the only major deviation [of the Malagasy constitution] from the classic socialist model is its presidentialism, which gives the head of state the prerogatives that in the Soviet Union are given to the Presidium of the Supreme Soviet'. As well as being head of state and commander in chief of the armed forces, the Malagasy leader presides over the meetings of the National Front for the Defence of the Revolution and the Supreme Revolutionary Council, the two top political institutions of the regime, and names the members of the CSR. He also names the prime

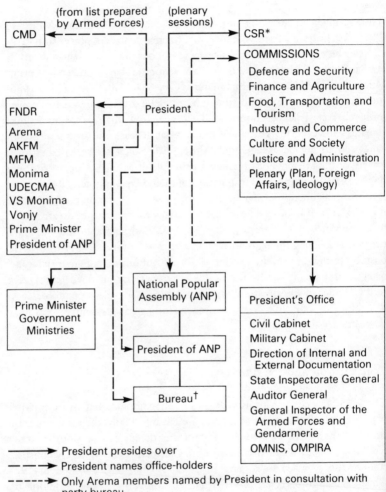

Figure 5.1 State organization under the Constitution of 1975

minister and the other ministers, as well as the heads of the armed forces and the members of the Supreme Court. He controls the agenda of the CSR, its secretariat, and the number, composition, and activities of the commissions that do most of its work. He also names the members of the Military Development Council. In addition to the CSR Secretariat, he has an extensive office of his own, with both a military and civil cabinet, and a secretariat charged with oversight of the bureaucracy. The DGID, the most important internal intelligence service, is located in the President's office, as is OMNIS, the military-run organization that controls several important economic sectors (see Calvet, 1976; de Gaudusson, 1976, which includes comparisons with previous regimes; Serre and Rasoarahoana, 1981; Panter-Brick, 1979). In spite of its presidentialism, the constitution also creates a large number of executive, legislative and advisory bodies. These bodies perform a multiplicity of functions. They connect the regime with its bases of support, provide arenas in which it must confront opposition, offer a large number of posts with which to reward the faithful or buy off opponents, and by their very number give the regime the possibility of playing one set of institutions against another.

The Supreme Revolutionary Council

Like many socialist systems, the Malagasy Republic has an executive divided between political and administrative bodies. The Supreme Revolutionary Council is the formal political executive, charged with the task of assisting the president in the 'conception, orientation and oversight of national policy and the preservation of internal and external national sovereignty' (Constitution, Article 7; see *Afrique-Asie*, 12 January 1976). Composed originally of military officers, it was enlarged in 1976 to include civilians and is now largely a civilian body with approximately twenty two members. As 'the expression of the FNDR at the summit of the state' (Calvet, 1976, p. 332) it includes the leaders of the parties belonging to the Front (with the periodic exception of Monja Jaona) with, of course, a pronounced majority of Arema representatives. Regional balance is scrupulously observed in appointments as is balance between the different branches of the armed forces. Some members of the Council of Ministers sit on the CSR, and there is some movement back and forth between the two bodies. Most of the work is done in its seven commissions, whose importance varies according to the tasks the President assigns them. For example, the Economic Commission and particularly its head, Rakotonirina, has been encouraged to play an important

Table 5.3 CSR Commissions*

---

(1) Plenary (Plan, Foreign Affairs, Information and Ideology)
(2) Defence (Military commissioners only)
(3) Finance and Agriculture
(4) Food, Transportation and Tourism
(5) Industry and Commerce
(6) Culture and Society
(7) Judiciary and Administration

---

* As in 1986. The number and activities of the commissions change periodically.
Source: Thompson, 1987.

role in contacts with foreign investors and creditors as a counterbalance to the less 'trustworthy' Ministry of the Economy.

Evaluations of the importance of the CSR vary. In recent years it has been used in part as a semi-retirement post for figures like Rakotomavo-Razakaboana and Tiandraza whom the regime wanted to remove from active political life but who were too important to be completely alienated. Cadoux and de Gaudusson argue (1980, p. 362) that 'the population is mainly interested in the CSR in the measure that networks of personal and family ties permit it to get some advantages, even if only the speeding up of the bureaucratic decision-making process'. However, this remark also indicates the importance of the CSR as one of the main arenas in which the allocation of benefits to the diverse components of the regime's political base is decided. Disagreements over policy have increased since 1980, a change that might be one reason why discussion of policy issues has been, at least in part, moved elsewhere (see also *Le Monde*, 5 November 1982). The CSR is not, and never has been a collective leadership body, but it is important as an arena for the raising and settling of disputes among the different elements of the regime coalition.

The FNDR

The FNDR, or National Front for the Defence of the Revolution, is charged by the Constitution with the task of 'guiding the revolution and inspiring the actions of the state'. As the embodiment of the 'unity of the country's masses' it is the only legal forum for political activity. The 'revolutionary organizations' (in practice political parties: attempts of unions to join independently have been refused) who compose it must accept the Revolutionary Charter, the principle of democratic centralism, and state oversight of their activities (Calvet, 1976). However, the Front does not have the institutional structure to carry out its mission: there are no local units of the Front and no formal lines of articulation between the Front and the other state institutions. One reason for its lack of integration in the system is that it is the institution over whose composition the President of the Republic has the least control. Although he approves new organizations, the parties name their own representatives, and, with the exception of Monima, party delegations are composed of their top leadership, all people with political bases independent of the regime. Each party names three delegates, and while the fact that the President, Prime Minister, and President of the National Assembly (all Arema) belong ex officio doubles Arema's representation on the Front, this is still not enough to allow the regime party to dominate the body (see Table 5.4).

Table 5.4 Composition of the FNDR (National Front for the Defence of the Revolution)

President of the Republic
Prime Minister
President of the ANP
Parties (3 delegates each)
AKFM
Arema
MFM
Monima
UDECMA
Vonjy
VS Monima

The Front was intended to be a substitute for, and possible precursor of the single party that Ratsiraka had hoped to create. Instead, like the CSR, it has become an arena for conflict and negotiation among its members. The parties that compose it continue to lead separate existences and to be divided by 'doctrinal quarrels, personal animosities and international ties' (see *Afrique-Asie*, January 1979; *Le Monde*, 5 November 1982). Relations between the parties and the regime are also often difficult. While Chaigneau's argument that the only characteristic the non-Arema members of the Front have in common is that 'they officially support the regime in the hope of succeeding it when it falls' is an exaggeration, it does capture the ambiguity of the relationship between the regime and the other 'revolutionary organizations' (1983a, p. 21; see also Cadoux and de Gaudusson, 1980, pp. 358–62). Under these circumstances the Front is not an arena for the discussion of major policy decisions. However, it does serve a function besides that of providing another setting for conflict. By joining the Front, Madagascar's parties have registered at least a formal acceptance of the regime and its objectives, and of responsibility for its policies and their results. While this implication in the regime's activities does not eliminate their criticisms and opposition, it does limit their ability to express their reservations in public. On several occasions Ratsiraka has been able to use the Front to elicit reaffirmations of support for his regime: in 1980 the parties of the Front published a declaration of their intention to continue a socialist development strategy in spite of the economic crisis, and in 1982 all the parties but Monima supported his presidential candidacy. The Front's existence allows the regime to have some sense of the opposition to its policies without having to deal with public opposition. As Cadoux and de Gaudusson argue, even if the Front is not the spearhead of the Malagasy revolution, it is at least a line of defence against counter-revolution (1980, p. 362; see also Calvet, 1978, p. 340).

The Government

If the FNDR and CSR are not the centres of political decision-making that their constitutional descriptions might suggest, the Council of Ministers, composed of the Prime Minister and other ministers is more than the group of technocrats the constitutional division between political and administrative executives seems to imply. Several of the ministries are highly 'political' and headed by figures of considerable political standing. The most obvious is the prime ministership held since 1978 by Désiré Rakotoarijoana, a former lieutenant-colonel in the gendarmerie, named minister of finance by Ratsimandrava, a member of the 1975 Military Directorate, and a founder of Arema. The Ministry of the Interior, which controls the territorial administration, the ordinary police, and one of the country's intelligence networks is headed by Ampy Portos, an associate of Ratsiraka's in the Ministry of Foreign Affairs from 1972–5, and, like Rakotoarijoana, an Arema founder. The Ministry of Food, Transport and Tourism, which is responsible for maintaining adequate supplies of rice, has been under Joseph Bedo, formerly head of the President's Office, since 1978. (Bedo was also in charge of the DGID in the last years of the Tsiranana regime. For a more complete description of the backgrounds of key regime figures see the section on regime dynamics.) Another Arema founder, Georges Ruphin, heads the ministry in charge of relations with the administration. In all, of approximately twenty ministries (periodic reorganizations change the number from time to time) one-third to half are held by major political figures. The others, mainly economic, are held by people who are more clearly identifiable as technocrats, whose tenure is much less secure, and who do not have the political weight of the 'old guard' (*LOI*, 29 October 1983). The government also includes representatives from other parties in the FNDR, most notably the AKFM and Vonjy. Like the technocrats these people tend to come and go, with the exception of Gisèle Rabesahala, one of the founders of the AKFM and one of its key Marxist ideologues, who has been minister of culture and revolutionary art since the regime was established.

As Table 5.5 shows, there is considerable overlap between ministerial jurisdiction, particularly in economic and social affairs. In addition, the same areas are covered by the CSR commissions and the President's Office. This leads to confusion and territorial disputes, but has the advantage of giving Ratsiraka considerable flexibility in the allocation of specific tasks, and the movement of control over specific policy areas from one ministry to another or out of the government altogether is one of the persistent characteristics of the system. Defence, for example, moves from the presidency to the Prime Minister's office to the government. (The current Minister of Defence is Raveloson-Mahasampo, one of Ratsiraka's brothers-in-law.) Various sections of the ministries of finance and economy, especially the planning bureau, are occasionally moved to the president's office. Occasionally the subject matter is moved without a formal transfer. Foreign affairs is a presidential domain when Ratsiraka wishes, while the 1983 transfer of Nirina Andriamanerasoa, a technocrat who has become a political figure because of his abilities and rapport with foreign economic negotiators, from the government to the president's office was part of the president's strategy for asserting his own control over those negotiations. (This is a continuation of earlier practices. See de Gaudusson, 1976.)

Like the other executive institutions, the government is an arena for conflict as well as cooperation. Ministers, most notably Rakotomavo-Razakaboana and Tiandraza, have tried to use their position to build an independent political base. Some of the 'old guard' are heavily involved in the black market and similar activities, and Ratsiraka either will not or cannot

Table 5.5 List of Ministries (1986)

Culture and Revolutionary Art
Posts and Telecommunications
Justice
Finance
Transport, Food and Tourism
Civil Service, Labour and Social Affairs
Population and Social Welfare
Defence
Health
Interior
Secondary and Primary Education
Higher Education
Information, Ideology and Cooperatives
Foreign Affairs
Youth
Industry and Energy
Commerce
Public Works
Agricultural Production and Agrarian Reform
Animal Production and Forests

dismiss them, in spite of the complaints of the IMF and other creditors (see *LOI*, 29 October 1983). On the other hand, there are claims that several ministers tried to resign as the economic crisis and political conflict grew worse, only to have their resignations turned down by Ratsiraka on the grounds that 'we're all in this together' (see Cadoux and de Gaudusson, 1980).

Other Institutions

The Malagasy constitution creates two assemblies: the elected legislature, the ANP (National People's Assembly) and the appointed, consultative CMD (Military Development Council). The ANP is composed of 137 deputies, in general one per *fivondronampokontany*. (For terms, see the section on subnational government. Urban *fivondronampokontany* elect several deputies.) The 1976 ordinance establishing the ANP warns its members against 'illegitimate ambitions' and the powers of the assembly are limited both by law and by the political balance of power. (See Calvet, 1978; *Afrique-Asie*, June 1976.) The legislature meets for only four months a year, and follows an agenda set by the President of the Republic in consultation with the president and political bureau of the assembly. The executive is the main source of legislation and between ANP sessions the President and CSR can pass 'ordinances' that have the effect of legislation. The regime's control of the assembly is further reinforced by Arema's domination of the legislature (currently 117 of the 137 deputies), a domination that is reflected in the political longevity of its president, Lucien Michel Xavier Andrianarahinjaka, a major political figure who has held the post since the ANP's first session. In spite of the restrictions on the assembly's powers, it is more than a rubber stamp for regime legislation. The secrecy of the commission meetings that do most of the ANP's work may limit its ability to serve as the public voice of popular discontent, but the same secrecy can make it easier to express opposition like that which delayed passage of the new investment code. During the years of economic crisis, the public sessions on the budget have also provided the occasion for open criticism of regime policies and their administration (see Cadoux and de Gaudusson, 1980).

Unlike the Tsiranana regime, which created quasi-permanent deputies and attempted to use them for the purposes of local political control, the Second Republic has followed the model of the 'citizen deputy', whose official position is a supplement to his regular occupation. Andrianarahin-jaka's description of the function of the deputy suggests a role as transmission belt between regime and population: 'the deputy is the only political agent in contact with the different levels of the Revolutionary Power, from the *fokonolona*, of which he is a member to the national level . . . and including the *firaisampokontany* that he must visit regularly, the *fivondronampokontany*, which he represents, and the *faritany*, of whose council he is also a member' [Calvet, 1978, p. 337]. However, the information available about ANP deputies suggests that they lack the central local position necessary to perform important linkage functions. Calvet's rough list of the occupations of members of the first ANP seems to indicate that they come from the lower level elites of their districts (see Table 5.6). In addition, the post has not been a permanent one since 1972. There was almost no carry over from the First Republic legislature to Ramanantsoa's CNPD and few members of that assembly were elected to the first ANP. The 1983 elections returned only 32 members of the outgoing legislature (*LOI*, 20 November 1983). The combination of minor local position and high turnover makes it unlikely that the deputies either have or are able to construct a local following that is linked to the regime through their activities. It is more probable that they

Table 5.6 ANP Deputies (total = 137)

Teachers (both public and private systems)	45
'Cultivators'	33
Bureaucrats (mainly junior)	20+
Employees and artisans	10+
Doctors	9
Clergy	6

Source: Calvet, 1977, p. 327. The average age of the deputies was 45, and there were four women deputies.

serve as general communicators of regime policy to their constituents than as specific intermediaries.

The CMD

The Malagasy political system has few institutions that can be characterized as façades, but the Military Development Council probably comes closest to the image of an institution whose imputed activity really occurs elsewhere. Officially, the CMD is the parliament of the Malagasy armed forces, composed of fifty members chosen by the President of the republic from lists submitted by the different services. It meets twice a year, and the brief mentions of its secret discussions either do not do them justice or lead to the conclusion that intra-military political issues are debated in other arenas. Its first agenda included a condemnation of the manufacture of *toaka* (bootleg rum), a consideration of the future participation of the armed forces in road building and flood control, and a discussion of 'the role of the revolutionary soldier' (Calvet, 1977). The president of the CMD has always been either a minor regime figure or a personality that the regime wanted to remove from active political life. (See *LOI*, 15 December 1984 for the transfer of head of the armed forces at the time of the 1984 Kung Fu riots, to the presidency of the CMD.)

The Constitutional Court

Another institution that is less important than the list of its functions indicates is the constitutional court. Named by the president from lists submitted by the ANP, the court judges constitutional cases, electoral disputes and jurisdictional disputes between the decentralized collectivities. It also reviews the constitutionality of executive ordinances passed between ANP sessions. As Cadoux and de Gaudusson point out (1980, p. 360), 'it could hardly, even if formal law demanded the action, veto the acts of popular revolutionary will as embodied in the executive'. However, it did overturn several Arema victories in the 1983 legislative election, and it has played an important role in defining the relative spheres of competence of the lower levels of government.

The Decentralized Collectivities

The Malagasy system of local government is strongly marked by the tension between local autonomy and attempted centralization that has characterized successive regimes from the time of the Merina monarchy. The current regime inherited a project, embodied in Ratsimandrava's '*fokonolona* reform' in which the tendency to local autonomy dominated. Ratsiraka has opposed this orientation, and the 1976 Charter of Decentralized Collectivities redressed the balance to such a degree that de Gaudusson (1978b) has characterized it as 'the revenge of the State'. However, the original reform had aroused such enthusiasm that the framers of the Charter were obliged to preserve at least its institutional outline, rebaptising the lowest level '*fokontany*', the name of the geographic unit rather than '*fokonolona*', the name for the community of inhabitants. (In fact, both terms are used. See Figure 5.2.) There are four levels of government, the *fokontany*, corresponding to the village or urban neighbourhood; the *firaisampokontany* or district; the *fivondronampokontany* or region; and the *faritany*, or province (Calvet, 1976; Andriamirado, 1977a; Givelet, 1978; Rajaona, 1980). Each level has roughly the same structure. At the *fokontany* level the population elects a council, which chooses an executive committee whose president is in turn elected by the general population. Elections to the other councils are indirect, with the people's council at each level sending delegates to the council at the next level. The *faritany* council includes the ANP deputies from the province as well as delegates from the regional level. The decentralized collectivities also

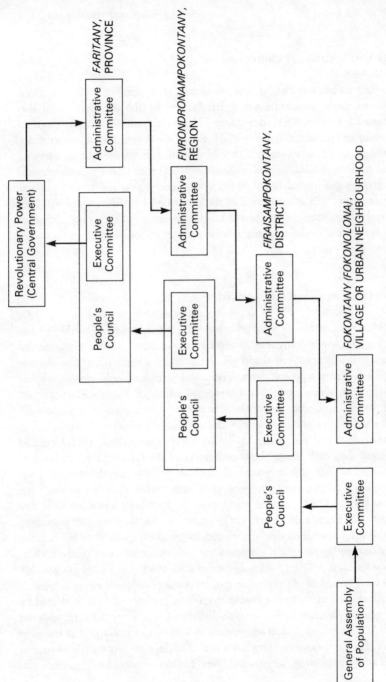

Figure 5.2 The decentralized collectivities

have elected administrative committees charged with coordinating the collectivity's relationships with the administration and economic committees which are reponsible for the planning and direction of economic activities (see also Camacho, 1981; Prats, 1977; Rabevazaha, 1981; Serre-Ratsimandisa, 1978).

The collectivities' duties are similar to those of local government units under previous regimes: the maintenance of local peace and security, the enforcement of health measures, the provision of social assistance, and the conciliation of quarrels in the community (de Gaudusson, 1978; see Covell, 1974 for a discussion of the activities of the *fokonolona* under previous regimes). The major change is the increased responsibility for economic activities but here, too, there is a tendency to use the collectivities as tools for the administration of policies created at the level of the central state: a lack of will and of funds has prevented them from functioning as autonomous economic units (Rabevazaha, 1981; Serre-Ratsimandisa, 1978). The actions of the collectivities are closely supervised. The Ministry of the Interior has direct oversight of the provinces and urban areas, and indirect oversight of the rest. The Ministry of Information and Ideological Animation also has a directorate responsible for the collectivities and the President's Office has two. Elected local officers can be and have been removed by the central authorities if their performance is not satisfactory (de Gaudusson, 1978b; Cadoux and de Gaudusson, 1980). On the other hand, officials considered to be too corrupt or too closely identified with unpopular policies have been subject to attempts by the local population to remove them from office. Although Calvet argued (1976, p. 322) in 1976 that the heads of the local executive committees could turn into the 'new local bosses' of the system, the position has proven to be a difficult one, caught between the attempts of the state to turn the decentralized collectivities into an instrument of administration either of influence on the state or of closure against the state (see *LOI*, 13 March 1982; Leymarie, 1975).

The Administration

The Malagasy administration has a multi-faceted political importance that goes beyond its function as an instrument of rule. Not only is it an interest group in its own right, the state administration has always had a collective identity separate from that of its political 'masters' and this sense of independent existence has been reinforced by the post-1972 changes of regime (Andriamirado, 1977a). Bureaucratic posts have been a major type of reward that successive regimes have offered their followers, and the size and shape of bureaucracy reflect this consideration at least as much as they reflect the technical requirements of rule. Moreover, because bureaucrats constitute a, if not the, major component of the political class, they form a large proportion of the other groups the regime must deal with. In spite of its sense of corporate identity the administration is divided both by the conflicts prevalent in the larger political system and by its own cleavages. Many of the bureaucrats recruited for political reasons were hired outside the normal civil service framework, and the relationships between regular and 'irregular' civil servants, who may constitute as much as half the total administration, are often difficult (de Gaudusson, 1976). Differences also exist between pre-1972 bureaucrats, those from the 'revolutionary generation', and those for whom the revolution is ancient history. The bureaucracy is also divided between the functional ministries and the territorial administration. In Antananarivo the functional ministries, with their degree-holding technocrats, have the greater prestige, but in the countryside the territorial administration is numerically and politically superior.

The relationship between the regime and the administration is a complicated one. Because the bureaucracy is both political base and instrument of rule, the regime cannot alienate it by policies that would make it more a responsive and effective instrument. None of the post-1972 regimes has conducted a thorough-going purge of the bureaucracy. The current regime requires bureaucrats to undergo indoctrination sessions on the tenets of the Revolutionary Charter, and urges them to join Arema, but the party has not been used as an overseer of the bureaucracy. (For a parallel situation, see Halliday and Molyneux, 1981, p. 150, who argue that the response of the Ethiopian administration to the revolution was 'to bow to the inevitable, but to preserve relatively intact its personnel, institutional structure and, it would seem, its political preferences'. The Malagasy administration has done the same, under considerably less pressure.) The same considerations that limit the regime's ability to shape the bureaucracy politically prevent it from acting against the self-enrichment activities of the bureaucrats that thwart the application of so many official policies. Indeed, the regime's use of the bureaucracy as a source of reward gives a tacit consent to the practices. (See Rabemora, 1985; Callaghy, 1983; Gould, 1980.) The economic crisis has worsened an already difficult relationship by lowering the standard of living of most bureaucrats and causing the virtual disappearance of several preferred items of consumption from the open market. Overt opposition has probably been prevented by the results of the 1979 civil servant's strike, which took place over the issues of salaries and a proposed reform that would among other changes have integrated many of the 'irregular' civil servants into the regular hierarchy. The regime won, using the army and TTS squads to break up the strike. It has also abolished the National Administration School, with the result that aspiring bureaucrats must either take their degrees abroad or go through the administrative section of the Antsirabe Military Academy. This demonstration of regime strength has discouraged further direct resistance but has not lessened the wilful inertia that can be even more damaging than open opposition (Calvet, 1977; Cadoux and de Gaudusson, 1980; De Barrin, 1985).

The Armed Forces

The armed forces are another group that is at the same time a power base for the regime, an instrument of rule, an interest group and a potential source of opposition. Although the regime has some of its historical roots in the 1975 Military Directorate, and several important regime figures were, or still are, soldiers, the regime is not an emanation of the armed forces or representative of the military as an institution. On the contrary, it is an alliance between selected factions of the armed forces and their civilian counterparts. The relationship between the regime and the armed forces grew more distant as leading regime figures civilianized themselves, and the distance does not appear to have been lessened by Ratsiraka's 1983 resumption of his commission (*LOI*, 17 December 1983; see also Radu, 1983, pp. 26–7: 'once in power the 'progressive' leadership transferred its loyalty from the military to the party [in the Malagasy case, simply to itself] . . . once this transfer of loyalties is completed, the army becomes an instrument of the [regime] . . . the army maintains influence by providing support for various factions within the [regime] itself. Some of the most serious challenges to [regime] leadership come from factions supported by the military'). There have been several attempted coups since 1975, and the failure of the military to intervene in the Kung Fu battles with the TTS in 1984 demonstrated the degree to which the armed forces do not consider the regime's survival to be identical with their own interests. The regime has attempted to control the armed forces through several strategies including indoctrination, reorganization, weapons acquisition and task manipulation. Direct intimidation, as exemplified by the 1983 officers' trials, is also used.

The Revolutionary Charter identifies the armed forces as one of the five 'pillars of the revolution' but also warns that they must be 'reconverted' into an instrument adapted to the political and military tasks proposed for them.

In part this reconversion has involved direct indoctrination in the principles of the Charter, but in even larger part it has taken the form of a major reorganization. The size of the military has doubled since 1978, to about 30,000 (D. in *Sudestasie* argues that the real number of soldiers is nearly triple the official figure, 1982, p. 37) and the budget has more than doubled, to take up about one-third of the national budget. Most of the officers of the generations preceding the one that took power in 1975 were retired at an early stage in the reorganization. The forces themselves have been reorganized on the linked bases of task and loyalty. The gendarmerie was the least touched by the changes, growing in size from 5,000 to about 8,000, gaining a second training school at Antsirabe, and getting new weapons, but not a significantly higher level of armament than it had previously enjoyed. The other forces, rebaptized the National People's Army, have been radically restructured. The largest branch, the Development Army, groups the old infantry, the Civic Service, and the Engineering Corps. The Development Army shares rural police duties with the gendarmerie, and undertakes agricultural projects, road building and the running of the National Military Service. This service was extended to women in 1974 and is used to fill the gaps in the public education system. (See Archer, 1976; Serre and Rasoarahona, 1981. Calvet, 1979, estimates that between 1973 and 1978 13,253 went through the service, 6,954 women and 6,299 men. In 1977, of 4,964 conscripts (including 2,985 women) 4,244 went to teach in the primary system and 135 to the secondary schools, 346.) The Development Army has been used to help with bringing in the harvest and with the collection and distribution of rice.

The other units are all much smaller and equipped with a more sophisticated level of weapons. The air force and navy have been merged and have, if anything, decreased in size since 1975. An elite 'Intervention Force', recruited from former paratroopers and naval artillerymen on the basis of personal loyalty to Ratsiraka, has been created and is directly commanded by the president. Also attached to the President's Office are the President's Security Guard, which according to *Le Monde* protects the Presidential Palace with armored vehicles and Soviet artillery, and the Presidential Security Regiment, recruited from Arema members and commanded by North Korean officers (*Le Monde* 24 February 1982; see also Serre and Rasoarahona, 1981). For all these branches of the armed forces the regime has invested heavily in weapons, training, and technical assistance from Eastern Europe and North Korea (see Cadoux and de Gaudusson, 1980, p. 374; *Année politique*, 1981).

The main military task, strictly speaking, of the armed forces is defence against attack or infiltration from South Africa. However, it is clear that its

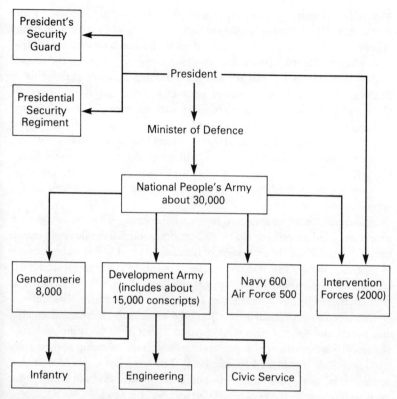

Figure 5.3 Armed forces, 1987

Source: Figures are from a variety of sources, and should be treated as *estimates* only. Some sources, e.g. D. *Sudestasie*, 1982, argues that the real numbers are twice the official figures

internal functions far outweigh its external role. First, as I have indicated, it undertakes a large number of economic activities. Especially since the economic crisis its transportation and communications system is the most reliable in the island, and it has taken over much of the responsibility for the transportation of crops and goods from the state societies, whose stock of vehicles is almost useless (see D., in *Sudestasie*, 1982; Ramaro, 1980). In 1979, in response to the failure of other ventures, the Ompira (the Military Office for Agricultural Production) was created and given responsibility for the '100,000 hectares' rice project. Since then it has expanded, with North Korean assistance, to the cultivation of coffee, vanilla and groundnuts (Ramaro, 1980, D., 1982). It was preceded by Omnis (the Military Office for

Materials of Strategic Interest) which is administered directly by the President's Office. Omnis is responsible for research and exploration in the area of strategic materials and was involved in the search for offshore oil that took place in the mid-1980s. It is also responsible for running the former arsenal at Antseranana, and the chromite mining industry that furnishes Madagascar's only strategic export (see Serre and Rasoarahona, 1981; de Gaudusson, 1979). In addition, military officers serve in several of the nationalized companies. This expanded economic role reflects several considerations: it gives the enlarged army something to do; it makes use of an institution that, for all its reticence, is still more directly under the regime's control than the administration or general population; and it gives the military access to the benefits created by the expanded state role in the economy.

The armed forces are also used for internal policing. This has always been true of the gendarmerie but since 1972 the other forces have also been drawn into police work and the repression of internal revolts. In 1984, in response to the increase in banditry two coordinated command structures were set up: the *état major de conception* that includes the President and Prime Minister as well as the Ministers of Defence, Justice and the Interior, the defence commission of the CSR (all officers) and the heads of the army, gendarmerie, and police, and the *état major mixte operationel* that joins the commanders of the army, gendarmerie and police and formalizes the blending of their roles (see Figure 5.4; and *LOI*, 2 March 1984). The army has a special unit that specializes in putting down riots, but other units have also been used for the purpose, most recently in the 1985 attacks on the Kung Fu headquarters. Although the current Malagasy regime is not 'military', its survival does depend on the willingness of the armed forces to continue defending it.

There are several sources of tension in the relationship between the regime and its armed forces, but in many cases these issues also divide the armed forces themselves. The gendarmerie has not profited to the degree that it might have expected from its support of the regime, the French-trained older generation of officers distrusts the Moscow–Havana–Pyong-Yang trained younger generation; those whose training has been limited to Madagascar are jealous of those trained abroad, and all resent the superior privileges and weapons of the elite regiments (D. in *Sudestasie*, 1982; Chaigneau, 1983a; De Barrin, 1985). However, while these resentments might lead to incidents like the assassination of two members of the Presidential Guard, whose bodies were found outside the Gendarmerie Officers' Mess in Antsirabe, and while they might have contributed to the armed forces' reserve in 1984, military issues alone have not presented the greatest dangers to the regime. The plots

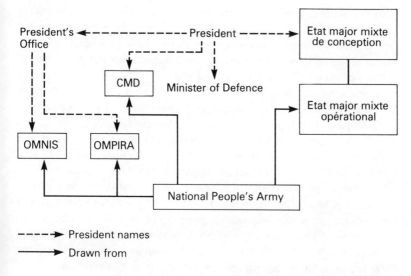

Figure 5.4 Organization of defence and security

uncovered so far have involved both soldiers and civilian opposition groups, indicating that the fragmented boundaries and cross-boundary alliances already characteristic of the Malagasy armed forces in 1972 are, if anything, even more important today. Moreover, the military participants in these plots acted as individuals. There is no indication that whole units were involved, let alone the military as an institution. While these events are always difficult to predict, it appears that the regime has more to fear from alliances between civilian and military opposition groups than from opposition by the armed forces as a whole.

Parties

Arema

Madagascar differs from the expected pattern of Marxist states both in the characteristics of its party system and in the nature of the regime party, Arema. While Arema is clearly the dominant party in the system, neither by law nor in the opinion of the other parties does it have a monopoly on guardianship or definition of 'the Revolution'. If anything, the party system is more competitive now than it was under the Tsiranana regime in terms of the numbers of existing parties, the share of the vote the parties gather, and their degree of influence on political decisions. The formal adherence of all parties to the principles of the Revolutionary Charter has not prevented the emergence of considerable ideological diversity.

Arema itself has become more a 'party-nation' than a vanguard party (Cadoux and de Gaudusson, 1980, p. 366). Characterized by Chaigneau as a catch-all party' (1982, p. 114, in English in the original), Arema has moved into the organizational if not the ideological space vacated by the elimination of the PSD. This is true in terms of its strength in the rural areas, based on a symbiosis with the territorial administration, and its relative weakness in the cities, particularly the capital (Lefèvre, 1969). It is also true in terms of membership, both at the top, where several of the party's founders had PSD connections, and at the bottom, where local notables who had been PSD members 'ex officio' simply transferred their allegiance to the new 'party of the *fanjakana*'. However, Arema is more than simply a reincarnation of the PSD. If not itself a revolutionary vanguard, it does contain a core of revolutionary ideologues. It has recruited among traditional urban strata who had boycotted the PSD and among the emerging administrative-technical elite that is largely the creation of post-1972 government policy. In the countryside it has absorbed many of the 'new men' who emerged after 1972. As a result, Arema has, if anything, a more diverse social composition and a broader ideological range than its predecessor in the role of regime party. This may give the regime a broader base, but diminishes the utility of the party as a revolutionary weapon or even as an instrument of rule (see also Leymarie, 1982; Moine, 1981; Ravaloson, 1983). Ratsiraka has made several attempts to deal with the problem. After the presidential elections, party discipline (in part defined as loyalty to the president) was tightened with the vanquishing of 'right Arema' and the 1983 revision of the party's political bureau. (Several members, including Rakotovao-Razakaboana, leader of the dissident group, and Robert Koto, who had attempted to run for president himself, were removed and nine new members, 'like them ethnically but more loyal' were added. *LOI*, 25 March 1983.) At times Ratsiraka has had to draw on other parties in the Front, most notably the AKFM and occasionally the MFM, to build a more ideologically homogeneous coalition in support of policies that had aroused opposition in his own party (see *LOI*, 5 February 1983; 26 October 1984).

Arema's party statutes follow a fairly classical outline, beginning with cells at the *fokontany* level, and continuing with 'sections' at the *firaisampokontany* level, 'unions of sections' at the *fivondronompokontany* level, and 'federations' at the *faritany* level. A national party congress, composed of the existing central committee and the political bureaux of the federations is to meet every four years to elect a new central committee, national political bureau, and secretary general, (Calvet, 1976, p. 365). However, the statutes give only an imperfect picture of Arema's organization and functioning. A secretary-general (Ratsiraka, more commonly referred to as the party's president) and political bureau were named in 1976, pending the party's founding congress. This congress has never been held, and the 1983 changes in the political bureau were made by Ratsiraka himself. The Central Committee has no visible activities or existence and in many areas the intermediate level party units were only put into place at the time of the 1982 and 1983 elections (*LOI*, 3 April 1982; see also Moine, 1979; Chaigneau, 1982). There has never been a detailed accounting of Arema members: the party claimed to have 90,000 members in 30,000 cells in 1977 (Calvet, 1978, p. 341) but the figure has never been verified or updated (Chaigneau, 1983c, gives a figure of nearly a million members). The party does maintain formation centres that dispense instruction on the principles of Marxism–Leninism and of 'decentralized Malagasy socialism', as well as training for trade union and cooperative officials and publications like the 'Guide for the Arema militant' (Malley, 1982a). There are several auxilliary organizations: youth groups, 'young pioneers', 'revolutionary' women, students, artists, and a party-led union, now the country's largest. The most important appears to be the Revolutionary Women led by Ratsiraka's wife Celine and her sister, Hortense Raveloson-Mahasampo. In addition to the expected round of social activities, itself of considerable significance given the importance of social and family ties in the system, the Revolutionary Women undertake social welfare activities like the establishment of child care facilities. The party also runs cooperatives, particularly in fokontany where the state cooperatives are dominated by the AKFM or the MFM (Camacho, 1981).

Arema-State Relations

There is no formal articulation between Arema and the state; rather, the task of giving ideological guidance to the institutions of government belongs to the FNDR, of which Arema is, of course, the dominant member. The party also lacks a structure paralleling that of the administration that would allow it to be used for the supervision of the bureaucracy. However, there is some degree of overlapping membership. The proportion of administrators who are party members is not known, although possession of a party card is generally considered to be an advantage in the pursuit of a bureaucratic career. At the top, several members of the Council of Ministers and the CSR are also members of the party's bureau, and nearly half the members of the bureau are or have been ministers (see Table 5.7). Most of these are founding members of the party; for the rest, holding a ministerial post has usually preceded 'promotion' to the political bureau. In general the relationship between party and government is one of mixed division and duplication of

Table 5.7 Arema Political Bureau, 1983

	Council of Ministers	CSR
Members of original Bureau		
L. M. X. Andrianarahinjaka*		
(President, ANP)		
Theophile Andrianoelisoa*		×
Indrianajafy Georges*		×
Simon Pierre	×	×
Rabezandrina Raveloarimefy		
(President, Foreign Affairs		
Commission, ANP)		
Laurent Radaody Rakotondravao		
Désiré Radimiharison		
Rajaofera		
Désiré Rakotoarijaona	× (P.M.)	×
Justin Rakotoniaina		×
Didier Ratsiraka	President of the republic	×
Christian Remy Richard	×	
Georges Ruphin	×	
Zakariasy Albert (ANP)		
Joined between 1977 and 1983		
Tahiry Fidison		
Ampy Portos	×	
Rakoto Ignace	×	
Moise Rakotosihanaka		

Table 5.7 *(cont.)*

	Council of Ministers	CSR
Hortense Raveleson-Mahasampo (Head, Revolutionary Women)		
Noro Robinson		
Joined in 1983		
Oliva Andrianasola		
Fara Eloi		
Vazaha Evariste*		
Jean-Claude Rahaga		
Honoré Rakotomanana		
Roland Ramahatra		
Armand Ramambazafy		
Voantio Tsifanahy		
Aristide Velompahany		

Note: Five members of the 1977 bureau politique were no longer members in 1983, having been expelled during the 'right Arema' dispute. Remi Tiandraza was a member in 1983, but was expelled early in 1985 after the Kung Fu riots.

* Former minister

Sources: Calvet, 1977; *LOI*, 26 March 1983.

function rather than hierarchical oversight. Each presents Ratsiraka and his associates with an alternate set of institutions and resources for maintaining power and directing policy. Rather than serving as directing force or organizational focus for the system, Arema resembles Linz's authoritarian party which

is not a well organized ideological organization which monopolizes all access to power. . . . A considerable part of the elite has no connection with the party and does not identify with it . . . . The party is often ideologically and sociologically heterogeneous. Far from branching out into many functional organizations in an effort to control the state apparatus and penetrate other spheres of life . . . it is a skeleton organization. [Cited in Collier, 1982, p. 150]

Arema's failure to develop into a revolutionary party of mobilization is in part the result of internal obstacles such as a lack of resources and the ideological diversity of its top leadership, but it also reflects the success of the other parties in maintaining and even expanding their role in the system.

The AKFM

The AKFM has gained under the Second Malagasy Republic what it desired so much in the First, a chance to influence government policy and participate in the exercise of power. However, the extent of its influence is not always clear, and the party has paid a price for its close support of the regime. The price was most evident in the elections of 1982 and 1983. The traditional 'party of Antananarivo' was unable to deliver the capital in the 1982 presidential election and was fourth in votes in the 1983 ANP election, while over half its local representatives lost their positions in the decentralized collectivities elections (*LOI*, 20 November 1982; 15 October 1982. See Table 5.8). The party has lost its role as the articulator of urban opposition to Monima, it has never regained the audience among the younger generation that it lost in the final years of the Tsiranana regime, and its base in the middle and lower middle classes of the capital is largely eroded (see Calvet and de Gaudusson, 1980; *Le Monde*, 10 November 1982; *LOI*, 3 March 1982). The party is still led by its founding generation, with no obvious successors behind it.

Table 5.8 Election results, 1983

Party	Fokonolona Councils (% of seats)	National People's Assembly (% of vote)
Arema	65.5	64.8
AKFM	12.5	8.7
MFM	9.7	11.1
Vonjy	9.5	10.6
Monima	2.3	3.7
UDECMA	0.3	—
VS Monima	0.1	—

Source: LOI, 8 March 1983, 15 October 1983.

However, the party's usefulness to the regime does not rest only, or even principally, on its popular support. Despite the waning of this support, and the electoral defeat of many of its lower level personnel, the AKFM still has a stronger organizational structure than the other parties in the system. Ideological affinity and willingness to offer at least publically unconditional support to the regime in general and Ratsiraka in particular have made it a useful part of the ruling coalition. As an ally the party has consistently supported the centralization of power. It is the only non–Arema member of the FNDR willing to discuss the establishment of a single party, it has argued for the abolition of the private press, and in 1982 it proposed that the president be chosen by an electoral college rather than by direct elections. Although it has maintained its links with the international communist movement and its affiliated organizations, it does not perform the function of linkage with the regime or Arema, which have developed their own relationships in this area. Rather, its importance lies in the contribution it makes to the internal balance of forces (see also *LOI*, 3 April 1982).

Monima

All Malagasy parties are dominated by a single leader: in the case of Monima, it is almost accurate to say that the leader is the party. This domination has been even stronger since the party split into two wings, Monima-Kamiviombio, led by Monja Jaona himself and Vondrona Socialista Monima, formed by members who resented his 'dictatorial' methods. Monja Jaona's appeal lies in his nationalist past and his consistent opposition to every Malagasy regime from the French to the present republic. His continued criticism of the regime, undiminished either by periodic membership in the FNDR or by recurring house arrest, has made Monima the new party of urban opposition, particularly in the capital. However, Monja Jaona's popularity has not been matched by organizational growth. The party's rural structures, never very strong, have collapsed with the ageing of its founding generation and the party has lost most of its original base in Toliary province. The loss of the rural base has in part been compensated for by the development of an audience in the cities, where easier communications make organization less important. However, the lack of organization does limit the party's effectiveness. Monja Jaona's 1977 and 1982 appeals for a general strike led to rioting in Antananarivo and the provincial capitals but not to any coherent action, and the party's score in the 1983 elections fell far short of the 23 per cent of the vote its leader had won in 1982. (It should be noted that the 1983 total almost certainly underestimates Monima's strength, but it is part of a pattern of overall decline that began in the mid-1970s; see Table 5.9 and Cadoux and de Gaudusson, 1980; *Le Monde*, 5 November 1982; Chaigneau, 1983a; *Afrique-Asie*, 3 January 1983; De Barrin, 1985.)

The party, through Monja Jaona, has appealed to a range of urban groups. It lost one generation of university students and professors to the MFM, but has been able to recruit from subsequent generations who have been critical of the MFM's involvement with the regime and who see greater opportunities for influence in a party with an ageing, non-intellectual leadership. The party also had links with the groups involved in the Kung Fu movement, and Monja Jaona used Kung Fu members as his security guard in the 1982 election (*LOI*, 15 December 1984). Monja Jaona's repeated criticisms of 'the barons of socialism and their associated boot-lickers' and of their dependence on the Soviet Union and the IMF articulate public resentment of sufficient proportions that the regime hesitates to move definitely against their author. Moreover, the criticisms provide more than a useful safety valve in that they are attacks from the left, in the name of a more radical revolution. When Monja Jaona is not attacking the regime he has offered Ratsiraka support and the latter once characterized their relationship as that of '*mpiziva*'; friends and rivals (*Le Monde*, 5 November 1982). The relationship is strained now, but combines with Monja Jaona's prestige to protect him from thorough-going retaliation.

The MFM

The MFM is another party whose relationship with the regime is charged with ambiguity. Formed at the beginning of the Ramanantsoa period by the radicals of 1972, the party was committed to a long-term strategy of working through existing institutions where possible and against them when necessary, expecting the process to culminate in a violent social and political revolution (see Bouillon, 1973, for an early description; Archer, 1976; Althabe, 1980; Camacho, 1981). The MFM formed part of the left front that supported Ratsiraka in 1975, but viewed his regime as only one stage in the proletarian revolution, and refused to join the FNDR until 1977. While the MFM and its leadership have been an important source of support for Ratsiraka in the Front and in his quarrels with opponents in Arema, the party has been involved in several incidents of violent opposition to regime policies and personnel. The party abandoned its commitment to the necessity of armed struggle in 1980, but maintained its commitment to the acquisition of power (Cadoux and de Gaudusson, 1980; *LOI*, 21 January 1984).

In 1975 Serre described the MFM as an intellectual led party that used the

Zoam as shock troops and that had not succeeded in establishing a rural base in spite (or because) of its attempts to mobilize the population against the territorial administration and its associated *notables* (p. 217). Since then both the strategy and audience of the party have changed, at least in part. Since joining the Front the party has run in elections and openly organized groups such as unions, but also continues to maintain a semi-clandestine character. (Information about its internal organization is almost non-existent, and official meetings of its executive organs are rare. Cadoux and de Gaudusson, 1980; *LOI*, 26 October 1984.) It has lost its base in the urban lumpen-proletariat to Arema and Monima but has been able to gain a sufficient audience among rural and urban middle sectors to achieve relative success in the 1983 elections everywhere but in the capital (*LOI*, 5 February 1983; 19 March 1983; 15 October 1983). However, open organization and electoral activities have not completely replaced non-electoral activities and links with groups like the Kung Fu.

Vonjy

On the 'right' of the Front, Vonjy has provided a home for many former PSD figures (André Resampa was a Vonjy candidate in the 1983 *fokonolona* council elections) and has inherited that party's links with the Socialist International and the French Socialist Party. The party is strong in its leader's home region of south-east Fianarantsoa and among the more conservative urban administrative and commercial groups attracted by its emphasis on 'pragmatic' rather than 'ideological' socialism (Cadoux and de Gaudusson, 1980; Serre, 1975; *LOI*, 3 April 1982, 2 April 1983; 3 September 1983). Although the party supported Ratsiraka in 1982 and did better than expected in the 1983 elections, its ideological distance from the core of the regime and links with Ratsiraka's conservative opposition within Arema have diminished its influence.

UDECMA

Characterized by Cadoux and de Gaudusson (1980, p. 362) as 'a marginal formation tolerated, or perhaps accepted 'by charity' by the other members of the Front', UDECMA is the latest of a series of unsuccessful attempts to establish a radical Christian Democratic party in Madagascar. The party is not supported by the Church hierarchy, and received very few votes in the 1983 elections. However, its leader, Solo Norbert Andriamorasata, is a long-time participant in Malagasy politics with considerable personal prestige (see also Calvet, 1977).

Opposition and Security

Officially there is no opposition in Madagascar. All legal political activity requires adherance to the principles of the Revolutionary Charter and partisan political activity requires membership in the FNDR. However, in spite of these restrictions, opposition of various types is widespread and constant, and regime attempts to control it are not always successful or even whole-hearted.

Classic schema divide opposition according to its object: individual policies, the occupants of government office or the regime itself (see, e.g., Dahl, 1966). However, in a personalized authoritarian regime like the Malagasy Second Republic, the one so often shades into the other that it is perhaps more useful to distinguish opposition by its location: excluded groups, support groups and members of the ruling coalition (see Jackson and Rosberg, 1982; Ilchman and Uphoff, 1969). In Madagascar, opposition can be found in all these locations. Formal, and even real, participation in the regime does not preclude opposition to regime policies, doubts about Ratsiraka and his close associates and (much the same thing) preparation for the coming of a successor regime. Contacts among the various groups are also not uncommon and can be dangerous to the regime. For example, the Kung Fu movement involved excluded groups like the youth who joined the clubs, support groups including some of the parties in the FNDR and, according to rumour, key members of the ruling coalition in the armed forces.

Excluded Groups

These include the peasants and urban poor, whose opposition takes forms ranging from withdrawal to riots to outright attacks on local administrators and elected officials. Students, particularly at the university level, where Monima is well implanted, must also be considered an excluded group, and practically a permanent opposition. Their tactics include the demonstrations and riots of the previous groups, as well as more elaborate techniques of semi-clandestine organizations, pamphlets and graffiti.

Members of the 'Merina oligarchy' who have not found an accommodation with the regime also constitute an excluded group, but one with more impressive powers of opposition given their money, personal contacts with each other and with members of regime support groups, and in many cases access to foreign contacts. (One member of this group, the owner of an important Antananarivo factory that closed under suspicious circumstances, was tried and convicted in 1983 for illegal possession of firearms and for training commando units for an eventual attack on the regime, with the assistance of some members of the gendarmerie. See *LOI*, 19 November 1983.)

Politicians from the Tsiranana regime constitute another excluded group. Many went into exile in France, where they have joined other Malagasies resident in France to keep a critical eye on the regime and its policies. Jacques Rabemanajara, Minister of Foreign Affairs under Tsiranana, went into exile after 1972. The 1983 arrest of Monja Jaona led him to speak out against the 'increasing repression' of the regime and to criticize the results of its 'catastrophic experiment' (Thompson, 1987, p. 536). Other Malagasies resident in France, most notably the members of the 'Committee of Malagasy Democrats', have also criticized the regime for violations of human rights (see *LOI*, 14 November 1984, for a description of an article by Alexis Bezaka, a Christian Democratic politician of the Tsiranana period, on 'Le TTS et le terrorisme d'état'). However, the exile groups are relatively small, given the number of Malagasies, of varying attitudes to the regime, who live in France.

Support Groups and Opposition

These include the churches, the state apparatus, and most members of the FNDR, of whom only the AKFM has given the regime anything approaching unconditional support. Several of these groups maintain contact with more intransigeant opponents, and some have at least flirted with the idea of a change of regime. While all give at least verbal support to the ideological direction of the regime, some, like Vonjy, would prefer a non-Marxist brand of socialism, while others, like Monima and some groups in the MFM, suspect the regime of lacking true commitment to the revolution.

Opposition in a support group is, by its very location, threatening to the regime. The international contacts of the groups are also threatening given the very tactical nature of the commitment of the regime's international partners. All of the churches have international affiliations, parties like Vonjy have political friends in France, as do other groups, including the older generation of the armed forces, and Monima and the AKFM have independent contacts with various communist countries and parties. The tactics of these groups have included verbal attacks like the successive 'bishops' letters' of the Catholic church and the speeches of Monja Jaona, arguments within fora like the FNDR and the CSR, and the utilization of external sources of pressure (see Chaigneau, 1983c). Opposition from support groups can change the course of government action, or at least delay it. Ratsiraka's 'read the Bible' speech, and the delays in publication of the new investment code both reflect the pressures of opposition from different support groups.

Core Groups

The most dangerous opposition, and the least known, comes from the groups most closely associated with the regime. That it exists can be seen from Ratsiraka's 'Judas and Simon Peter' speech, and from his appointment of his brother-in-law to the post of Minister of Defence after the death of his old friend Guy Sibon in 1986. There are several sources of this opposition. One is ideological, and has become particularly important with the changes in policy since the 1980 economic collapse. Quarrels within the president's entourage about the desirability of the 'liberalization' that has been undertaken since the collapse are reported largely through rumour, but the rumours are frequent and persistent. Another source of division is disagreement over the strategy to follow in dealing with other sources of opposition. Some, including most members of the President's family, urge a narrowing of the regime and a hard line against opposition groups, while others urge concessions and reconciliation. Finally, potential opposition exists in the core group because some of its members joined the ruling coalition for self-enrichment. When Ratsiraka and the regime can no longer deliver, or if their disappearance appears imminent, these people are likely to desert, and even to participate in an overthrow.

These opposition groups have not yet been able to combine. They are divided by ideology and foreign contacts, and fragmentation and mutual suspicion have prevented the construction of a counter-coalition that would be capable of changing the policies of the regime or of presenting an alternative. Ratsiraka himself still has considerable prestige and, ironically, benefits from the country's current problems. The groups that would be most capable of replacing him are intimidated by the situation they would face in his stead.

Control

In addition to the means afforded by the territorial administration, the judicial system, the police and armed forces, the regime uses other means of control of opposition, most notably the various security services and censorship offices. The most important of the security services is the DGID (Direction Générale d'Information et de Documentation) located, as under the First Republic, in the President's Offices. This service has extensive powers, including the legal possibility of holding suspects in secret for fifteen days (and the practice of holding them for longer periods). It was responsible for investigating and assembling the evidence in the trials that followed the 1982 plot discoveries and interrogated several members of the right Arema, including ministers, after the 1982 presidential elections. Its methods have been criticized by human rights groups and by the Malagasy judiciary itself (see Cadoux and de Gaudusson, 1980; *Le Monde*, 24 February 1982; *LOI*, 1 October 1983). Criticisms of the DGID led to the removal of Raveloson Mahasampo in March 1985, as part of Ratsiraka's campaign of reconciliation with support group opposition (*Africa Research Bulletin*, March 1985).

There are other intelligence and security services attached to the army, gendarmerie, Ministry of the Interior, and other ministries, especially those that have a mandate that includes island-wide travel. Many have East German or North Korean 'technical assistants' attached to them. In addition to secret services, both the *fokonolona* executive committees, and the Arema committees (often the same people) have a responsibility for keeping an eye on political activities at the village level. Finally, the TTS and groups like them have been used to break up demonstrations or to turn demonstrations into riots that can then be broken up by the police and armed forces.

Censorship

Censorship is also used to control the expression of opposition and criticism, and in a more thoroughgoing way than under the Tsiranana regime. The Malagasy press has historically been unusually important and active, although its circulation was largely limited to the capital (*Lumière*, 1, 8 May 1966). In 1972 there was a single island-wide newspaper, the *Courrier de Madagascar*, French owned and so supportive of the regime that its building was burned in the course of the May uprising. There was a French language weekly journal of political commentary, *Lumière*, published under Jesuit auspices in Fianarantsoa. *Lumière* was considerably more critical of the government than the *Courrier de Madagascar*, and was widely read among the elite for the accuracy of its commentary. Another Catholic journal, *Lakroan' i Madagasikara* was published mainly in Malagasy and its editor, Ralibera, was an important political as well as religious figure. In addition, there was a numerous press of journals published in Malagasy, largely in Antananarivo, with circulations ranging from 1,000 to 5,000, with a possible total of 30,000 (*Lumière*, 1, 8 May 1966). There was also an underground press of journals like *Ny Andry*, published irregularly by the clandestine opposition.

The events of 1972 at first increased the flow of print as various groups in the movement either started journals or began open publication of clandestine journals. The *Courrier de Madagascar* reappeared after a six-day pause as *Madagascar Matin* and persists, still French owned and still either apolitical or pro-regime in its commentaries. However, the Ramanantsoa period and even more the 1975 change of regime also brought more stringent censorship and greater organization and regulation of journalistic activity. The press associated with the May 1972 movements either disappeared or returned to clandestinity. Licensing of journalists and the creation of an 'Order of Journalists' under the authority of a Minister of Press and Information (after 1975 the Minister for Ideological Animation) was begun in 1973 (*Afrique-Asie*, June 1976: Chaigneau, 1983a).

In August 1975 the regime established its own censorship law, whose form followed the Revolutionary Charter's description of news reporting (p. 4) as 'a privileged means of education of the population ... which should incite them to apply the measures taken by the authorities in the interests of the masses'. The law permits the suspension of any journal that is 'harmful to public order, national unity, or morality' and publications are checked and double checked for infringements of law. The Ministry of Information and Ideological Animation has a section that gives publications a first check, while a panel of Arema officials reviews disputed cases. In addition, the presidency has its own press review service that calls the others to order when it considers them too lax (Chaigneau, 1983b, pp. 301–2).

Under the circumstances, *Lumière* ceased publication in 1975, and even *Madagascar Matin* is occasionally censored. The smaller newspapers of the capital have decreased in number, and it is almost impossible to get the permission necessary to start new ones (see *LOI*, 5 December 1981 and 13 February 1982). *Lakroa* continues to publish, and has been able to maintain its stance of mingled support and criticism, in part because of the personal position of its editor (Chaigneau, 1983a). This journal and the others have, as Andriamirado puts it, had to rediscover the uses of allegory and allusion practised under the colonial period and to a degree under the first republic (Andriamirado, 1977a, p. 21). Controls are also tight on foreign journals. The tone of Andriamirado's articles in *Jeune Afrique* resulted in the banning of the importation of that periodical in 1980.

Radio and television are government run, as they were under previous regimes. As under the Tsiranana regime many journalists find it prudent to be members of the governing party. (According to Chaigneau, 1983b, ninety-six of 211 registered journalists are employed by the government.) In addition, the government nationalized film distribution in 1975, and has made an attempt to substitute production of Third World or socialist countries for 'Maciste, Kung-Fu and other B-films' (interview with head of film office, *Afrique–Asie*, June 1976, p. 32). As the rise of Kung Fu inspired groups in the early 1980s suggests, the effort has not been completely successful.

The efficiency and weight of this apparatus are hard to evaluate. Chaigneau (1983c, p. 344) argues that an extensive secret police network is one of the bases for the regime's continuation in power. Certainly the apparatus is more extensive than that of the First Republic (although probably not more dominated by foreign technical assistants). However, it is also true that the range of permitted political activity is much greater than it was under the Tsiranana regime. The persistence of overt opposition and the ability of the Kung Fu groups to assemble a large armed force suggest that Madagascar is far from being a rigidly controlled police state. Cadoux and de Gaudusson (1980, p. 378) point out that the secret police is also obliged to cope with the networks of personal relationships that often connect opposition figures and groups with powerful members of the regime.

The Bases of the Regime

Given the ambiguity of the support of most groups, it makes more sense to analyse the basis of the regime in rather personal terms, and to look at it as a group of people more or less connected to Ratsiraka, using 'instruments of rule' of varying reliability, and acting in concert with other groups whose goals coincide with theirs in some respects but not all. The most important connections, often overlapping, are those of family, region and personal contact at earlier stages of Ratsiraka's career. The importance of these personal connections has increased as the political difficulties of the past several years have increased suspicions of the loyalty of other members of the ruling coalition.

Regime figures in both party and state have been drawn from Ratsiraka's family and his home region of Toamasina. His brothers-in-law were useful supporters in the days of the Military Directorate, and have continued to be closely associated, his sister-in-law Hortense plays an important role in the organization of Arema women, and his wife Celine has challenged ministers and won. The family are considered to be among the regime's main 'hard liners'. Among the regime figures from Toamasina are Joseph Bedo, a presidential councillor in 1975 and now head of the crucial Ministry of Food Supplies; Jean Bemananjara, in the government since 1975 and now Minister of Foreign Affairs; Jean-Jacques Seraphin, Minister of Health since 1975; and Georges Solofoson, head of Ratsiraka's civil cabinet in 1975, and now Minister of Commerce. Etienne Mora, now retired, but formerly an important figure in Arema, is also from the province.

Another source of regime personnel was Ratsiraka's time in the navy, and the Ramanantsoa government. The late Guy Sibon, Minister of Defence from 1977 to 1986 was an old associate from the navy. Of the thirteen ministers Ratsiraka named when he first took office in 1975, five had been on the team that renegotiated the cooperation accords in 1972 (Calvet, 1977). Ampy Portos, Minister of the Interior since 1976, was the director of the Foreign Ministry under Ratsiraka from 1972-5; Solofoson was a councillor; Justin Rakotoniaina, Prime Minister in 1976 and one of the builders of Arema, was ambassador to Algeria. Others were military men, many of whom gave Ratsiraka crucial support in the 1975 Military Directorate. These include Sibon and Désiré Rakotoarijaona, Prime Minister since 1977.

Military rank has generally not in itself been a road to power without the intervening personal connection. A more important qualification is a period as a direct presidential councillor. Bedo and Solofoson were both presidential advisers at the beginning of the regime; Georges Ruphin, another architect of Arema, Minister of Information and Ideological Animation, and now Minister of the Civil Service was also an early adviser, as were L. M. X. Andrianarahinjaka, another Arema founder and President of the National Assembly since 1977, and Simon Pierre, the current Minister of Information and Ideological Animation.

The reliance on family and the Toamasina region means that many regime figures have been drawn from the old PSD. Ratsiraka's father was connected with the PSD leadership through his earlier membership in PADESM, and both Ratsiraka and his brother Etienne are married to daughters of prominent PSD members, while Etienne was Director General of the Ministry of the Interior from May to November 1972, a time when there were still many Resampa followers there. Figures with PSD connections include Bedo, who was a councillor of Tsiranana and head of the DGID after 1970, Portos, who was Resampa's chief adviser in 1971, the late Raymond Maro, a long-term Ratsiraka adviser and member of the Bureau Politique of Arema, who had extensive connections in the PSD, and Ruphin, who was director of the PSD party study centre.

The introduction of people drawn from Ratsiraka's time in the navy and the Ramanantsoa government has served to expand the geographical bases of support, most notably to Firanarantsoa. Andrianarahinjaka, Rakotoniaina and Simon Pierre all come from the province, as does Ignace Rakoto, Minister of Higher Education since 1977. Other parties are also represented, but more officially through the close association of figures like the AKFM's Andriamanjato and the MFM's Manadafy Rakotonirina with the regime.

These figures, and their corresponding networks overlap with, and connect the regime to, its more distant support groups. The relationship between the regime core and these groups is characterized by the tension between participation and criticism on the part of the groups, and between closure and inclusion on the part of the regime. Particularly since the crises of the early to mid-1980s there has been increasing pressure to closure and a tendency to rely on the most loyal, without regard for ideological inclinations. Ratsiraka's family has maintained if not increased its importance, as exemplified by the reappearance of his brother-in-law, Raveloson Mahasampo, as Minister of Defence. In addition, the regime has relied on its East German and North Korean security advisers to an increasing extent. The most visible sign of this was the construction, under North Korean supervision, of a concrete presidential 'bunker' at Iavoloha, outside Antananarivo. (The above-ground part of this heavily fortified installation is a replica of the royal palace in Antananarivo, an act of *lèse majesté* that did not please the inhabitants of the capital. Ratsiraka has not yet taken up residence in the bunker.)

On the other hand, closure is not yet complete. There are disadvantages to relying on the most loyal, who are not always the most competent or the least corrupt, and Ratsiraka has encouraged the development of a counterbalancing group of younger advisers, many trained in Moscow or East Europe (see *Le Monde*, 7 November 1986; Chaigneau, 1983c). The importance of personal connections and the real support that the groups often provide to the regime also create a countervailing desire for inclusion. Moreover, the groups themselves or, rather, their leaders are powerful enough to resist exclusion from political influence. Ratsiraka's personal discretion is far from absolute (for a contrast, see Callaghy, 1983). Much of the arena in which he must operate was shaped by the activities of previous regimes and he has not been able to impose a totally new agenda or list of participants. The fact that Ratsiraka can dominate but not monopolize political activities, means that compromise, whether desirable or not, is still an essential part of the political system.

6 Economic Policy

Malagasy economic policy since 1975 can be divided into three distinct phases, succeeding each other against a background of continuity of problems, and often policies, inherited from pre-1975 regimes. The problems include low productivity in both agriculture and industry, a growing population that must be fed and employed and a mutually reinforcing lack of articulation in the economy and lack of coordination in economic policy. The country is tied to the international trade system by the current need to import essential products and the consequent need to export to get the exchange to pay for them. The first phase of the current regime's economic policy, which began under the Ramanantsoa regime, attempted to lay the bases for economic independence via first a state capitalist and, after 1975, a socialist organization of the economy. The second, 'all-out investment' phase was linked to the first only by the predominant role given to state economic initiative and represented an attempt to solve the regime's problems by massive injections of money. It ended in the near collapse of the economy across all sectors. The third phase, which began in 1980-1, is that of attempted recovery and represents at least a partial return to the policies of previous regimes, including a reliance on external partners.

Agriculture

Agriculture is central to the Malagasy economy for two reasons. First, the country depends on agriculture to feed the population, and particularly to provide the daily 400 plus grams of rice that are considered the minimum for civilized existence. Second, the country derives over 80 per cent of its foreign exchange earnings from agricultural products (see Table 6.1). The regime inherited production levels whose growth was not keeping pace with increases either of population or of imports and structures of state intervention in rural areas that were at best ineffective and at worst counterproductive, because of the corruption they encouraged and the peasant resentment they created. The first attempts to improve agricultural production involved changes in these structures. Under the Ramanantsoa regime state societies were created to handle the collection of important commodities, and the first *fokonolona* reform was launched. The post-1975 regime kept these new

Table 6.1 Production of selected agricultural
products ('000 tons)*

	Average 1964–8	1970	1975	1980	1984
Rice	1,739	1,946	1,972	2,109	2,112
Coffee	70	69	84	80	81
Cloves	5	14	5	12	13
Vanilla	1	2	7	3	5

* Exports in 1982 included coffee (29.3 per cent), cloves (25.4 per cent) and
vanilla (18.3 per cent).
Sources: Area Handbook, 1973; World Bank, 1978; *LOI*, 1986.

institutions, with some modifications and added rural credit banks, cooperatives and a measure of land reform.

The state societies, SINPA (Société d'Interêt National de Commercialisa-
tion des Produits Agricoles) and SONACO (Société National de Commerce
Extérieure) were established in 1972 and operational by late 1973. SINPA
took over the collection and distribution of rice, previously dominated by
networks of Malagasy, Chinese, and Indian collectors who were, with some
justice, suspected of underpaying sellers, overcharging buyers, and engaging
in large scale usury (Archer, 1976, p. 88; Serre, 1975). They were also part of
the PSD clientele network and, as Ratsiraka said later, 'if the Ramanantsoa
government had left the monopoly of a political product like rice in their
hands, it wouldn't have lasted a month' (*Afrique-Asie*, 27 September 1972,
p. 44). SINPA absorbed the personnel and equipment of several pre-existing
organizations, including the *syndicats des communes*, hardly an auspicious
beginning given those organizations' records of corruption and mismanage-
ment (Calvet, 1976, p. 343). SINPA did not break the tradition and its
problems contributed to the crisis that led to Ramanantsoa's resignation.
After 1975 SINPA was placed under the authority of the Ministry of
Transport and Food Supplies, a ministry headed since 1977 by Joseph Bedo,
an important political figure in the current regime. The organization's
performance did not improve, and it was not well placed to withstand the
post-1980 crisis in production and distribution that resulted from a
combination of natural disasters and economic collapse (see also Cadoux and
le Gaudusson, 1980, p. 371). Drought in 1978 and 1979, and cyclones in 1981

and 1982 cut production (it was estimated that the 1982 cyclones destroyed half of the Antananarivo province rice crop) and the deterioration of the road system, the disappearance of replacement parts for SINPA's fleet of trucks and shortages of items as basic as sacks to hold the rice hindered the collection and distribution of what was produced (see, for example, *Afrique-Asie*, 1982, pp. 53–4). Under these conditions the black market flourished, with prices five times the official price, creating further problems of collection. Rationing did not solve the problem, since the supplies available on the official market often were too small to provide the amounts promised (see Rabevazaha, 1981). Imports and gifts of rice have partially filled the gap, but have not solved the problems of collection and distribution.

The same problems have characterized the operations of SONACO, established at the same time as SINPA, and given the responsibility for organizing the collection of most cash crops and the importation and sale of items like cooking oil, tyres, cement, batteries. Like SINPA, SONACO was designed to replace the non-Malagasy middlemen who had dominated this sector of the economy. Also like SINPA, it did not represent a complete break with the past since many of these middlemen continued in their old function, working under contract for the state enterprise rather than on their own (Camacho, 1981, p. 640; Rabevazaha, 1981, p. 448). In its early years SONACO made a profit, in spite of large scale diversions of funds. (SONACO's first director-general went to prison for 'economic crimes'. See Calvet, 1976, p. 344; de Gaudusson, 1979, p. 221.) However, the problems were serious enough that when the three French commercial companies that handled the overseas sales of cash crops were nationalized in 1976 their functions were not given to SONACO, but divided among the Caisse de Stabilisation de Prix (Fund for Price Stabilization established in 1966), the External Exchanges Bureau of the Ministry of the Economy and three new state enterprises (de Gaudusson, 1979, p. 222). Given its functions, SONACO was particularly hard hit by the post-1980 import restrictions, since many of the commodities it handled were among the imports banned.

Land Reform and Cooperatives

Although some degree of 'land reform' has taken place since 1975, extensive redistribution of land has not been a major part of the regime's agricultural policy. There are two reasons for this. First, it is the frequently expressed view of Ratsiraka and other important personalities that the biggest problem in this area of reform is not inequality of land tenure, but rather the division of agricultural land into large numbers of small holdings. Allied to this opinion is a belief that individual peasants are not capable of the 'dynamism' necessary to produce on a scale equal to national requirements (see the *Revolutionary Charter*, p. 62; de Gaudusson, 1978a, p. 279; Prats, 1977, p. 20; Calvet, 1976, p. 347). Secondly, the main area where land inequalities and absentee landlords are an important characteristic of rural society is the province of Antananarivo, particularly around the capital, where the rural elites and urban-based landlords are an important source of support for both the AKFM and Arema (see *Area Handbook*, 1973, p. 236, for a discussion of land holding patterns and Camacho, 1981). These two considerations reinforced each other and led to a land reform policy based on the nationalization of abandoned colonial concessions with some real expropriation of foreign occupied plantations. This occurred especially in the south-eastern region of Fianarantsoa, where the same plantations had been one of the main targets of the 1947 rebellion (de Gaudusson, 1978a; Prats, 1977). The lands were claimed, without success, by the local *fokonolona*, the decendants of their former owners, and the sharecroppers and employees actually working them. The regime has preferred to run them as state farms or give them to the cooperatives to manage (Calvet, 1976, p. 349; de Gaudusson, 1979, p. 230).

The organization of socialist cooperatives in the countryside was seen as a major element of the regime's agricultural policy. *Les Options Fondamentales pour la planification socialiste* (1978, p. 20) argued that they should handle 50 per cent of agricultural production. From another perspective, the cooperatives are one in a series of attempts by successive regimes to 'rationalize' the structures of rural production. An early critic argued that without adequate support 'the socialist cooperative will appear to the Malagasy peasant as just one more episode, following the Peasant Sectors, Autonomous Rural Communities, Communal Agricultural Societies, Productivity Groups, Development Societies, 1960s style cooperatives, State Farms, Communal Unions, and Major Projects' (H. de Laulanie in *Lakroan'i Madagasikara*, cited in Calvet, 1978, pp. 349-50; see Desjeux, 1979, for a critical review of these and other attempts to 'rationalize' and 'dynamize' the Malagasy rural population).

The 'socialist cooperative' went through several versions. The first model, inspired by the North Korean example, and outlined in the 1977 'Charter of the Socialist Cooperative Movement' proposed collective ownership of both land and tools. As Calvet remarked, it seemed better suited to a society of landless peasants than to the actual Malagasy rural society, dominated by individual landholders (1976, p. 349). A second model, proposing collective exploitation of individual landholdings proved no more attractive and in

1978 a third model, which was to become the dominant type, was published. This model proposed a more thorough organization and an extension of traditional mutual aid, joint purchase of equipment and the creation of work teams to help bring in the harvest (de Gaudusson, 1978a, p. 278). A 'pilot cooperative' was established at Laniera near Antananarivo, with the President and various groups from the capital coming out to help in agricultural tasks (see Camacho, 1981, p. 326). Even the scaled-down third model has had problems. These include the overlapping of the cooperatives' activities with the economic functions of the *fokonolona*, the attempts of the AKFM and MFM to use the cooperatives as power bases, with the subsequent formation of and competition from Arema cooperatives, and the reluctance of rural credit organizations to lend them money since they have no land to seize in the (not uncommon) event of default (see Camacho, 1981, for a description of several cooperatives and a criticism of the whole project; see also Rabevazaha, 1981; *Le Monde*, 6 November 1982 for critical evaluations).

Recent Policy

Calvet has pointed out that the projects undertaken during the 'all-out investment' period 'occurred alongside the main social forces of the country rather than in symbiosis with them' (1978, p. 431) and this refusal to rely on cooperation with the population was particularly true of the few agricultural projects carried out. Investments went to existing state-run projects like the army's '100,000 hectares of rice' scheme or to the creation of new state dominated activities like the soya bean project rather than to the improvement of existing agriculture (see Ramaro, 1980, p. 24, for an interview with Ratsiraka on the topic). This pattern of investment reflects the not so glamorous nature of the latter, but is also the result of the regime's lack of confidence in the peasant producer, a lack of confidence reinforced by difficulties in earlier policies like the setting up of cooperatives. The main impact of the 'outrageous investment' policy on Malagasy agriculture came in its aftermath, when the transportation system almost ceased to operate and essential inputs like imported fertilizer disappeared.

Under the circumstances current policy is directed at restoring the production and collection of existing crops rather than the development of new projects. This 'rehabilitation' includes the road network (in 1982 the Minister for public works estimated that it would take until 1987 to repair the existing roads. See *Afrique-Asie*, October 1982, p. 53), the revival of some export crops like Cape Peas that have disappeared from the market, the renewal of others, like coffee, whose bearing stock has been neglected, and the revitalization of market-oriented livestock raising, as well as improvements to rice production. There have been some increases in agricultural output, but since Malagasy production historically follows a fluctuating pattern, it is impossible to say whether these increases will be permanent (see *LOI*, 1986, esp. pp. 42–3).

In addition there has been some reorganization and 'liberalization' of government agencies and policy in response to the demands of the country's creditors. SINPA has been reorganized yet again, and the Ministry of Agriculture, notorious for its division into warring clientele networks, has been split in two. The field of crop collection has been re-opened to private collectors, floor and ceiling prices have been substituted for a single government set price and there are plans to turn some state farms into mixed enterprises or to 'privatize' them altogether (*LOI*, 1986; see also *Le Monde*, 6 November 1982). These changes may lead to some increases in production, but do not deal with the fundamental problem that has characterized Malagasy agriculture not only under this regime but also under all its predecessors: the fact that agricultural policy has been conducted by and for almost eveyone but the peasant. Agricultural policy has been used to build political networks, and, as Camacho argues, to demonstrate the power of a technocracy (1981, p. 326). Dejeux's critique of colonial policy (1979, p. 127), that 'agricultural policies' often claim they are made to augment peasants' revenues and improve their conditions of life but usually only 'rationalize' agricultural production in the interests of cities in the case of food products and following the logic of capital in the case of export crops, can also be applied to the Merina empire and the Tsiranana regime. In spite of efforts like the *fokonolona* reform, a mitigated version of this criticism can still be made.

Industrial and Commercial Policy

In 1972 Madagascar's industries were largely geared to import substitution and were largely in the hands of non-Malagasies: de Gaudusson estimates that Malagasy-owned companies, including state enterprises, accounted for about 5.1 per cent of total production (1978a, p. 274). The state ran the railway system, held 51 per cent of the capital of Air Madagascar, and 67 per cent of utilities, and participated in some mining companies. The assertion of national control over the economy was one of the demands of all groups involved in the 1972 uprising, and one of the most important, although later one of the most controversial, policies of the Ramanantsoa regime.

In keeping with the state capitalist orientation of the regime, direct state takeovers were rare. Three state enterprises were created (SINPA, SONACO, and SNTP, although the latter was not put into operation) and the French company that controlled the remaining 33 per cent of utility production was nationalised, as was the arsenal at Antseranana. The state took majority participation in several banks and established a mixed textile corporation (Calvet, 1976; Hugon, 1977; de Gaudusson, 1979). The 1974–7 plan, never implemented, projected the establishment of state control over the 'key sectors' of banks, energy, insurance, mining, transportation, foreign trade, pharmaceuticals and film importation and distribution (de Gaudusson, 1979, p. 219). When Ratsiraka took power in June 1975, the state controlled, in one way or another, about 13 per cent of industrial and commercial economic activity (Hugon, 1977, p. 49; see also Table 6.2). Other steps taken to assert national control over the economy included the departure from the franc zone (although the Malagasy franc remained unofficially 'pegged' to the French franc) and the passage of an investment code that required firms to establish a local headquarters and encouraged local participation in management and ownership.

If the policy initiative of the Ramanantsoa regime laid the bases for many of Ratsiraka's actions, they also contributed to the economic crisis his regime inherited in 1975. Some of the problems arose from the nationalization

Table 6.2 Estimated state control of economic activity (per cent)

Sector	June 1975	1978
Banking	25	100
Insurance	15	100
Imports	20	60
Exports	–	78
Sea transport	14	14
Water and energy	100	100
Internal trade	30	70
Industry	18	33
Total	13	61

Source: de Gaudusson, 1979, p. 219.

process itself. At a very practical level, companies that feared they might be nationalized reduced their activities (see *Europe- Outremer*, 1974). Moreover, the functioning of the Malagasy economy had always depended in part on the existence of a network between local industry, the commercial companies, the banks, the transportation companies and overseas buyers. With the nationalization of some of the links, the network disappeared (Camacho, 1981, p. 653). Other problems came with the nature of the Ramanantsoa regime itself. Disagreement, or simply a lack of any idea, about what the state should do with its new 'control' over the economy combined with other crises to bring investment to a halt and slow other activities, with the result that production declined between 1972 and 1975 (see *Afrique-Asie*, June 1976; Hugon, 1977; World Bank Report, 1979).

From Nationalism to Socialism?

Ratsiraka's assumption of power was accompanied by a series of nationaliza-tions designed to establish the socialist credentials of his new regime and to satisfy the members of the left front that had supported him. (The title of this section is taken from De Craene, 1977.) In June 1975 the state took over the banks, insurance companies and film distribution companies. At the end of the month the state also took 51 per cent participation in the Société Malgache des Transports Maritimes and the refinery and port operations of Toamasina. By 1978 the three commercial companies had been nationalized, and state control in one form or another had been extended over petroleum distribution, the chrome mining industry, the country's two biggest textile factories and the island's sugar refineries (see Table 6.2; for greater detail, see de Gaudusson, 1978a, 1979; Calvet, 1976; Hugon, 1978; Leymarie, 1978; Roux, 1980). Although many of the sectors involved had been on the Ramanantsoa regime's list of 'key sectors' there were differences between the two regime's policies that went beyond the more explicit ideological basis of the post-1975 nationalizations. The longer list indicated a strategy of direct state control of the economy, rather than a 'commanding heights' approach, as did also the greater importance of outright nationalizations. However, there were limits to the policy of direct control: a pro-nationalization strike at the Bata shoe factory was ignored by the regime (see Calvet, 1976, p. 351).

A May 1978 decree attempted to organize the state-controlled activities into fifteen 'economic sectors', each with a governing council, but the decree was never implemented (de Gaudusson, 1979). A reorganization of the banking system that created specialized banks to deal with agriculture, industry and commerce was completed and steps were taken to transform the Antseranana arsenal to production of tools and equipment for the domestic market (see Calvet, 1977, p. 350; Camacho, 1981, pp. 478–80; *Afrique–Asie*, 1978). In general, the political activities of the period prevented the implementation of any announced economic policy, including the 'Plan for the year 2000' and the short-term plans published at the end of 1977. This meant that when the 'all-out investment' policy began in 1979 there was an outline of priorities to guide it, but little in the way of structure to enforce the priorities, and what little there was gave way before the volume and momentum of the new investment policy (see Cadoux and de Gaudusson, 1980, p. 368).

The policy itself corresponded to the view outlined in 'Options for Socialist Planning' that industry, rather than agriculture, should receive priority in investment, but financing via large-scale external borrowing contradicted the plan to have most of this investment financed from internal sources, including the profits from state enterprises (OFPS, 1978; ITOM, 1979; Calvet, 1977). Moreover, with the exception of investments in the transportation infrastructure and the Andekaleka dam, which would depend on the higher level of economic activity supposed to result from the other investments, the other projects emphasized industrial production for the export, as well as for an internal market. These projects included two fertilizer factories, textile mills and a pharmaceutical factory. In addition, many of the industries would require imported raw materials to function at their projected capacity (see *Le Monde*, 6 November 1982; *LOI*, 1986, pp. 140–2). The only project that could be considered as directed at establishing the bases for self-sufficient development was the feasibility study of oil-bearing shale deposits at Bemolanga (conducted mainly by a company that was also the island's largest supplier of imported oil; see *LOI*, 1986). Overall, by tying investment financing to Western sources of capital, emphasizing projects that, even if successful, would have left the economy dependent on importing raw materials and exporting finished products, the 'all-out investment' policy compromised both the goal of economic independence and the political goal of alliances with 'progressive forces' (see Calvet, 1978, p. 424).

Collapse and Attempted Recovery

As it was, the policy was not successful: before most of its projects were completed, and even before some were begun, the government was applying to the IMF for aid in meeting its balance of payments deficits. Not only did the new projects not provide the hoped for economic breakthrough, but lack of foreign exchange to import the necessary raw materials and replacement parts combined with nearly ten years of previous neglect to bring about the near collapse of existing industrial production. Production declined in almost all industries and all but stopped in others (see Table 6.3). As part of its negotiations with the IMF and other aid donors, the government has established a Programme of Public Investments for the period from 1984–7, a programme that was approved by the World Bank Consultative Group for

Table 6.3 Industrial production (tons, except where otherwise specified)

	1974	1978	1982
Food	136,148	129,894	88,591
Beer (hectolitres)	182,825	257,037	190,071
Tobacco	3,332	4,259	3,706
Textiles			
Cotton ('000 metres)	80,617	78,184	72,889
Other products	6,665	5,320	3,683
Paper	17,018	21,563	25,707
Chemical			
(Soap, candles, paint)	19,272	24,592	13,800
Matches ('000 boxes)	53,816	68,949	6,088
Petroleum refining (cu.m.)	732,061	414,587	476,740
Cement	61,447	66,044	35,921

Source: World Bank and Plan, *LOI*, 1986, p. 108.

Madagascar at the end of 1984. (Originally planned for 1983–5, the programme was delayed by several breakdowns in Malagasy–IMF negotiations; see *LOI*, 1 December 1984.) The plan's major emphasis is on attempts to revive and rehabilitate existing industries and infrastructure and on arranging the completion of some of the 'all-out investment' projects (see also *Afrique-Asie*, October, 1982). Improvements to the transportation system account for some 28.8 per cent of the total of public investments under the programme and rehabilitation of rice production another 15 per cent. The energy sector, oil-producing plants, and cotton production are other major targets for investment (see *LOI*, 1986, for details).

Although the public investment programme has received the overall approval of organizations like the World Bank Consultative Group, there are several reasons to question whether it will attain even its limited goal of restoring the economy to previous levels of production. The first cause for doubt is simply the scope of the collapse and the discrepancy between the money needed and the money available to put things right. For example, the programme budgets about US$10 million for the restoration of the Toamasina oil refinery (some estimates place the sum required at $30 million). So far only half the $10 million has been raised (*LOI*, 1986, p. 103). Overall, only 44 per cent of the projected public and private foreign investment has taken place. Secondly, the programme does not cover the whole economy: important projects, like those connected with the textile industry, remain outside its scope and compete with it for government and other investment. Thirdly, in addition to the lack of coordination this implies, there are further problems created by the method of financing. Although the programme was approved as a whole, it has been financed on a project by project basis, with some individual projects denied the World Bank approval. This means that some projects that have found donors will not have the desired effect because other projects have not been carried out. For example, Rumania has agreed to contribute to the restoration of the naval repair facility at Antseranana, a restoration that will have little effect until the harbour itself is repaired. Other problems include the 'drainage' caused by continued corruption. Most important, questions can be raised about the whole conception of the programme. The improvements themselves will require the continued importation of material, thus worsening the country's balance of payments problem, while the international 'rescue' operation, which consists largely of rescheduling old loans and extending new ones, simply postpones the problem (see *LOI*, 1986; D. in *Sudestasie*, 1982, p. 34; as Calvet noted at the beginning of the crisis, Madagascar's story resembles that of many underdeveloped countries. 1978, p. 430).

7 Foreign Policy

'We are a very small country on the Cape Route, in the middle of an ocean that smells of petroleum . . . . It is for this reason that we are non-aligned: so people will bloody well leave us alone' (qu 'on nous fiche la paix).
Interview with Ratsiraka in *Afrique-Asie*, *Special Madagascar*, June 1978, pp.7–8

Of course, the goals of Malagasy foreign policy are more complicated than that. They do include an attempt to achieve independence from the larger powers of the East and West, or at least to maintain a balance of dependencies, but the government of the island has also attempted to play a role in the politics of the Indian Ocean and of the non-aligned movement. In addition, Malagasy foreign policy has internal objectives, including that of discouraging potential attempts to replace the regime by demonstrating the support of essential foreign allies. Contacts with socialist countries have been used to reinforce the ideological options of the regime and to furnish substitutes for internal agents that were felt to be unreliable or lacking in expertise. Since the economic collapse of 1980, the regime has become increasingly reliant on its relationships with Western powers for simple economic survival, and this has complicated both the task of maintaining balanced dependence and the pursuit of an active policy in the Third World.

The background to Malagasy foreign policy has been shaped by the increasing strategic importance of the western Indian Ocean. When Ratsiraka became foreign minister in 1972, a year before the first oil shock, the great powers were already giving the region increased attention. Construction of the American installations at Diego Garcia had begun, and the Soviet Union had begun to assert a 'regular naval presence' in the Indian Ocean (Braun, 1983; Laforge 1982). When the Democratic Republic of Madagascar was proclaimed in 1975, the Ethiopian coup had already begun the process of realignment in the Horn of Africa and the independence of Mozambique had placed a fellow Marxist regime on the other side of the Mozambique channel. By the end of the decade, the second oil shock had occured, the Carter Doctrine had declared the Persian Gulf an area of strategic interest to the United States and the Soviet invasion of Afghanistan had sharpened great power confrontation in the region. If the western Indian Ocean is tense internationally, external complications can also threaten the domestic position of the region's governments. The period since the establishment of the Second Republic has seen continuing destabilization in

Mozambique, a successful mercenary-led coup in the Comoro Islands and an attempted one in the Seychelles (Allen, 1984; Braun, 1983; Bowman, 1981).

Madagascar occupies a position of middling strategic importance in its region. Most of the shipping that carries oil from the Persian Gulf to Europe via the Cape route goes through the Mozambique Channel. The harbour of Antseranana, at the northern entrance to the Channel, is one of the best natural harbours in the western Indian Ocean. However, Madagascar does not have the strategic centrality of a country like Ethiopia. It is not totally necessary for the oil tankers to pass through the channel. Moreover, the west coast of Madagascar is underpopulated and isolated from the rest of the country, and it is difficult to imagine what Madagascar itself could do to threaten shipping. In addition, the Malagasy strategy of refusing to align itself definitively with one or the other side in the great power rivalry in the Indian Ocean has reduced its significance to either. As a result, Madagascar's strategic position has given the country some bargaining power but has also set limits to it (Gomane, 1981; Labrousse, 1980).

From Neo-Colonialism to Non-Alignment

Ratsiraka's assumption of the post of Foreign Minister in 1972 marked the beginning of a major redirection of Malagasy foreign policy. This change not only included the ending of the special Malagasy–French relationship, the adoption of a radical stance in international politics and the cultivation of contacts with other radical states of the Third World, it also included the beginning of interaction with Marxist states (see Leymarie, 1973). This interaction was intensified when Ratsiraka took power in 1975 and declared Madagascar itself to be a Marxist state. However, the change has not consisted simply of substituting the Soviet Union for France in a similar type of relationship. Madagascar has diversified its ties within the socialist bloc, and integration in the 'socialist commonwealth' has been limited by the refusal of Madagascar to commit itself militarily to such an alignment, by its unwillingness to forgo economic ties with the West, and, recently, by its increased dependence on Western economic aid. Soviet refusal to commit large amounts of resources to the economic assistance of the island has also reduced the attractions of total allegiance (see *Le Monde*, 6 November 1982 for the Soviet refusal to finance a 'second Cuba' in the Indian Ocean).

The relationship with the Soviet Union has revolved around military assistance, development aid and cultural affairs. Discussions to open diplomatic relations began in October 1972, and a Malagasy–Soviet Union Cooperation Commission was established after the formation of the Second Republic. The relationship has centred around aid much more than around trade (see Table 7.4). The exact amounts of aid are difficult to estimate. In 1984, *LOI* estimated that total development and military aid had reached US$300 million, with a further US$55 million provided in assistance for the Malagasy balance of payments (*LOI*, 11 February 1984).

Military aid is a major part of the total package. In 1987 the Malagasy armed forces are almost entirely equipped with Soviet weapons, particularly in the air force, and there are at least 150 Soviet technical assistants attached to the armed forces. The most spectacular instance of Soviet–Malagasy co-operation was the Soviet construction of, and planned technical assistance in the running of, a series of surveillance/intercept stations along Madagascar's Mozambique Channel coast. (There had been some discussion of giving the commission to the French. See *LOI*, 12 December 1982; 7 January 1984.) Built in 1983, the installations caused extreme concern among the Western nations with whom Madagascar was dealing at the time and the stations were eventually dismantled.

Soviet economic aid is also often channelled through the armed forces, with particular emphasis on the development of mineral resources in cooperation with OMNIS (Calvet, 1977, Wild and Pineye, 1979; Laforge, 1982; *LOI*, 2 February 1984). Other projects have included aid for road reconstruction. Although the Soviet Union refused to furnish the money to rescue Madagascar from its economic difficulties and dependence on IMF aid, it has agreed to the rescheduling of its share of the Malagasy debt and provided some emergency oil supplies when the Iran–Iraq war cut deliveries from Madagascar's major oil supplier, Iraq. It also provided some emergency food aid after the series of cyclones that hit Madagascar in the early 1980s and cement for reconstruction. (See *LOI*, 20 October 1984, for a comparison of Soviet and American aid.)

Cultural affairs, including the provision of Russian professors to teach at the University of Madagascar and the granting of scholarships for study in the Soviet Union to Malagasy students, are another important area of aid. In 1984 *LOI* estimated that about 2,000 Malagasy students had studied at Soviet universities since 1975 (*LOI*, 2 February 1984). Other socialist countries also provide assistance, notably in the transportation system and in agriculture. Cuba has provided assistance in the education system. There are persistent rumours of Cuban military assistance, but most sources discount them (Calvet, 1977; Laforge, 1982).

Aside from the Soviet Union, North Korea is the socialist state with whom

Madagascar maintains the closest relations and the one on which it relies most heavily for internal political assistance. Ratsiraka has expressed an admiration for the self-reliance principles of Juche and a personal friendship for Kim Il Sung, (see, for example, the interview with Simon Malley, 1978a; Cadoux and de Gaudusson, 1980, and the annual surveys in the APOI.) North Korea has provided personnel to train and run the President's personal security forces, and to build his bunker at Iavoloha. It has also supplied anti-aircraft weapons, and lent Madagascar a MiG while it was waiting for delivery of aircraft ordered from the Soviet Union. North Korean assistants direct some of the army's agricultural projects and the North Korean model was used for the first version of rural cooperatives.

In general, there seems to be a clear differentiation in the type of aid received from various socialist countries. Countries with a higher degree of technological development, like the Soviet Union, provide aid in the more technologically advanced areas, including the armed forces and the university, while members of the 'socialist Third World' like North Korea provide aid in areas that are less technically advanced, but more politically central. Other 'radical' but not explicitly Marxist regimes, especially Algeria, have also provided models if not assistance.

In spite of the importance of these relationships, Madagascar considers itself a non-aligned state and there is no indication that it has been pressed to move into a position of closer alignment with the Soviet Union and its allies. Madagascar established diplomatic relations with the Republic of China at the same time as with the other 'socialist camp' and has maintained them throughout the period, although they are clearly of lesser importance (Laforge, 1982). Madagascar has always refused the use of its ports, not just as bases, but also as stopping points, to warships of all powers. The relationship has not prevented Ratsiraka from engaging in public criticism of socialist countries. At the 1983 Non-aligned Summit, while he agreed to the thesis that the socialist states were the natural allies of Third World countries, he also criticized them for failing to furnish the aid necessary to help those countries in the common struggle against capitalist imperialism, and for attitudes that were themselves often tinged with imperialism (*Afrique-Asie*, 28 March 1983). For its part, the Soviet Union maintains its contacts with other Malagasy political groups like the AKFM and limits its economic support.

Relations with the West

If Madagascar's refusal to ally itself completely with international socialism has cost it in terms of the reciprocal limitation of commitment on the part of the Soviet Union and its allies, the ambiguous nature of the relationship has given the country a margin of manœuvre in its relations with the West. Here the practice of the regime has been to cultivate relations with Britain and the United States and, to a lesser degree, Japan, to counterbalance the resumption of its relationship with France, a relationship that is, on both sides, complicated psychologically as well as politically.

Relationships with the West underwent a period of coolness after 1972 and even more after 1975. Attempts to establish a new relationship with France were unsuccessful, the British closed their embassy as an economy move in 1975 and suspicions of American involvement in the *lycéens'* riots of that year led the Malagasy government to refuse the appointment of new American ambassadors. In addition, Ratsiraka's desire to move into the radical camp of the Third World led him to take positions on several issues, including French interventions in Africa, which he attacked, the Vietnamese invasion of Cambodia, which he supported, and the Soviet invasion of Afghanistan, on which Madagascar abstained in UN votes, which were counter to the positions of the Western powers. (See the succession of interviews with Simon Malley, 1978a.)

Events in the late 1970s led to attempts on both sides to reopen relations. Visits of officials between Madagascar and France increased, a new American ambassador was named and accepted in 1980 and the British embassy was reopened in December 1979. Ratsiraka paid a visit to President Reagan in 1982 and in 1983 the two countries devoted considerable fanfare to the celebration of the 100th anniversary of the first Malagasy–American friendship treaty (*LOI*, 26 March 1983). The World Bank opened an office in Antananarivo in 1983. On the Malagasy side there has been a muting of verbal assaults on Western policies, a change that in conjunction with more concrete acts represented, for the next American ambassador, 'an evolution to a position of real nonalignment'. (At his confirmation hearings the ambassador also described to the Senate committee the strategic position of Madagascar on the Indian Ocean sea-lanes. See *LOI*, 9 July 1983; Thompson, 1986.) There is no evidence that Madagascar has been pressed to furnish military facilities; the main goal of Western policy appears to be the denial of Malagasy facilities to the Soviet Union rather than the acquisition of the facilities for Western use (Allen, 1982).

It is the resumption of relations with France that has been both the most crucial element in Madagascar's attempts to re-establish its economic position and the most difficult. Although the 'special relationship' was formally ended in 1972, the practical and psychological consequences of the colonial period mean that relations between the two countries are more intense than the diplomatic norm. There are debates within the French foreign policy establishment about the credibility of Ratsiraka's 'real non-alignment', and in Madagascar about the degree to which better relations with France and the specific changes that have followed the rapproachment compromise the basic goals of the regime. (See Ratsiraka's reaffirmation of his commitment to socialism and non-alignment in Malley, 1982a.)

The continuing French presence in the western Indian Ocean has been resented and feared by Madagascar. The maintenance of French control of Mayotte when the other Comoro Islands became independent led to Malagasy protests and support for Mayotte independence movements. The island of Réunion remains a French overseas *départment*, and became the headquarters of the French Indian Ocean Forces after their departure from Antseranana. Réunion radio and television broadcasts cover the whole of the region and, at several levels, contain a message contrary to that of the Malagasy services. The French also maintained a military presence in Djibouti when that territory became independent (see Braun, 1983; Gomane, 1981).

In addition to general objections to the French military installations in the region, Madagascar has also objected to the continued French occupation of the 'scattered islands' of the Mozambique Channel: Europa, the Glorieuses, Juan de Nova, Bassas da India and Tromelin. These islands were administered from Madagascar during the colonial period, but were detached from the island in 1960, just before the granting of full Malagasy independence, and are now part of the Réunion administrative area (see Dadanaivo, 1978; Gomane, 1981; *Afrique-Asie*, 1981; Laforge, 1982). They have obvious military significance, and are located in areas that give promise for deep-sea mining. The French have installed some military facilities there, and in 1978 declared a 200 mile economic zone around them. (Madagascar had already declared a 1,000 mile economic zone around its perimeter.) Resolutions of the OAU and the UN have demanded their return to Madagascar, but without success, and the issue remains at stalemate. As part of the 'normalization' of its relations with France, Madagascar has stopped pressing the issue, but without formally accepting the French position.

Madagascar has changed its position on other issues. Negotiations for an increase in cultural cooperation have been undertaken, compensation for the expropriation of the Marseillaise company has been agreed on, and other French firms assured of a welcome (see *Le Monde*, 7 November 1986; the Marseillaise was expropriated without compensation after Ratsiraka took power). Negotiations have begun for a possible return to the franc zone. In return, French aid has increased and France has played a crucial role in mediating between Madagascar and its international creditors. (Aid doubled between 1981–2, to make Madagascar the second most important recipient of French aid in Africa, after Senegal. See Chaigneau, 1983a.) However, there are limitations to the new relationship. There has been no resumption of military cooperation, in spite of some discussions. Madagascar has attended meetings of 'la Francophonie', which includes countries like Canada and Belgium, but still boycotts the Franco–African meetings that group only France and its former colonies.

Trade and aid contacts with other countries have been pursued in an attempt, partially successful, to dilute the importance of ties with France. In 1972, Madagascar sent 65 per cent of its exports to France and bought 75 per cent of its imports there (*Area Handbook*, 1973). By 1985, while France remained Madagascar's most important trading partner, her role was greatly diminished (see Table 7.1). There are limits to the diversification. The EEC as a whole occupies nearly the position France did as a customer in 1972, and much of the change in the pattern of imports is the result of the increases in oil prices rather than of government policy. Trade with the Soviet Union and other socialist countries is almost stagnant. The same pattern is repeated in aid. France is still the most important donor. While the country does not have the near monopoly it once did, in combination with the rest of the EEC it still dominates. Aid from Japan has increased to about half the French total and OPEC countries have become another important source (OECD, 1984). However, French influence is increased beyond the monetary amount of its aid by the access the connection with France gives to the EEC and the circle of international creditors.

Other Relations

One of the goals of post-1972 Malagasy foreign policy was the development of a strong and radical Malagasy presence in Third World international relations. The steps taken to create this presence included the establishment of relations with the 'radical' countries of the Third World and increased activity in the OAU and the non-aligned movement, as well as such steps as the breaking of ties with Israel and the declaration of support for the PLO.

Table 7.1 Trading partners, 1985

	% of total
Exports	
France	25.0
Other EEC	32.3
United States	15.7
Japan	8.9
USSR, Eastern Europe	3.5
Indonesia	1.8
Imports	
France	25.8
Middle East (Bahrain, Qatar, Saudi Arabia)	25.6
Other EEC	11.8
United States	7.6
Thailand	3.4
Japan	2.4
USSR, Eastern Europe	2.0

Source: Direction of Trade Statistics Yearbook, 1986.

(The Tsiranana regime did not belong to the non-aligned movement and was not enthusiastic about the OAU, preferring the exclusively Francophone and more conservative OCAM. See Goguel, 1972.)

Indian Ocean

The change in Malagasy policy can be seen clearly in its activities on the Indian Ocean Peace Zone proposal. A United Nations resolution calling for the demilitarization of the ocean was passed in 1971 and a 1974 resolution called for a conference on the subject and established a committee to discuss the question. The conference has not yet been held, in part because the great powers, whose activities in the region have been the main target of successive resolutions, have not been eager to expose themselves to such a forum. (See Towle, 1981. The Soviet Union has been more enthusiastic about the idea since it was expelled from its bases in Somalia in 1977. See also Fernando, 1979; La Bayle, 1980.) Since the Soviet invasion of Afghanistan the United States and its allies have refused to consider demilitarization without also discussing the withdrawal of Soviet troops from Afghanistan.

Under the First Republic, Madagascar was one of the countries that voted against the 1971 UN resolution. Since 1972 the Malagasy government has been a consistent proponent of demilitarization and has used meetings of the OAU and the non-aligned movement to pursue conference proposals, offering Antananarivo as a possible site. Madagascar has abstained on resolutions condemning the Soviet invasion of Afghanistan and refuses to consider withdrawal a precondition to discussions of demilitarization. At the 1983 Non-aligned Summit in New Delhi the issue was revived, and the idea of a conference proposed again. Madagascar offered itself as an example of a country that had unilaterally refused militarization (*Afrique-Asie*, 28 February 1983; *LOI*, 19 March 1983).

Madagascar has also attempted to organize the 'progressive forces' of its region, notably the other islands, on the issue. The current regime's interactions with Mauritius, the Seychelles and the Comoro Islands have varied both in intensity and in the degree of cooperation and conflict involved (see Thompson, 1986; *Afrique-Asie*, 28 February 1983; Laforge, 1980; Allen, 1982). Relations with the Comoros were suspended after the mercenary-led coup that toppled the Ali Swali regime, and were not fully regularized until 1985. Relations with the Seychelles warmed after the 1977 radical coup in that island, and Madagascar sent some troops to form part of the Seychelles presidential guard after an attempted counter coup. The victory of the left in the 1982 election in Mauritius added another member to the 'progressive forces' in the western Indian Ocean, but internal disputes in that island's ruling coalition have complicated its relationships with the other states of the region. The three islands established an Indian Ocean Commission to discuss the creation of a common market, but as yet Madagascar's economic exchanges with the Seychelles are minimal and with Mauritius and the Comoros non-existent. Paradoxically, its greatest trade is with the least ideologically congenial island of the region, Réunion (see *Direction of Trade Statistics Yearbook*, 1981; Calvet, 1978; Laforge, 1982).

In Africa as in the Indian Ocean, the reversal of policy began in 1972. Madagascar cut the ties developed with the Republic of South Africa under the Tsiranana regime and established relations with states like Algeria and Libya. Support was given to the liberation movements of Southern Africa and the Western Sahara. However, Madagascar has diminished its activities in Africa. In part this is the result of the redirection of attention to the requirements of economic survival, but the divisions of the OAU, and in particular the failure of socialist brotherhood in the Horn of Africa have led to a certain disillusionment. Ratsiraka himself attempted to play the role of mediator in the Somali–Ethiopian dispute, proposing the establishment of a 'confederation of socialist states' that would group Ethiopia, Somalia, Djibouti, and an autonomous Eritrea, with an evident lack of success. In general, Madagascar has preferred to concentrate on individual African states of similar ideological point of view and on the non-aligned movement rather than working through the OAU (see Calvet 1978; Thompson, 1987). It was elected to the 'radical African' seat on the Security Council of the United Nations in 1984, but largely as a compromise candidate when Ethiopia and Somalia both demanded the place.

In the non-aligned movement, Ratsiraka has attempted to establish Madagascar as one of the leading countries of the group's radical wing. Madagascar has used the forum provided by the movement to push for its goal of demilitarization of the Indian Ocean, and has received support for its demands for the return of the Mozambique Channel islands. Ratsiraka has generally supported the argument that the socialist bloc countries are the 'natural allies' of the Third World, but has also been critical of the lack of concrete economic aid forthcoming from that group. He has also been critical of the non-aligned movement itself, and at the New Delhi Summit he gave an extended speech that included a call for an exercise in individual and collective self-criticism (*Afrique-Asie*, 28 March 1983; Ratsiraka, 1983, pp. 163–98 gives excerpts from the speech). However, Ratsiraka's desire to see Madagascar play the same type of leading role as countries like Algeria and India has been frustrated by the small size and isolation of the island. 'He should be president of a larger country', is a frequent comment.

8   Conclusion

The establishment of a Marxist regime has brought important changes to Madagascar, but the history of the new regime has itself been conditioned by important continuities imposed by the Malagasy environment. The political life of the Democratic Republic of Madagascar has also been affected by changes that have occurred in other African countries, whatever their ideological coloration. These include the economic crisis made visible by increased debt loads, the 'shrinking' of the state, the sharpening of political antagonisms, and an accompanying increase in the degree of violence in political life (see, for example, Chazan, 1983; Callaghy, 1984; Young, 1982a). This interaction between change and continuity, general trends and particular circumstances, has shaped the politics, economy and society of the island, and the results tell us much about the possibilities and consequences of creating Marxist or socialist regimes in an African setting.

Malagasy Marxism

To what degree does Madagascar correspond to models of socialism, whether those proposed by outside observers or by its own leaders? There are, as I argued in the introduction, many available models of socialism, a situation that in itself reflects the increasing diffuseness of the phenomenon. Most recent studies of Third World Marxist regimes do not insist on immediate conformation to a single set of criteria, but emphasize the process of transition and what Colin Leys has called 'convergence' rather than exact similarity (1982, p. 116).

The editor of this series, Bogdan Szajkowski, has put forth a multi-stage model of the transition to socialism based on the degree of domination by the working class and the extent of economic change undertaken by the regime. The transition begins with an 'anti-feudal, anti-imperialist or anti-fascist movement partially led by the working class', and ends with 'the assumption by the proletariat of its leading role in the society' and a transition to full socialist revolution (Szajkowski, 1982, p. 3). Writing more specifically about African socialism 'as it exists (not as it is hoped to become)', Leys notes, 'clear areas of convergence' in the policies of African socialist states. These include public ownership of strategic industries and state or cooperative trading, limits on foreign investment and a redirection of foreign economic contacts, restraints on the emergence of indigenous capitalism and inequalities of private consumption, efforts to promote collective or cooperative farming, and '*most important of all in the long run*, efforts to foster popular participation in local as well as national institutions' (Leys, 1982, p. 116, emphasis added).

The explicit ideology of the Malagasy regime shares some characteristics with these models, but it also diverges from them in several significant ways. Like the external models, it draws on a wide range of sources. The Soviet Union is not the only, or even the primary external referent, being replaced as 'role model' by Third World Marxist regimes like North Korea and non-Marxist socialist regimes like Algeria and Tanzania (Serre, 1975, p. 184; Calvet, 1976, p. 359; Andriamirado, 1977a, p. 5; see also Young, 1982b, pp. 25–7). The ideology also emphasizes its links with national traditions and the need for adaptation to the national context. However, while the external models give some role to international relations, 'anti-imperialism' and the creation of links with other socialist countries, Malagasy ideology emphasizes anti-imperialism as *the* most significant aspect of its socialism. Anti-imperialism includes both the elimination of the dependent relationship with the former colonial power, and, more generally, support for liberation movements and for a revolution in the position of the Third World in the international system. (The collection of Ratsiraka's speeches cited in the bibliography (Ratsiraka, 1983) is subtitled 'From the Third World to the third World Power'.)

The Malagasy version of Marxism also differs from the models in the small role it gives to immediate popular participation in the construction of socialism. Rather than popular mobilization *against* internal class enemies or state structures, the revolution is to involve mobilization *by* newly strengthened state structures. In the Malagasy model socialism is seen as a way to strengthen the state and enlist the population in the development effort. As *Options for Socialist Planning* argues, 'socialism requires discipline of a sort that neither the population nor the state apparatus are very accustomed to' (OFPS, 1978, p. 5). Marxism is, therefore, seen largely as a strategy for conducting a strong nation with a strong state. It is this instrumental view of the ideology, as well as brute necessity, that explains the modifications in policy undertaken since 1981. If a strong Madagascar and a strong regime can be built by other means, they might well be tried.

Policies and Change

Given the predominant role of anti-imperialism in the Malagasy conception of Marxism, it is not surprising that regime policies correspond most closely to the external and to its own models in the area of foreign affairs. (This is not uncommon; see Harding, 1981, pp. 28-9; Radu, 1983, p. 17.) The changed relationship with France, the establishment of relationships with Marxist and non-Marxist socialist countries, and the adoption of radical Third World positions in international affairs constitute a clear break with the policies of the First Republic. The break is less clear in economic relations. While Madagascar is less dependent economically on France, to a large degree the relationship has simply been transferred to the Western economic system as a whole, a diversification rather than an elimination of dependence. Trade with other socialist countries has not increased greatly, and aid only slightly more. The dependence on Western trade and aid has, of course, increased since the debt crisis, and the need to maintain the relationship has affected political foreign policy and economic domestic policy.

There are several reasons for the incompleteness of the change and the relapse since 1980, aside from the relative capacities of the potential partners. Both the structure of the world economy and internal economic and political factors that include the requirements for maintaining the cohesion of the ruling elite make it very difficult for Third World countries to redirect trade and aid relationships away from their usual partners. Total reorientation would require adjustments and change on such a scale that they would probably be acceptable only after a crisis similar to that which faced Cuba after Castro took power. Failing such a stimulus from the outside, a reorientation of the type Madagascar has undertaken, that of maintaining economic relations with the West while taking military aid and political assistance from the East is probably the maximum, and certainly the most common change.

Internally, the most important change has been the enlargement of the state economic sector to include most industrial and commercial activity. Again, the change is incomplete. Significant economic activities, most notably agriculture, but also many forms of trading, remain largely in private hands, while the growth of the black market can be seen as an extension of the private sector. Moreover, state ownership of the economy is not the same as state 'control', which implies a capacity on the part of the state that the current Malagasy regime has not always possessed. The measures of economic liberalization introduced since'1981 can be seen as a retreat from earlier positions, but their implementation has been no more complete than that of the socialist policies.

It is in its political development that the regime corresponds least to its own or others' images of what socialism entails. While the FNDR can be presented as the type of alliance common to the early stages of the emergence of many Marxist regimes, Arema is far from being a vanguard party or even an alliance of 'progressive' elements, and the role of director of the alliance is played by Ratsiraka and a group of allies including members of other parties rather than by Arema itself. Although it has added a new type of personal link in the form of ideological affinity, the introduction of socialism has not yet changed the diffuse, personalistic nature of political relations at the top of the Malagasy political system. If anything, personal relations have become more important during the current crisis. Bienen (1985, p. 368) describes similar failures on the part of the populist military regimes he discusses. It is one of the supposed advantages of the Marxist model that it is less personalistic than populist socialism, but Madagascar's experience suggests that this is not inevitably the case.

The area in which there has been least change is that of state–society relations, although there has been some extension of access to social benefits, especially education. Attempts to change the nature of employment relationships via the Charter of Socialist Enterprises and the nature of relations between the peasant and the economy via state trading firms and banks can hardly be considered a success, while the record of the decentralized collectivities even given their limited goals in the matter, is mixed. In spite of official attempts to limit income differentials, all evidence suggests that they are increasing (Camacho, 1981, p. 1; de Gaudusson, 1978a, pp. 271–2).

Theories that emphasize the role of class conflict in the transition to socialism would argue that this increase does represent movement in a socialist direction, although hardly one planned by the regime. The same can be said of another characteristic of state–society relations, the increasing resistance to state demands and policies, whether in the form of withdrawal from contact with the state or that of demonstrations and riots. The 'instability' of the Malagasy population does represent increased expectations of the state as well as the disappointment of those expectations. Given the real conflicts that exist in Malagasy society itself and between the society and the state, even violence has to be better than the morbid passivity of the post-1947 period (Leys, 1982, p. 119; Serre, 1975, p. 76).

An Ambiguous Revolution

If our models tell us to look at the process of transition, then it must be both admitted and argued that, at twelve years of age, the Malagasy regime is at a very early stage of the transition. However, there are reasons for the very mixed nature of the Malagasy regime that go beyond the specificity of its own model of socialism or the short time that the regime has been in existence. These include the mixed origins of the regime and the mixed motives for the adoption of a Marxist ideology. Finally, the environment in which the regime operates has had an influence on both the policies adopted and their results.

The circumstances under which a regime is created have an effect on 'what happens next', especially in the short term. Although Madagascar belongs to the category of African Marxist regimes of military origin, it is not this characteristic of the regime that is the main reason for the ambiguity of socialist policies and their implementation. The regime constitutes at least a partial exception to the common pattern in which military Marxists discover both the content and the utility of the ideology after their arrival in power (Decalo, 1979; Szajkowski, 1982, p. 60). Although Ramanantsoa and many in his regime did not have a clear political ideology, and a figure like Ratsimandrava does correspond to the picture of a soldier politicized while governing, others in the army were involved in civilian political debates, and certainly by 1975 an ideologically aware 'progressive party' grouping military and civilian actors had been put together. Moreover, as the history of Arema suggests, a 'vanguard' party or at least one constructed in the way Arema was, can be at least as heterogeneous as an army, and contain as many 'counter-revolutionary' elements.

It is possible that the main danger of staging a revolution based mainly on a military takeover is that it makes the process too easy and eliminates the need to build a critical mass of like-minded supporters. Certainly, one important characteristic of the origin of the Democratic Republic of Madagascar lies in the fact that the 'progressive front' did not take power by itself in 1975, nor did it proceed to construct the regime as the Ethiopian Derg did by eliminating those who were unwilling to accept its ideology or monopoly on power. (See Markakis and Ayele, 1978, p. 112, for a description of the process in Ethiopia.) The group was too weak to do this, and had come to power with, as part of its mandate, the avoidance of civil war. As a result, the Second Republic came into existence led by a coalition, symbolized by the FNDR, many of whose components did not share the commitment to Marxist socialism or, indeed, to socialism of any recognizable variety. (As Chaigneau,

1983c, p. 116, points out, many of the founding groups and parties of the Second Republic were anti-communist and/or anti-Soviet.) The coalition was assembled in part in spite of the adoption of Marxism, through modifications in the ideology, the offering of material inducement and the threat of force. The result was a heterogeneity of attitude that necessarily complicated regime policies.

Functions of Ideology

A second reason for the ambiguities of the regime lies in the mixed motives of the members of the progressive front themselves. The version of Marxism they developed did correspond to the analysis they made of their internal and external political situation and to their goals of national independence and development. No account of Malagasy Marxism would be complete if it ignored this. However, there were 'functions' of the adoption that must also be taken into account. Ideological disputes provided much of the currency of the struggle for power that occurred in 1975. Rivals for power espoused different ideologies and different ideological convictions fed political rivalries. The proponents of the Marxist alternative had the advantage of the fact that the country had, since independence, experimented with and discredited most of the other available ideological alternatives, including capitalism masquerading as social democracy, state capitalism and radical populism.

Marxism also provided the outline of a set of techniques for establishing and maintaining power and, in the elitist version adopted in Madagascar, a justification for its concentration and for state domination of the population similar to the justification provided by the ideology of 'modernization' in the Tsiranana period (Camacho, 1981; *Etudes*, 1985, p. 590). While it seems unreasonable to doubt the commitment of many of the actors of 1972 and 1975, it should be pointed out that their conception of a Marxist revolution did not exclude the maintenance of their own power, the perpetuation of their standard of living and the continuing material advancement of themselves, their family and their friends. This mixture of motives is a major cause of the ambiguities of government action, but does not make the ideological commitment unreal. It is simplistic and unreasonable to demand that people be either 'sincere' ideologues or 'cynical' opportunists. (The same point has been made earlier in the study of African nationalism. See Lonsdale, 1981, p. 193; Schatzberg, 1980.)

Constraints

The regime has been further handicapped by the lack of interest of the 'instruments of rule' in the socialist option, the fragmentation of state power, and of the society itself, and by the popular appeal of competing ideologies, most notably the notion of 'Malagasy rule' as local freedom from all outside authority, and the anti-state populism that is related to it.

As Chazan points out, 'instruments of rule' like the administration and army have an existence and will of their own and cannot be treated as simple extensions of the political component of the state (1983, p. 24). In some new socialist regimes, a lack of commitment on the part of one instrument of rule can be compensated for by control of another, or by the creation of a dominant political party that overrides all other instruments. This has not happened in Madagascar. The administration and army were not reshaped, and Arema was put together as a broad coalition rather than the vanguard party its name suggests. The failure of the regime to replace the personalistic nature of Malagasy politics with a more institutionalized base means that the fragmentation of state power remains, and is a decisive obstacle to state action. As Archer claims, in the Third World it is easier to seize state power than to use it (1976, p. 9).

Another obstacle to socialist transformation lies in the diffuse nature of Malagasy society itself. There are no well-organized groups, and even less classes through which the population could be mobilized. It is difficult to criticize a regime for 'not making the correct class alliances' when the correct classes do not exist, or exist only in embryonic form. If the Malagasy state is weak, Malagasy society lacks the levers through which state power could be multiplied—or, rather, the levers are the old village elites put in place by previous regimes and firmly attached to the status quo. Changes since 1972 have not totally replaced this group or altered the relation of village intermediaries to the state.

It is likely that the same fragmentation of society and lack of committed organizational instruments at the state level would also have defeated a more populist form of socialism. The history of Peronism in Argentina and the incomplete 'Rawlings revolution' in Ghana indicate that radical populism is no easier to achieve than state socialism. However, the choice of a state-centred form of socialism did make mass mobilization difficult, both by precluding a direct appeal to the population and by disappointing popular expectations of change in the role of the state. The increasing corruption and incapacity of the state have also served to increase rather than decrease popular suspicions of its promises.

While corruption and declining state capacity have not been as dramatic in Madagascar as in other African countries, both have occurred. The two phenomena are not only characteristic of socialist regimes (or African regimes) and in Africa seem to be related to more general characteristics and processes including the concentration of state power, the lack of other sources of enrichment, and the processes of class formation that are occurring to one degree or another in all African states (Sklar, 1979). (See also Young, who argues that corruption 'thrives on the decay of the state' (1982a, p. 86).) The significance for socialist development of the type attempted in Madagascar is two-fold. First, corruption diminishes state capabilities and the Marxist–Leninist model of the transition to socialism lays a special burden on the state. Second, most models of socialist development emphasize intense state–population interaction, whether initiated from the top or from the population itself, and corruption not only increases alienation from the state, it also distorts the relationship by giving advantages to those with monetary resources and increasing income differentials (see D. in *Sudestasie*, 1982, p. 39; Gould, 1980, p. 29).

State–Society Relations

Can a state be fragmented and shrinking, and yet oppressive at the same time? Seen from one angle, the Malagasy 'state' is composed of groups with such disparate and conflicting goals and has so little control over not just distant but central components that one might question the very applicability of the term to the Malagasy political system. From another point of view, that of the population contemplating the *fanjakana* in all its manifestations, a state exists and its components behave in uniform and sadly predictable ways.

Of course, the angle of vision is critical to the perception. Looked at by themselves, most states are composed of conflicting groups, and are, as Lonsdale argues, not 'things' but 'channels of action', and 'cockpits of conflict' (1981, pp. 153 and 156; Callaghy, 1984, pp. 53–4). Seen in relation to their societies, however, states can provide the groups that compose them with preferred access to resources, and with a base from which to squeeze those resources out of the rest of the population (see also Halliday & Molyneux, 1981, p. 146). When a state is operating in a context of class formation under circumstances of extreme scarcity, the conflict of interest between state and society and the degree of real and felt oppression will be even greater than normal.

Modernization from above, contained in both Marxist and non-Marxist conceptions of development, adds further strains. Although the Malagasy population has engaged in the common reaction of at least partial withdrawal from contact with the state, it is one of the legacies of 1972 and 1975 that the population has increased expectations of the state, expectations that increase the violence of reactions against state policies, but that also prevent complete withdrawal. (See Hyden, 1980. His argument that withdrawal gives the population the power to resist state demands has been contested. See, for example, Anthony, 1980.)

To Be Continued

In spite of the gap between regime policies and external or internal models of socialism, the Democratic Republic of Madagascar is clearly not just a replay of the liberal capitalism that characterized the First Republic, and is much closer to a Marxist model than the state capitalism of the Ramanantsoa period or the radical populism proposed by Ratsimandrava. There has been change since these regimes, and in many cases in a 'socialist' direction. The history of the regime does illustrate the difficulties of creating socialism in a situation where both the organizational resources and the popular basis for such a regime are deficient. However, it would be excessively deterministic to criticize the regime for taking power when and under the circumstances it did. Power was there to be taken, and it could be argued that the responsibility of an aspiring revolutionary in such a case is to take it and do the best possible under the circumstances, not to turn away because 'the time is not ripe'.

In many ways, of course, the regime either falls short of the goal, or displays negative characteristics that have to be considered as the result of its pursuit of that goal. However, just as it is unreasonable to expect African states to follow a smooth path to liberal democracy that was not, in fact, followed by today's developed states themselves, so it is unreasonable to expect a smooth transition to socialism. If it is true that early capitalism was filled with conflicting and contradictory developments. and was not particularly 'nice', none of the examples of actually existing socialism that we have suggests that early socialism is any freer of contradictions or any 'nicer' (Leys, 1982, p. 108).

The expression 'transition to socialism' implies a smoothness and unilinearity to the process that does not, in fact, exist. Conflict seems to be an essential part of the changes involved, and the oppressive processes of state formation are as well. In addition, socialism in an African country must occur under conditions in which all the other pressures are to the formation of an elite stratum at the top of society, if not an actual bourgeois class. The emphasis on the state found in socialism of the type pursued in Madagascar might even further those processes. The international environment is not propitious and seems to force a choice between socialism and 'development' as the West and many socialist leaders themselves conceive of it. Finally, the fragility of African states means that regimes and their policies are easily reversible.

For these reasons, it is difficult to predict the future development of Madagascar. A coup involving anti-socialist elements in the army, in alliance with the still numerous anti-socialist groups in civilian life, is perfectly possible, as is an attack on the regime by groups that are not opposed to socialism but either doubt the capacity of the current regime to bring it about, or that would prefer a more 'Malagasy' type of socialism rather than the current Marxist variety. In spite of the increase in social differentiation and popular alienation, a popular uprising is not too likely, although the Kung Fu incident indicates that it is a real possibility for the future. Finally, it is perfectly possible that the regime will persist. As the history of Benin, the Congo, Somalia and Ethiopia suggests, Marxist military regimes often do settle down, after a period of early turmoil, to a long if ambiguous existence.

Appendix

Who Killed Colonel Ratsimandrava?

There are several points to be made before discussing specific possibilities. First, the field of suspects is very extended: the nearly three hundred defendants at the 'trial of the century' were merely representatives of larger groups who were threatened by his coming to power. Not only did Ratsimandrava's proposed programme threaten large and important groups of interests, but he also scorned compromise and political manœuvres. It is probable that several groups were planning assassinations in February 1975 and that had the first one failed or not taken place, others would have been tried. The event itself, like many assassinations, is surrounded by mysterious details, including the persistent rumour that Ratsimandrava was killed in his office, rather than at the scene. However, two of his bodyguards and two of the commandos were killed at the scene, although the survivors claimed not to have fired any shots themselves. The surviving commandos claimed that their intention had been only to kidnap the colonel, and that they had acted on orders from two higher officers. These, not unnaturally, denied ever having given such orders. There is differing testimony about whether Rabetafika was the first officer on the scene or the fourth, and about who the other officers were. Ratsimandrava's car apparently was marked with bullets on both sides, although the ambushers were hidden on only one side of the street. Finally, the colonel's briefcase was delivered to his house—empty—several hours after the body (see Archer, 1976; Andriamirado, 1975; Molet, 1977).

Archer identifies three groups of most probable suspects: Ratsiraka and his supporters, who had been excluded from power by Ratsimandrava; Tsiranana, Resampa and their supporters in the GMP, attempting to re-establish their power; and the groups threatened by Ratsimandrava's promises of further nationalizations and continued investigations into corruption; the commercial companies and a number of fellow officers, including his rival, Rabetafika. There are problems with all of Archer's 'hypotheses' (see Archer, 1976, pp. 108–15). Ratsiraka was only a potential beneficiary of the assassination, and in fact it took him four months to impose his leadership on the Military Directorate (see also Escaro, 1983). The hypothesis of a Tsiranana-Resampa plot seems more plausible, since these were the only ones of the suspects with strong ties to the GMP, from whom the immediate assassins were recruited. However, Archer argues that the two PSD leaders would have been foolish to assassinate Ratsimandrava, who could easily have been replaced by a revival of the Ramanantsoa-Rabetafika alliance that was much more hostile to their goals and interests than the colonel had been (Archer, 1976, p. 109). The hypothesis of an attack organized by Rabetafika rests on several elements, including the previous enmity between the two men, and Ratsimandrava's threat to use his new power to expose Rabetafika's role in the regime's corruption. However, this theory involves the unlikely scenario of Rabetafika convincing members of the GMP to assassinate Ratsimandrava when they were much more likely to want to shoot *him* for his role in promotions and in destroying their December coup. Archer does mention the possibility of a joint Rabetafika-Tsiranana plot, the link again being provided by the corruption investigations. In fact, it is quite probable that all of these people were conspiring against Ratsimandrava, and that the release of the defendants at the trial reflected not common innocence but common guilt, with only chance having determined who got to him first.

Bibliography

Allen, Phillip M. 1975. 'Madagascar: the Authenticity of Recovery' In John M. Ostheimer (ed.), *The Politics of the Indian Ocean Islands*, New York, Praeger.

—— 1984. 'The Indian Ocean: Rocks between Hard Places', *Africa Contemporary Record*, vol. 25, pp. A168–79.

Althabe, G. 1969. *Oppression et libération dans l'imaginaire*. Paris, Maspéro.

—— 1972. 'Les manifestations paysans d'avril 1971', *RFEPA*, June 1972, pp. 71–7.

—— 1980. 'Les luttes sociales à Tananarive en 1972', *Cahiers d'Etudes Africaines*, vol. 20, pp. 407–47.

Andriamirado, Sennen 1977a. 'Madagascar, ou l'unité des contraires', *Spéciale Jeune Afrique*.

—— 1977b. 'Heures et malheurs du fokonolona', *Autogestion et socialisme*, September 1977, pp. 51–64.

Anthony, C. 1980. 'Peasant Power, State Power; Tanzanian Socialism Revisited'. *Africa Today*, 1980, pp. 51–4.

Archer, R. 1976. *Madagascar depuis 1972*. Paris, Editions de l'Harmattan.

Area Handbook for the Malagasy Republic. (H. D. Nelson *et al*.) 1973. Washington, D.C., The American University.

Atlan, R. and Magnard, P. 1972. 'Le président Philibert Tsiranana par lui-même', *RFEPA*, June 1972, pp. 104–14.

Atlas de Madagascar 1969–70. Association des Géographes de Madagascar. Tananarive, Institut Géographique National.

Bastian, G. 1967. *Madagascar: étude géographique et économique*. Tananarive, Nathan.

Bates, R. H. 1974. 'Ethnic Competition and Modernization in Contemporary Africa', *Comparative Political Studies*, vol. 6, pp. 457–86.

Bemananjara, Z. 1986. 'Les langues et l'enseignement à Madagascar'. Paper presented to the International Colloquium on Language Management, Ottawa, Canada, 26–9 May 1986.

Berg, G. M. 1981. 'Riziculture and the Founding of the Monarchy in Imerina', *Journal of African History*, vol. 22, pp. 289–308.

Bezy, F. 1979. 'La transformation des structures socio-économiques à Madagascar', *Cultures et Développement*, vol. 11, pp. 83–116.

Bienen, H. 1985. 'Populist Military Regimes in West Africa', *Armed Forces and Society*, vol. 11, pp. 357–77.

Blardone, G. 1984. 'Madagascar: le développement du sous-développement', *Croissance des Jeunes Nations*, December 1984, pp. 10–13.

Bloch, M. 1971. *Placing the Dead: Tombs, Ancestral Villages, and Kinship Organization in Madagascar*. London, Seminar Press.

—— 1983. 'La séparation du pouvoir et du rang' comme processus d'évolution: une

170   *Madagascar*

esquisse du développement des royautés dans le centre de Madagascar' in Raison-Jourde (ed.), 1983, *Les souverains de Madagascar*.

Bouillon, A. 1973. 'Le MFM malgache', *RFEPA*, November 1973, pp. 46–71.

Bowman, L. W. and Clark, I. (eds) 1981. *The Indian Ocean in Global Politics*. Boulder, Westview Press.

Braun, D. 1983. *The Indian Ocean: Region of Conflict or 'Peace Zone'?* London, C. Hurst and Company.

British Overseas Board of Trade. 1984. Tropical Advisory Group. Trade Mission to the Democratic Republic of Madagascar. *Report*.

Bukarambe, B. 1985. 'Zone of Peace or Strategic Primacy: Politics of Security in the Indian Ocean', *Bulletin of Peace Proposals*, vol. 16.

Cadoux, C. 1969. *La République Malgache*. Paris, Berger-Levrault.

—— 1980. 'Gabriel Ramanantsoa: 1906–1979'. *Encyclopedia Universalis, 1980*.

—— and de Gaudusson, J. du Bois 1980. 'Madagascar, 1979–1981: un passage difficile', *APOI* vol. 7, pp. 357–87.

Callaghy, T. M. 1979. 'The Difficulties of Implementing Socialist Strategies of Development in Africa: The First Wave' in Rosberg & Callaghy 1979, pp. 112–29.

—— 1983. 'External Actors and the Relative Autonomy of the Political Aristocracy in Zaire', *Journal of Commonwealth and Comparative Politics*, vol. 21, pp. 61–83.

—— 1984. *The State-Society Struggle: Zaire in Comparative Perspective*. New York, Columbia University Press.

Callet, F. n.d. *Histoire des rois d'Imerina*. Tananarive, Académie Malgache.

Calvet, J. L. 1976. 'Madagascar', *APOI*, vol. 3, pp. 347–93.

—— 1977. 'Madagascar', *APOI*, vol. 4, pp. 305–70.

—— 1978. 'Madagascar: chronique politique et constitutionnelle', *APOI*, vol. 5, pp. 319–46.

Camacho, M. 1981. 'La problématique de la construction du socialisme à Madagascar: Bilan de cinq ans de transformations sociales'. Unpublished thesis, Paris, Institut d'Etudes Politiques.

Campbell, G. 1981. 'Madagascar and the Slave Trade', *Journal of African History*, vol. 22, pp. 203–28.

Chaigneau, P. 1982. 'Un mode d'orientation socialiste à la périphérie du socialisme: le cas de Madagascar', *Pouvoirs* vol. 22, pp. 109–16.

—— 1983a. 'Madagascar: la crise économique face aux vicissitudes politiques', *L'Afrique et l'Asie modernes*, no. 138, pp. 12–24.

—— 1983b. 'La presse pré-coloniale', *Les Cahiers de la Communication*, vol. 3, pp. 283–317.

—— 1983c. 'Le système des partis à Madagascar', *Recueil Penant*, no. 781–2, pp. 306–45.

—— 1985. 'Politique et franc-maçonnerie dans le Tiers-monde: l'example de Madagascar', *L'Afrique et l'Asie modernes*, no. 145, pp. 10–18.

Chazan, N. 1983. *An Anatomy of Ghanaian Politics: Managing Political Recession, 1969–1982*. Boulder, Westview Press.

Collier, R. B. 1982. *Regimes in Tropical Africa: Changing Forms of Supremacy, 1945-1975*. Berkeley, University of California Press.

Condominas, G. 1960. *Fokonolona et Collectivités Rurales en Imerina*. Paris, Berger-Levrault.

Covell, M. 1974. 'Local Politics and National Integration in the Malagasy Republic'. Unpublished doctoral dissertation, Yale University.

D., J.-P. 1982. 'Madagascar: une économie en crise', *Sudestasie*, vol. 26, pp. 32-44.

Dadanaivo, A. 1978. 'Quatre petites îles . . .', *Afrique-Asie* 2 May 1978, pp. 29-30.

Dahl, R. H. 1966. *Political Opposition in Western Democracies*. New Haven, Yale University Press.

De Barrin, J. 1985. 'Madagascar: la révolution en panne', *Le Monde*, 21, 22, and 23 March, 1985.

Decalo, S. 1976. *Coups and Army Rule in Africa: Studies in Military Style*. New Haven, Yale University Press.

—— 1979. 'Ideological Rhetoric and Scientific Socialism in Benin and Congo/Brazzaville' in Rosberg and Callaghy (eds), 1979, pp. 231-64.

De Craene, P., (ed.) 1977. 'Madagascar: du nationalisme au socialisme', *Le Monde*, 28 December, 1977.

De Gaudusson, J. du Bois 1976. *L'administration malgache*. Paris, Berger-Levrault.

—— 1978a. 'Madagascar: révolution socialiste et réforme des structures administratives et économiques. Premier bilan', *Année Africaine*, 1978, pp. 269-85.

—— 1978b. 'Propos sur les aspects idéologiques et institutionnels des récentes réformes des fokonolona: le fokonolona en question', *APOI*, vol. 5, pp. 15-36.

—— 1979. 'Madagascar: des entreprises publiques aux entreprises socialistes' in F. Constantin (ed.), *Les entreprises publiques en Afrique noire*, vol. I, pp. 197-285. Paris, Pedone.

De la Guérivière, J. 1971. 'Madagascar: "Zizanie" à Tulear', *RFEPA*, May 1971, pp. 12-14.

Delcourt, A. 1969. 'Les relations extérieures de Madagascar', *RFEPA*, April 1969, pp. 47-66.

Délivré, A. 1974. *L'Histoire des rois d'Imerina: Interprétation d'une tradition orale*. Paris, Klincksieck.

Delval, R. 1977, 1978. 'Les Musulmans à Madagascar en 1977', *L'Afrique et l'Asie modernes*, vol. 115, pp. 28-46; vol. 116, pp.5-20.

Democratic Republic of Madagascar 1976. *Constitution*. Dobbs Ferry, N.Y., Oceana Publications.

Deschamps, H. 1972. *Histoire de Madagascar*. Paris, Berger-Levrault.

Desjeux, D. 1979. *La question agraire à Madagascar: administration et paysannat de 1895 à nos jours*. Paris, Editions l'Harmattan.

—— 1981. 'Réforme foncière et civilisation agraire à Madagascar', *Le Mois en Afrique*, no. 184, pp. 55-61.

Direction of Trade Statistics Yearbook, 1986. Washington, International Monetary Fund.

172   *Madagascar*

Donque, G. 1971. 'Tananarive', *RFEPA*, July 1971, pp. 29–40.

Ellis, S. 1980. 'The Political Elite of Imerina and the Revolt of the Menalamba: the Creation of a Colonial Myth in Madagascar', *Journal of African History*, vol. 21, pp. 219–34.

—— 1985. *The Rising of the Red Shawls: A Revolt in Madagascar*. Cambridge, Cambridge University Press.

Escaro, A. 1983. 'Les militaires et le pouvoir politique à Madagascar de 1960 à 1975', *Le Mois en Afrique*, nos. 211–2, pp. 48–53.

Etudes, May 1985. 'La Voix de l'Eglise à Madagascar', pp. 593–6.

—— 'Lettre pastorale publieé par la Conférence des Evêques de Madagascar, le 27 September 1984: Droits et devoirs de la vie en société', pp. 598–600.

Europe-Outremer, 1974. 'Le nouveau Plan malgache accorde la priorité à la culture du riz', pp. 41–6.

European Economic Community 1966. *Possibilités d'industrialisation des Etats africains et malgaches associés: vol. 5 Madagascar*. Brussels, European Economic Community.

Feeley-Harnik, G. 1978. 'Divine Kingship and the Meaning of History among the Sakalava', *Man*, vol. 13, pp. 402–17.

—— 1982. 'The King's Men in Madagascar: Slavery and Citizenship in Sakalava Monarchy', *Africa*, vol. 52, pp. 31–50.

—— 1984. 'The Political Economy of Death: Communication and Change in Malagasy Colonial History', *American Ethnologist*, vol. 11, pp. 1–19.

Feit, E. 1973. *The Armed Bureaucrats: Military-Administrative Regimes and Political Development*. Boston, Houghton-Mifflin.

Fernando, B. J. 1979. 'Comité spécial de l'Océan Indien', *Désarmement*, vol. 2, pp. 27–36.

Gendarme, R. 1962. *L'économie de Madagascar, diagnostic et perspective de développement*. Paris, Cujas.

Gimoi 1972. 'Trois jours qui ebranlèrent Madagascar', *RFEPA*, June 1972, pp. 44–50.

Gintzburger, A. 1983. 'Accommodating to Poverty: the case of the Malagasy Peasant Communities', *Cahiers d'Etudes Africaines*, vol. 23, pp. 419–42.

Givelet, N. 1978. 'Le fokonolona malgache, ou l'expression d'une âme collective', *Cérès*, vol. 63, pp. 31–40.

Goguel, A. M. 1972. 'La diplomatie malgache', *RFEPA*, January 1972, pp. 78–103.

Gomane, J.-P. 1981. 'France and the Indian Ocean' in Bowman (ed.), op cit. 1981, pp. 189–203.

Gonidec, P. F. 1981. *African Politics*. The Hague, Martinus Nijhoff.

Gould, D. J. 1980. *Bureaucratic Corruption and Underdevelopment in the Third World: the Case of Zaire*. New York, Pergamon Press.

Halliday, F. and Molyneux, M. 1981. *The Ethiopian Revolution*. London, New Left Books.

Harding, N. 1981. 'What does it mean to call a regime Marxist?' in Szajkowski, B., ed., 1981, pp. 20–33.

Heseltine, N. 1971. *Madagascar*. New York, Praeger.

Hugon, P. 1977. 'L'évolution économique de Madagascar de la 1ère á la seconde république', *RFEPA*, November, 1977, pp. 26–57.

—— 1978. 'Madagascar: chronique économique et démographique', *APOI*, vol. 5, pp. 423–33.

—— 1982. 'Le développement des petites activités à Antananarivo: L'example d'un procesus involutif', *Canadian Journal of African Studies*, vol. 16, pp. 293–312.

Hyden, G. 1980. *Beyond Ujamaa in Tanzania. Underdevelopment and an Uncaptured Peasantry*. London, Heinemann.

Ilchman, W. F., and Uphoff, N. T. 1969. *The Political Economy of Change*. Berkeley, University of California Press.

Industries et Travaux d'Outremer (ITOM), 1979. 'Le plan malgache 1978–80', pp.269–72.

Jackson, R. H. and Rosberg, C. G. 1982. *Personal Rule in Black Africa*. Berkeley, University of California Press.

Jowitt, K. 1979. 'Scientific Socialist Regimes in Africa: Political Differentiation, Avoidance, and Unawareness' in Rosberg and Callaghy (eds), *Socialism in Sub-Saharan Africa*, 1979, pp. 133–73.

Kent, R. 1970. *Early Kingdoms in Madagascar*. New York, Holt, Rinehart.

Knauss, P. R. 1980. 'Algeria under Boumédienne: the Mythical Revolution, 1965 to 1978' in Mowoe (ed.), *The Performance of Soldiers as Governors*, 1980.

Koerner, F. 1974. 'Le Front Populaire et la question coloniale à Madagascar', *Revue française d'histoire d'outre-mer*, vol. 62, pp. 436–57.

Kottak, C. P. 1980. *The Past in the Present: History, Ecology and Cultural Variation in Madagascar*. Ann Arbor, University of Michigan Press.

L., Ph. 1973. 'Madagascar: consolidation du regime', *RFEPA*, November 1973, pp. 17–20.

La Bayle, H. 1980. 'L'Océan indien, zone de paix: le désenchantement', *APOI*, vol. 7, pp. 289–309.

Labrousse, H. 1980. 'L'Europe et l'Océan indien: perspectives géopolitiques et stratégiques', *APOI*, vol. 7, pp. 17–31.

Laforge, A. 1982. 'L'Océan indien, zone de déséquilibre et de conflits', *Est et Ouest*, vol. 34, pp.14–19.

Langellier, J.-P. 1982. 'Madagascar: l'éléction de la colère', *Le Monde*, 5, 6 November 1982.

Latrémolière, J. 1980. 'Situation économique et stratégique de Madagascar', *Problèmes économiques*, 5 March 1980.

Le Monde Diplomatique, May 1975.

Lefèvre, J. 1969. 'Le Parti Social-Démocrate de Madagascar', *RFEPA*, April 1969, pp. 67–84.

Lefort, R. 1981. *Ethiopia: An Heretical Revolution*? London, Zed Press.

Lejamble, G. 1963. *Le fokonolona et le pouvoir*. Tananarive, Centre de droit publique et de science politique.

Lettre de l'Océan Indien 1986. *Madagascar: les secteurs-clés de l'économie*. Paris, Lettre de l'Océan Indien.

Leymarie, P. 1969. 'Madagascar: la tentation sud-africaine', *RFEPA*, December 1969, pp. 22-5.

— 1972. 'Les accords de coopération franco-malgaches', *RFEPA*, June 1972, pp. 55-60.

— 1973. 'Madagascar: une "seconde indépendence"?', *RFEPA*, July 1973, pp. 21-3.

— 1974a. 'La nouvelle diplomatie malgache', *RFEPA*, January 1974.

— 1974b. 'La magachisation en question', *RFEPA*, January 1974, pp. 29-40.

— 1975a. 'Le fokonolona: la voie malgache vers le socialisme?', *RFEPA*, April 1975, pp. 42-67.

— 1975b. 'Madagascar: comment repartir?', *RFEPA*, August 1975, pp. 15-17.

— 1976. 'Madagascar: les années de l'espoir', *Afrique-Asie. Dossier*, 28 June 1976.

— 1977. 'L'armée malgache dans l'attente (1960-1972)', *RFEPA*, February 1977, pp. 50-64.

— 1978. 'Madagascar: L'an III de la révolution', *Afrique-Asie. Special*, 6 February 1978.

— 1979. 'Le Parti du Congres pour l'Indépendance de Madagascar (AKFM)', *RFEPA*, April 1979, pp. 44-59.

— 1982. 'Madagascar: la course de vitesse des socialistes', *Le Monde Diplomatique*, July 1982, pp. 16-19.

Leys, C. 1982. 'African Economic Development in Theory and Practice'. *Daedalus*, Spring 1982, pp. 99-124.

Lonsdale, J. 1981. 'States and Social Process in Africa: A Historiographical Survey'. *African Studies Review*, vol. 24, pp. 139-225.

M., S. 1978. 'Somalie-Ethiopie: la médiation de Ratsiraka', *Afrique-Asie*, 9 January 1978.

'Madagascar: la révolution embourbée', *Peuples du Monde*, March 1983, pp. 17-21.

Maestre, J.-C. 1968. 'Aspects originaux de la fonction publique malgache', *Annales de l'Université de Madagascar*. Série Droit, vol. 4, pp. 165-223.

Malley, S. 1978a. 'A coeur ouvert avec Didier Ratsiraka', *Afrique-Asie*, 9 January 1978, pp. 19-25.

— 1978b. 'Madagascar: quelles retrouvailles?', *Afrique-Asie*, 16 October 1978.

— 1979. 'Un entretien avec Didier Ratsiraka', *Afrique-Asie*, 19 February 1979.

— 1982a. 'Didier Ratsiraka: des vérités à dire', *Afrique-Asie*, 15 November 1982.

— 1982b. 'Ratsiraka: Haut la main!', *Afrique-Asie*, 22 November 1982.

Marey, G. 1980. 'L'Océan indien: théâtre de confrontation Est-Ouest', *Confidential*, vol. 6, pp. 17-37.

Markakis, J. and Ayele, N. 1978. *Class and Revolution in Ethiopia*. Nottingham, Russel Press.

Maynard, P. 1972. 'Le président Philibert Tsiranana par lui-même', *RFEPA*, June 1972, pp. 104-14.

Moine, J. 1975. 'Madagascar: les militaires s'accrochent au pouvoir', *L'Afrique et l'Asie modernes*, no. 105, pp. 56–62.

—— 1979. 'Océan indien et progressisme', *L'Afrique et l'Asie modernes*, 1979, pp. 3–23.

—— 1981. 'Madagascar: difficultés pour le Président Ratsiraka', *L'Afrique et l'Asie modernes*, no. 129, pp. 42–53.

Molet, L. 1977. '*Madagascar depuis 1972* (critique)', *L'Afrique et l'Asie modernes*, no. 113, pp. 39–51.

Mowoe, I. J. (ed.), 1980. *The Performance of Soldiers as Governors: African Politics and the African Military*. Washington, University Press of America.

Munslow, B. 1983. *Mozambique: the Revolution and its origins*. London, Longmans.

OECD (Organization for Economic Cooperation and Development) 1984. *Geographical Distribution of Financial Flows to Developing Countries*. Paris. OECD.

Les options fondamentales pour la planification socialiste 1978. République démocratique de Madagascar.

Ottaway, D. and Ottaway, M. 1981. *Afrocommunism*. New York, Africana Publishing Company.

Panter-Brick, S. K. 1979. 'Four African Constitutions: Two Models', *Government and Opposition*, vol. 14, pp. 339–48.

Pautard, A. 1972. 'Madagascar: une révolution ambiguë' *RFEPA*, June 1972, pp. 3–6.

Poirier, J. and Dez, J. 1963. *Les groupes éthniques à Madagascar*. Tananarive, Faculté des lettres et sciences humaines.

Prats, Y. 1977. 'Les nouvelles institutions socialistes du développement économique en République démocratique malgache', *APOI*, vol. 4, pp. 15–23.

Rabearimanana, L. 1980. 'Presse d'opinion et luttes politiques à Madagascar de 1945 à 1956', *Revue française d'histoire d'outre-mer*, vol. 67, pp. 99–121.

Rabemora, F. 1985. 'Dix années de socialisme à Madagascar', *Etudes*, May 1985, pp. 581–91.

Rabesahala, G. 1972. 'Madagascar Revolutionary Democrats', *World Marxist Review*, vol. 15, pp. 119–25.

—— 1974. 'Madagascar Looks Ahead', *World Marxist Review*, vol. 17, pp. 121–6.

Rabevazaha, C. 1981. 'Control of Development by the People: Regional Planning and Basic Needs in Madagascar', *International Labour Review*, vol. 120, pp. 439–52.

Racine, A. 1982. 'The Democratic Republic of Madagascar' in Wiles, 1982, *The New Communist World*, pp. 254–77.

Radu, M. S. 1983. 'Ideology, Parties and Foreign Policy in Sub-Saharan Africa' in Bissell, R. E. and Radu, M. S., *Africa in the Post-Decolonization Era*. London, Transaction Books.

Raison, F. 1970. 'Le catholicisme malgache: passé et présent', *RFEPA*, May 1970, pp. 78–99.

Raison-Jourde, F. (ed.), 1983. *Les souverains de Madagascar: L'histoire royale et ses resurgences contemporaines*. Paris, Karthala.

Rajaona, A. R. 1980. 'Le dinam-pokonolona: mythe, mystique, ou mystification?', *APOI*, vol. 7, pp. 145–67.

Rakoto, H. 1969. 'L'économie malgache, ou quatre ans d'exécution du premier plan quinquénnal', *RFEPA*, May 1969, pp. 66–105.

Rakoto, J. 1971. 'La crise de l'enseignement supérieur à Madagascar', *RFEPA*, November 1971, pp. 53–79.

Ramaro, E. 1980. 'Donnez-nous quinze ans', *L'Economiste du Tiers Monde*, November 1980, pp. 24–7.

Randrianarison, C. 1974. *La politique extérieure de Madagascar, 1960–1972*. Paris, Institut d'Etudes Politiques (mémoire).

Randrianja, F. S. L. 1983. 'La notion de royauté dans le mouvement d'émancipation malgache' in Raison-Jourde, op cit. 1983.

Ratsiraka, D. 1983. *Stratégies pour l'An 2000*. Paris, Editions Afrique, Asie, Amerique Latine.

Ravaloson, J. 1983–4. 'Madagascar: le socialisme aux calendes grecques' *Le mois en Afrique*, no. 215–16, pp. 139–44.

Razafindrakoto, J. 1968. 'Etude du village d'Ilafy', *Annales de l'Université de Madagascar*, Série Lettres et Sciences, nos. 8, 9, 3–15, 47–72.

République démocratique de Madagascar (RDM). Ministère auprès de la Présidence de la République chargé des finances et du Plan. Direction Générale du Plan. 1977. *Premier Plan*.

République malgache. Présidence de la République. 1967, 1968. *Rapport sur l'activité du gouvernement*.

République malgache n.d. Ministère des finances et du commerce. Institut national de la statistique et de la recherche économique. *Recensements urbains*.

Robert, M. 'Les musulmans a Madagascar et dans les Mascareignes'. RFEPA, June–July 1977, pp. 46–71.

Rosberg, C. G. and Callaghy, T. M. (eds), 1979. *Socialism in Sub-Saharan Africa: a New Assessment*. Berkeley, University of California Institute of International Studies.

Roquie, A. 1979. 'Le camarade et le commandant: réformisme militaire et legitimité institutionnelle', *Revue française de science politique*, vol. 29, pp. 281–401.

—— 1981. *La politique de Mars: Les procesus politiques dans les partis militaires*. Paris, Le Sycamore.

Roux, C. 1980. 'Le recentrage et la restructuration de l'économie malgache depuis 1974', *Le Mois en Afrique*, September, 1980, pp. 81–97.

Rucz, C. 1978. 'Les pays de l'Océan Indien et les organisations internationales', *APOI*, vol. 5, pp. 231–49.

Schatzberg, M. 1980. *Politics and Class in Zaire: Bureaucracy, Business and Beer in Lisala*. New York, Africana Publishing Company.

Serre, G. 1975. *Données politiques et institutionnelles du changement de régime à Madagascar*. Paris, Institut d'Etudes Politiques, Mémoire.

—— and Rasoarahona, C. 1981. 'Organisation militaire et revolution à Madagascar' in Roquie, 1981, op cit., pp. 179–95.

Serre-Ratsimandisa, G. 1978. 'Théorie et pratique du "Fokonolona" moderne a Madagascar', *Canadian Journal of African Studies*, vol. 12, pp. 37–60.

Simon, P. 1974. 'Au sujet de l'unité culturelle malagasy', *L'Afrique et l'Asie modernes*, no. 103. pp. 32–45.

Sklar, R. L. 1979. 'The Nature of Class Domination in Africa', *Journal of Modern African Studies*, vol. 17, pp. 531–52.

Spacensky, A. 1970a. *Madagascar: 50 ans de vie politique*. Paris, Nouvelles Editions Latines.

— 1970b. 'Dix ans de rapports franco-malgaches (1960–1970)', *RFEPA*, December 1970, 77–92.

Szajkowski, B. ed. 1981. *Marxist Governments: A World Survey*, London, Macmillan.

— 1982. *The Establishment of Marxist Regimes*. London, Butterworth Scientific.

Thompson, A. 1974. 'The role of firearms and the development of military technique in Merina warfare, c.1785–1828', *Revue française d'histoire d'Outre-Mer*, vol. 61, pp. 417–35.

Thompson, V. and Adloff, R. 1965. *The Malagasy Republic*. Stanford, Stanford University Press.

Thompson, V. 1987. 'Madagascar' in *Africa South of the Sahara*, 1987, pp. 614–36.

Tordoff, W. 1984. *Government and politics in Africa*. Bloomington, Indiana University Press.

Towle, P. 1981. 'The United Nations Ad Hoc Committee on the Indian Ocean: Blind Alley or Zone of Peace?' in Bowman, 1981, op cit., pp. 207–22.

Tronchon, J. 1974. *L'Insurrection malgache de 1947*. Paris, Maspéro.

— 1975. 'L'antagonisme Hovas-Cotiers: un cliché ambigu', *Le Monde* 29 May 1975.

Turcotte, D. 1981. *La politique linguistique en Afrique francophone: Une étude comparative de la Côte d'Ivoire et de Madagascar*. Québec, Centre Internationale de Recherche sur le bilinguisme.

Valette, J. 1969. 'Le Parti Social-Démocrate de Madagascar', *RFEPA*, September 1969, pp. 73–83.

— 1974. 'Les groupes éthniques à Madagascar', *RFEPA*, April 1974, pp. 31–40.

Veyrier, M. 1976. 'La Réunion, Madagascar: le droit des peuples', *Cahiers du communisme*, 1976, pp. 81–91.

Waller, M. and Szajkowski, B. 1981. 'The Communist Movement from Monolith to Polymorph' in Szajkowski, 1981.

Welch, C. 1980. *Anatomy of Rebellion*. Albany, State University of New York Press.

Wild, G. and Pineye, D. 1979. 'La présence économique soviétique en Afrique sub-saharienne', *Courrier des pays de l'Est*, December 1979, pp. 3–25.

Wiles, P. J. 1982. *The New Communist Third World: An Essay in Political Economy*. London, Croom Helm.

World Bank. 1979. *Madagascar: Recent Economic Developments and Future Prospects*. Washington, World Bank.

Young, C. 1982a. 'Patterns of Social Conflict: State, Class, and Ethnicity'. *Daedalus*, Spring 1982, pp. 71–98.

— 1982b. *Ideology and Development in Africa*. New Haven, Yale University Press.

xxx 1970. 'L'enseignement à Madagascar', *RFEPA*, April 1970.

xxx 1971a. 'Le filme des récents évènements à Madagascar', *RFEPA*, August 1971, pp. 92–8.
xxx 1971b. 'Rapport sur Madagascar', *Les Temps Modernes*, vol. 27, pp. 88–121.
xxx 1971c. 'L'attitude des églises malgaches face à la situation politique' *RFEPA*, December 1971, pp. 85–9.
xxx 1972. 'Le poids de l'assistance technique', *RFEPA*, June 1972, pp. 65–8.

Journals and Newspapers Consulted

Africa Confidential
African Economic Diary
African Research Bulletin
African Economic Diary
Afrique–Asie
Afrique contemporaine
Année politique
International Herald Tribune
Jeune Afrique
Lakroa
Lumière
Madagascar Matin
Le Monde
Madagascar Renouveau
Nouvelles Malgaches

Index